FROM THERE TO BACK AGAIN

FROM THERE TO BACK AGAIN

David Haight

FROM THERE TO BACK AGAIN
Copyright © 2024 by David Haight
Oprelle Publications, LLC

No part of this book may be reproduced in any form whatsoever, by photography or xerography, or any other means, by broadcast or transmission, by translation into any kind of language, not by recording electronically or otherwise, without permission in writing from the author, except by a reviewer, who may quote brief passages in critical articles or reviews.

This is a work of fiction. Names, characters, places, events and incidents are either the products of the author's imagination or used in a fictitious manner. Any resemblance to actual persons, living or dead, or actual events is purely coincidental.

For information address:
Oprelle Publications,
236 Twin Hills Rd.
Grindstone, PA 15442.

FIRST EDITION

ISBN: 979-8-9899015-4-8

To my wonderful wife Rachel, my stepdaughter Carys, my mother, and my beautiful daughter Morgan.

You're more than I could have ever imagined – this book is for you.

If they asked me, I could write a book
Rodgers and Hart

Chapter One
Blossoms and Blood

And love was creations' source, creation's ruler; but all love's ways are strewn with blossoms and blood, blossoms and blood.

Knut Hamsun (1969)
Victoria: A love story

PEERING out of the tiny rear window of the yellow 1976 Datsun 280Z at the browning corn pushed against the hard-blue sky as we headed towards the occasion of my sister's wedding rehearsal, I tugged at my rarely-worn corduroy skirt. We had been stuffed into this car for two and a half hours, and I hadn't uttered a peep. Not that the two of them noticed; the two being my father and, to his right, my older half-sister, the bride-to-be and his best friend, Adele. Normally, after an occasion like today's, I would go back to my dumb inconsequential life in Elmwood, working at Milton's cheese shop, continue raising my daughter, seeing my boyfriend Mark on the weekends, drinking too much, smoking too much weed, and little else; my father and sister would go back to their lives (whatever that consisted of I hadn't the imaginative power to visualize) only to convene on holidays the same way we had since I had been shoved resentfully off to college. I can't say this arrangement caused me an overt amount of distress, except for the fact that, for the first time in as long as I can remember, I had a favor to ask of my dad, which meant that in some loathsome way, I was asking it of Adele, too. Nine years ago, I aborted a child without ever telling the father. This same man sent me a letter the day before last. It was like a terrorist sleeper cell being summoned into action. He didn't indicate if he knew. But I needed my father to watch my daughter while I drove halfway across the country to confront him and all the ghosts from my past. It also meant I would miss Adele's wedding tomorrow. It was irrational and self-destructive, but I'd already told him I was coming. I continued to wait with predator's eyes for Adele to lower the can of beer away from the blond mustache that was born on her upper lip when she turned fourteen.

"Hey."

Without acknowledging me, she passed the beer back where I was positioned – in the back seat, head grating on the roof. I consumed its remainder in two swift gulps. My father, spying me in the rearview mirror, shook his head, satisfied. "Acorn doesn't fall far from the tree." Adele snatched the can from me, dropping it between her legs. Spending time with my father and sister was like crossing over into a foreign country; no different at twenty-eight than when I was a child of four.

After a moment, Adele resumed, "God, that's one of my favorite memories."

"How long ago was that?" Dad answered.

"Willow had just graduated college, I think. The best part..." she said, pausing to revel in the ancient recollection. "The best part was when we were all sitting at Butch's kitchen table: you, me, Stan, Mia, and Willow? Willow? Yes. Everyone else was downstairs in that epic, hours-long pool tournament. The one Jim lost and stormed off home before anyone could open presents," she added as an aside.

Our dad nodded. "He was always a poor loser."

"And a poor winner, actually."

She was telling the truth. I remembered a family bowling tournament where our younger cousin Jim threw his own match, tossing the ball wildly down the shining lane, clipping the seven-pin over and over in an embarrassing display, just to avoid being beaten by his own wife, marching off to the bar to drink wine and flirt with the dull, large-thighed women and pout. It couldn't have been a pleasant ride home for his wife, Billie, who hadn't an abrasive, or competitive, bone in her body.

"It was getting later. We were all shitfaced but gunning for more. And as always when we're together, we drank the place dry," she said with pride. "Willow and I checked the refrigerator, Stan and Mia dashed to the patio coolers, and when that turned up nothing, we all ran, I mean ran, to the refrigerator in Butch's garage. Finally, in a last-ditch hail Mary, we checked your trunk," she said, pointing at Dad, "for any emergency spares and reconvened at the table, sweaty and defeated. It was looking grim when, out of nowhere, Mia pulled a bottle of wine from her purse and set it in the middle of the table with a thud, smiling proudly. Everyone is excited except for Stan, who was furious. I mean, I thought he was going to have a stroke."

"That's not funny," Dad said.

"He pointed to it, his hands shaking like they always do, and was like, 'That's the bottle I brought!'"

Adele sat with wide-eyed astonishment at our father as if she wasn't the one who had just told the story or hadn't dozens of times. He nodded, the faintest trace of a smile ascending to the surface of his face. With that, Adele leaned back deep into her seat, satisfied.

"What do you mean?" I said.

"Oh, you drip," she said, pushing herself up from the bucket seats with her elbows. "She had slipped the wine into her purse to take home. Stan had brought it to the party, *for the party,* and she had swiped it for herself."

Our father shook his head from side to side, dismissing Mia's thievery with an ease devoid of judgment that comes from knowing someone their entire life. I glanced at the side of Adele's face but was unwilling (or unable) to see her without an overwhelming sense of resentment, which I knew was my father's fault.

"He was livid, *especially* since everyone was running around like rabid dogs trying to find more."

"But no one cared."

"No one cared," I repeated.

"She wasn't about to give up her prize if we happened upon more. But everyone just sat, glasses out, just happy there was more regardless of where it came from."

"That's why she's The Wheeze," Dad said, checking his side mirror. Leaning forward, I did the same. It was filled only with the negative space of the blank road trailing behind us.

"She's appropriately named. That's for sure."

"Wait," I said, perking up, leaning my head towards the front seat. "That's why she's called The Wheeze?"

"Yeah, why did you think she was nicknamed that?" Adele asked, disgusted, taking a sip from the can of beer.

"Because she is always coughing."

"It's short for weasel," Dad offered, checking the rearview and passenger side mirror before changing lanes. "Although, I'm constantly telling her that smoking will kill her."

"Really?" I asked, sincerely surprised, placing my hands on the side of the car, steadying myself.

"We've been calling her that for twenty years, and you never picked up on it? Get out of your bubble, Willow." She shook her head at me as she had a million times throughout my childhood, adolescence, and adulthood. Adele didn't really view me as her little sister, but as a child she never wanted. After a moment, she added, "I'm surprised you were even there."

Although she had never articulated what she thought of me, it was obvious; I didn't count. Not really, not truly. But like gravity, a gag reflex, or the boy who takes your virginity, I was a predictable inevitability that had appeared and couldn't be denied. Adele alone was entitled to being said acorn that fell from said father's tree: his love, approval, undivided attention, his money and property (after he died), and all those familial caveats that were supposed to amount to so much. And since these were not exclusively hers, she made most interactions with me intolerable, a tension that was heightened when our father was around, when any attention veered away from her flinging herself into a self-annihilating black hole. For all my sister's vaunted intelligence, she was just a jealous dog that acted out the second you stopped tossing the ball to her. It really meant that she wished I hadn't been born.

"What do you mean?" I said, easing myself back again, marveling at a Bur oak in bloom rising unexpectedly out of the middle of a field, not the least bit lonely or neglected or wanting. In a flash, it was behind us, and I was again left with the heat of my sister's indignation.

"Once you got your license, you always had some excuse why you couldn't make it to family events: you had to work, you weren't feeling well, your period was bad. 'It's killing me!' you'd scream and run upstairs, slamming the door behind you, which was all bullshit," she said, pounding her thighs in righteous disgust. "I remember when you had some nonsense story about having to work a double on Thanksgiving – like, who's open on Thanksgiving? All day? *All day?*" she asked.

"Stores are open. They want to get a jump on Black Friday," I protested, my eyes falling into my lap, noticing the shoelaces of my sneakers were two different colors, red and brown.

"Well, they weren't then. It was all a ruse. It was a boy. It was always a boy. There wasn't any problem in your life that you didn't try and solve with some new guy." She stopped and admired her engagement ring. "Do you remember what you did when we left that night? Of course not."

"I don't even want to hear. I'm sure it's terrible," I said, loathing the sound of my voice as it fell, like a wheel, into the well-worn rut of a perpetually put-upon teenager. It made no difference that I was a mother, had been a wife, had a job (of sorts). Around her, I was the maddening, moronic little sister who had to be put in her place whether she liked it or not, regardless of whether it was deserved or not.

"No, it was really funny. We were in the backseat of the car."

"Not this car," I said, drawing out each syllable. It was really unbearable.

"Obviously," she responded. "Sometimes I think you say things just to aggravate me. How would we be in this car, a car Dad didn't even have yet, ugh? Anyway, we were in the backseat of Dad's old car," she said, paused, and added, "You satisfied?"

I waited before answering, watching a hulking set of grey clouds like mourners shuffling across the horizon. It would rain soon. Far off, not affecting us. I imagined each drop of water, a single memory falling away, drifting into oblivion, never again able to be recalled, in no way resembling real life. The last time I had been to church, any church, was when my mother died ten years ago. I refused communion, taking a stand no one noticed or cared about. I haven't set foot in a church since. Not that there's been an occasion. Nor have I visited her grave. Actually, I didn't even know where her plot was located and was too embarrassed to ask.

"You weren't in the front seat? Will wonders never cease?" I asked, rolling my eyes.

"Oh stop. And take longer to answer. Anyway, Mia was with us. Or else I would have been," she said with a sarcastic chuckle, pleasing no one but herself. "All you could hear was the road and the wipers across the windshield. You were staring out your window, scraping at the frost, making little designs: a peace sign, making baby feet with the heel of your fist..."

"Making the toes with my fingers?"

"Of course, yes," she said.

"Dad would always get so pissed. Like out of proportion pissed."

"It smeared the windows," he said matter-of-factly. Somehow, I had forgotten he was in the car with us.

"And out of nowhere, you start going on in this really loud drunk voice, 'Dell, do ya think Dad knows I've been drinking?'" she said, imitating my slow sing-song voice that manifested when I was inebriated. "'I didn't mean to get so drunk. Dell, it just kind of got away from me. Things always get away from me.' You remember that, Dad?" she asked.

"I do," he said with a smile and a wink at me, taking a sip from a can of beer.

Out the window, the clouds had turned their back on us, making their way steadily onward, losing their grey, aged pallor. What was their ultimate destination? Did they wander aimlessly around our little blue orb in perpetuity until they were reabsorbed into the atmosphere? I suppose that's what we all do. It dawned on me that perhaps I had smoked too much weed before getting in the car with these two.

"I mean, you were going on and on. Willow, are you listening?"

"Yes."

"Same powers of concentration as always, I see. Anyway, you were going on and on. It was so obnoxious and loud. Not to mention hilarious, since you thought only I could hear you. Dad finally had enough: 'Willow, you're over twenty-one; you're allowed to drink'. You were so hungover the next morning you didn't even want to come out of your room and could barely open your presents. And you got good shit that year," Adele offered. "Better than me."

"Well…" my dad said suspiciously, eyes narrowing, his

head bobbing playfully from side to side.

"I do kind of remember that."

Adele whipped around and squinted hard, trying to confirm if I was telling the truth. Ignoring her, I refocused my glance back out the window until she let me be.

As I was saying earlier, spending time with my father and sister is like crossing over into a foreign country whose streets and buildings are set at awkward angles, whose customs perpetually rebuff me, and whose inhabitants speak a language I don't comprehend, leaving me unsettled and frightened.

It was no different at twenty-eight with a child of my own than it was a girl of four when I was loaded up in my mother's new Chevette and hauled across town to my father's house for the weekend for the first time. He lived in what could only generously be described as a landfill with access to twenty-four-hour sports. The foods were processed, quick, and forgotten once finished. Nothing was child-centric. Worst of all, I was forced to share a room with a person (five years older than me) I was told was my sister. She looked nothing like me, spoke harshly, and liked radically different things. I wondered how two people with the same father and different mothers could be sisters. I was too afraid to ask my mother, and my father, the reason for my presence in this wasteland, was largely absent. The constant in his life, I discovered, was work. He drove a delivery truck for a mid-sized furniture company during the week (whose hours were long and unpredictable) and did security on the weekends. If he was home, he was sleeping, and if he was sleeping, there was a one hundred percent chance we were going to wake him (despite the repeated warnings not to), and his loud tenor would be bellowing at us before his bedroom door was even opened. There was no time in the years I spent there as a child that I could honestly say I knew him.

The contrasts from living with my mother couldn't have been more striking had I gone to the moon. My mother woke early, fixed breakfast for me before I went to school, shared things from her world (adult things I hadn't the capability to comprehend), showed interest in my life, was a tireless housekeeper, and never raised her voice. And although it was an apartment rather than a house, it felt both expansive and more intimate. Why I needed this man with the thin-rimmed, thick-lensed glasses, I didn't understand, but having an a priori (and untainted) trust in my mother, I did as I was told every third weekend of the month and every other holiday. However, I was always astonished when I pulled open that creaky and rusted screen door, and a blood-river primordial feeling rose and overtook me, telling me that I loved this stranger unconditionally, almost wildly so.

"You two were delightful that night," Dad said, dragging me back into the present and a conversation I had forgotten about.

"Stupid is more like it," Adele scoffed, casually pointing out a car racing towards us at one of the rare crossroads that stretched in perpetuity in either direction like eternity's arms and you saw coming from miles away, as if in slow motion. He waved off her concern but accelerated through the intersection nonetheless, ignoring the stop sign and the oncoming car's muted horn. I closed my eyes until I was certain we were safe.

"Willow can understand," he began.

"What, because she has a kid?" Adele protested, whipping her head to the right, blinded by red-hot resentment, certain that I had hopscotched past her on some imaginary hierarchy in a completely unearned manner by my having a daughter. "Anybody can spread their legs," she had proclaimed more than once in a white-wine-fueled rage. Never, of course, in front of our father.

"You'll understand one day," he said.

"I've told you a million times, I don't want kids," she said.

"That bitterness will go away once you find out you're pregnant. Not even realizing how profoundly your life just changed. Forever. You'll stumble out of the bathroom with that silly-looking test in your hand, dumbfounded, and show it to whoever the lucky guy is—"

"Dad, think of where we are going," I said, my face shriveling in horror.

"You hate to hear it, but it's all true. All right, all right, I'll stop. But it's true," he said, lowering his voice and raising his eyebrows in that playful way she never appreciated. "Everything changed when I had you two, and the feeling never goes away. No matter what befalls you or how badly they disappoint you. It weathers all of that. Just like that night in the car. I can still see you," he said, nodding at me in the rearview mirror, "head against the window, hair down to your waist, scraping away, off in your special little world, always the dreamer. And you," he said, elbowing Adele, "fuming at every mumbled word. But that anger comes out of concern. No, it does. I know you weren't always the happiest that she came along. She cried when we told her," he said over his shoulder.

"I've heard the rumors," I said.

"But she was fiercely protective of you," he went on,

"eventually. Remember when she fell asleep in the back of my truck? You were worried sick. She was worried sick," he said to me, "racing up and down the neighborhood looking for you."

"Can you imagine if I was the one blamed for losing you?" Adele said.

"But love, the love of your sister and of that little bundle of joy when he or she arrives, cannot be denied. You'll see."

"I have an IUD in, Dad," she said, using those syllables like an axe dismembering an oak from the earth, happily tapping the fingers of both her hands on the dash.

"Don't tell me that, Dell," he said, his shoulders dropping.

A bitter phlegm gathered in the back of my mouth. Of course, McKenna wasn't enough. He wanted, needed, a grandchild from his firstborn. If you asked my father who he loved more, Adele or I, he would tell you to go fuck yourself. Forgetting that he had rescued Adele from an alcoholic mother and ex-wife but couldn't even bother to show up the day I was born. Not that I ever asked him about it. I just maintained a permanent low-grade rage that staved off any confrontation but ensured we never grew very close. That'll show him.

"Once your grandmother died, Christmas completely changed," he said. "The next year, Butch goes to Florida," he said with a flip of his left hand, "the following year, Mia stayed home with indigestion," he shrugged with a wave of his right. "Eventually, we all kind of did our own thing." His hands landed gently on the steering wheel like two large butterflies, followed by a long, weighty pause.

"I miss that," Adele said.

I did too.

"It's like the time your mother and I went to Niagara Falls."

"Which one?" Adele asked.

"There's only one Niagara Falls, darling."

"No, which mother... Jesus Christ, Dad," Adele moaned, pointing at the two of us. "How much have you had?"

"Oh, I don't know, that's not the point," he said and discreetly handed Adele the beer can.

"Don't know how much you've had to drink or which mother?" Adele asked, raising her eyebrows, finishing whatever was left in the can and smushing it, letting it fall at her feet. "Don't be calling me when you're too old to take care of yourself, old man."

They both smiled.

This joke was a tell of epic (and eventually heartbreaking) proportions. No doubt my father believes without giving it much thought that, when his time comes, and I do not necessarily mean when Mr. Bones comes knocking to collect his final bill, his eldest daughter will ease him into the final sunset. No, that would be too easy and merciful for my father (and especially Adele). God help them both should he be struck down by a stroke, Alzheimer's, or any number of ailments requiring extended care (and capital). For, when Dad reaches out his hand to Adele, that hand will be wound tight around the steering wheel of her car as she races off to Pittsburg or Orlando or any number of places, with (or more likely without) her new husband – anywhere but where my father is suffering. Even though Adele is the executor of his will and would be his first contact should he be diagnosed with some medical misfortune, their relationship has as much to do with familiarity as it does things in common.

"Anyway, there's this point you can go back, like, half a mile or a mile back from where the falls currently are, and they tell you that's where they used to stand."

"Erosion, right?"

"You could plant yourself there a hundred years watching, and you'd never see so incremental a change, but it's there, and it's earth-shattering. That's what your grandmother's death did to the family."

I remember when she passed. She was ninety-three and still living in the house where she raised my dad and his siblings when she fell. No one knows how or why she collapsed, although the phone was found beside her and around her neck dangled the life alert necklace with the little red button she refused (or so the family concluded) to press. Even at fifteen years old, it was obvious to me. *How do I not get permanently relocated to a nursing home after this?* When the universe offered its resounding silence, so goes my theory, she called it quits. Because the body always, always, knows before the mind.

There was a little more to it, of course. Her heart didn't stop, per her will, like shutting off a generator. Technically, she died in the hospital two days later after being found unconscious by my Uncle Stan and rushed to the hospital, where she lay for forty-eight mind-numbing hours while we said our goodbyes (mind-numbing for all of us as we took shifts, wept, strategized like a dutiful family acting out the last act of her drama as she, the protagonist waited off stage). Again, I'm convinced that was part of her plan, letting us all have our moment. She always thought of her family first. Then it was done.

It's strange. The memory I most often associate with her is not of her dying (even though I was there) or the Christmases or our chats over coffee at her little round table stuffed in the corner of her minuscule kitchen or any number of memories, but the way she insisted Adele and I kiss her on the mouth when greeting her. It was horrifying, beyond embarrassing. But there was no getting around it. If you tried to avoid this ritual, she would grab you by the cheeks, hard; I mean she would squish the hell out of your face and guide you right to her bright oval mouth (and she wore the loudest most obnoxious orange lipstick you can imagine) and lay a big fat wet one on you, those yellow conspiratorial teeth whispering about you as you approached her face. There are so many beautiful memories I have of that little woman, and my broken brain landed on that ugly, stupid one.

"That's your favorite metaphor, you know, that right?" Adele quipped, popping open a fresh can of beer, loudly slurping the excess contents gathered around the lip, some nesting on her mustache which she failed to wipe away.

"It really is," I added, trying without success to catch Adele's eyes. Instead, my view was dominated by a sagging, semi-dilapidated farm and a wind pump standing dutiful guard next to it, like a steel sunflower, its multi-bladed face lifting its chin to the crimson sun.

"What?" he asked, furrowing his brow in disbelief, first at Adele and then at me in the rearview mirror. "No?"

"From your divorce from Mom, Willow's mom, retiring after thirty years, blah, blah. It's always Niagara Falls; you'd swear it's the only place you've ever been. You have been to other places, right?" she asked with a sarcastic chuckle.

He stared helplessly at the road, sincerely distressed, the car decelerating briefly. His eyes narrowed in irritation before recalling his place atop the family tree, his face splitting into a big smile. "I guess I need some new material." The car soon regained its cruising speed.

"Or a vacation," I said, forcing the beer can from Adele. "You're in that house all the time."

"He's all right," Adele said, slapping his thigh and taking the can back. "We go up to the legion and play bingo every Wednesday, do the meat raffle, and Church on Sunday mornings."

"Blech," I offered.

"I'll win that raffle eventually," he said unconvincingly but without bitterness. "Speaking of which, did you see Tiger on Sunday?" my father asked, slapping his hands together enthusiastically before snapping them firmly back on the steering wheel. Adele groaned. "He was on point, his driving was solid, his putting yips have all but disappeared, and he didn't limp off the course."

I never recalled his going to Niagara Falls. There were no pictures in the photo albums that I remembered, or any stories about his having vacationed there with either of our mothers. It only became a topic of discussion after he retired, when the television became his primary companion. I know how lonely those cavernous and unending nights can be. Perhaps he saw a documentary about the slow erosion of the rock by water and it reverberated with him, reflecting how he now, in the final stretches of his life, viewed the world. In any case, the metaphor was the more vital part, giving his aging self a way to orient his life. It didn't matter if he ever traveled there or felt the cold mist of the mighty falls on his face.

"Since when did he start playing bingo on Wednesday nights?" I asked. The fact neither would think to invite me was simply a cold hard given.

"Eh," she said waving away his enthusiasm, and rolled down her window partway, dropping some unidentifiable object out that was picked up and sucked away by the highway wind. She rolled the window back up.

"He finished top ten in another major. It's only a matter of time."

"Do not say he's back," Adele said emphatically. "I've been hearing that garbage for ten years."

"You're being absurd. You are," he said, stopping what I could see as a torrent of protestations from Adele, no doubt from an argument they had been having for some time, although I had little idea what they were talking about.

"The guy is past his prime."

"You're waiting for him to be what he was in 2000 and 2001. That guy was a miracle, a once-in-a-lifetime occurrence…"

"Do not say 'from God.'"

"The things he did then – what he was – is incomprehensible even to him. Something he'll be chasing forever. Unfairly, I'll add. Really, it's a curse. Hand me that beer," he said, reaching for the can Adele had wedged between her legs.

"Okay, Dad, put it back in your pants," she said, doing as requested. "And don't try telling me he's a genius again. Because I'll freak the fuck out. O'Keefe, Plath, Amos. Not a guy who hits a little dimpled ball with a club."

"He is a genius," my father said with certainty. "He has too much talent, too much drive for you or anyone to write off," he said, taking a solid swig and handing it back after long consideration. "The mental concentration he has is unlike anything I've ever seen in 40 years of watching professional sports."

"You know what bothers me? Maybe you're right – although you're not. Maybe he's a genius – not at all. Perhaps he'll come back – not a chance. But it doesn't matter where he finishes, top ten or if he misses the cut, he's always the top story. Some poor guy wins a tournament, which is a terribly difficult thing to do, and he's an afterthought."

"You have a point," he said with a shake of his head, his brow furrowing.

"Let the new generation have some of the spotlight. He's like a dead oak in the forest; nothing under him can grow."

"All I'm saying is that to expect him to dominate like he did before is naïve. But mark my words – he has a lot of game still in him."

"Not to mention he's a fucking cheating creep," she added, taking a quick peek at her engagement ring again. If I were to guess what was going on in her mind, I would say she was trying (without success) to convince herself the diamond's cut wasn't shallow or that its clarity was flawless (in inverse proportion to her man no doubt) and that the carat better be a motherfucking heavyweight and other such nonsense. Happiness is a currency Adele doesn't deal in, directly or easily.

"That has nothing to do with anything. I don't give two shakes about his personal life. That's between him, his wife, and the lamppost."

"Ex-wife, his *extremely* wealthy ex-wife," Adele chimed in.

"I could live on a fraction of that," he chuckled.

"All that money," I said, seeing a chance to wedge my way into the conversation, feeling left out as I always did when they talked sports. "It contributes nothing to the fabric of society. Unlike teachers. Or social workers who get paid a drop compared to these people." This was an argument not worth having with these two. I could already see the two of them exhausted by me, and they hadn't uttered a syllable in response.

"The market decides these things. When people stop watching football games, athletes will stop getting multi-million-dollar paydays," Adele said, already ready to move on from my flaccid point.

In a more measured tone, my dad offered, "If you paid teachers what you paid athletes, you'd attract the wrong type of people into the profession. You want people who are teaching because they love it. Not people who are doing it for the money."

"You think paying teachers well is an argument against quality teachers? And pro athletes and entertainers aren't worth the millions they make, Dad."

"Of course not, but it's all about scale, honey. When Adele went to Nice and watched a guy play violin on the beach, she gave him a Euro. The difference is that when Tiger plays, he may have 10-20 million people watching him, so his compensation is naturally going to be on par with what companies are willing to pay in salary, in sponsorships. Is any one person ever going to be worth hundreds of millions? No. That's insane money. But that's how capitalism works."

When I thought about it that way, it kind of made sense. But I hadn't the heart to admit it – not with Adele in the car.

In reality, I just couldn't understand what they found *interesting* about sports. Such passion and concern. Over something they had no control over. For strangers who took money out of their pockets (directly or indirectly) and, as a rule, broke their hearts. It was incomprehensible to me. In fact, Brayden, my ex-husband, was frequently incensed at my attitude towards sports. Especially how it had rubbed off on our daughter, McKenna. *Sports are character-building. They build a sense of working together. You never encouraged her to try out for gymnastics, ballet, or even soccer like the other children.* In my defense, it wasn't like I discouraged her from playing athletics. I simply refrained from suggesting it as an option (which, as I've gotten older, I've realized may be worse. Just as a lie of omission can be much more destructive than an outright fabrication). It was the first thing he brought up for the brief nano-second we attempted therapy. He'd sputter words like *Teamwork* and *Synergy* at me like daggers, leveraging them to make a greater point about our marriage. *You're so dismissive. You eyeroll everything away, not just sports, but jobs, disagreements, our sex life, entire relationships, the death of your mother.* By the time we sat on the couch, you might as well have tossed a handful of dirt on the casket.

"In other words, don't hate the player, hate the game, Willow," Adele said bluntly. "And Tiger's not a genius."

"All right, honey."

The sun had worked its way back through the sky. There were no longer any traces left of those grey behemoths: no mourners, no rain, empty of memories. The great blue expanse reached to all sides as if stretching eternity to its limit. Saddled up to the very edge of the road was a homemade crucifix covered in flowers, notes pinned to its stubby, feeble arms. When I terminated my pregnancy, I thought I was being like my grandmother – making a choice, on my terms, clear-headed, resolute.

"Do you remember Chet?"

"Of course I remember Chet," Adele barked incredulously.

"I got a letter from him." I swallowed hard in anticipation of the short-fused fireworks I had just lit to go off.

"When? Recently?" she barked in rapid order, her radar already engaged for whatever nonsense I was introducing to her day, her week, her year, her wedding festivities. It was like when we were kids: Adele didn't get a birth-*day*, it was decreed we all got a week to celebrate the blessed event of her birth. Now, here I was, pulling the spotlight from her once again, as I did the moment I was conceived.

"A few days ago."

Even though it had been nearly a decade, I knew it was him just from the handwriting on the envelope. It was placed perfectly in its center, measured and controlled, yet compressed as if it had been composed on a much larger surface before being shrunk down.

"How antiquated," Adele moaned, trying to lock down the fury that was always bubbling right beneath the surface, to refrain from accusing me of making everything about me, of being unable to stand it when the sun cast its rays on her for even a moment. "What exactly did he want?"

"He didn't say."

"Yes, yes. Sure, sure. Mysteries solved are mysteries ruined."

"He enclosed his address but not his phone number," I said.

"Here I am, but we can't talk. Cute."

I knew the reason he withheld his number. Once we

split, he couldn't bear to hear my voice. It reminded him of the piano from Steely Dan's *Rikki Don't Lose That Number*. Or so he said when he called repeatedly, although I had no idea what that meant. In any case, I dared not say this aloud.

"He's not still doing all that stuff, is he? Because that shit got pretty weird. Intense."

"No, no. That was years and years ago."

"You remember that, Dad?"

Puffing his cheeks out like Dizzy Gillespie and exhaling hard (which said more about the tribulations of having daughters than any words could articulate), Dad asked, "Is he the one who would just show up and rake your yard or shovel your driveway in the winter without asking?"

"No, that was Jeff. He was a real prize too. He'd show up outside of her classes even after she gave him the heave-ho. Would call and send her presents even after she was married. I seem to recall a tin of meatloaf on more than one occasion."

"Then which one is Chet? They all run together sometimes. Meatloaf? Who brings a meatloaf to woo a woman?" he asked, twisting up his face in disbelief.

"Didn't Chet slam you up against a tree after you threatened to break up with him?" my sister added darkly. I knew having to ask this one favor would mean having to wade knee-deep in the shit of my unpleasant memories, not alone, as I already had the minute I received his letter, but with my sister and father as well. It was every woman's dream. I refused to answer.

"He's not doing that, now is he?" he asked, alarmed.

"Of course not."

"I wouldn't be surprised. Men can never take a hint,"

Adele said. "They force you to hurt them. And instead of being grateful for your time together, they flush any goodwill between you by taking their agony public," she added with increasing rancor. "Being a train wreck diverts attention away from them and makes you, the woman, culpable, freeing them of all accountabilities."

I thought about this for a hard moment. "I threw a tantrum over a man once, got a little stupid nuts, texting and calling a million times, crying on my knees outside a bar when one such upstanding young specimen dumped me for someone else," I said.

"Yeah, and what exactly happened, as if I don't know," she said.

"I was called a crazy bitch."

She nodded righteously.

"You live alone," our father said, interjecting, an ache gracing his face. He took a long gulp from the beer can, as if our conversation about my ex-boyfriends were a manifestation of every father's horror.

"That's sexist, Dad."

"Maybe, but you live alone, you're attractive, and you're small."

"I can't tell you how many things I object to in that sentence," I offered.

"And men don't abuse, misuse, and stalk married, unattractive, fat women?" Adele asked.

"Doesn't mean I'm wrong. Your safety comes first. Always."

"He lives in Salt Lake City."

"If he does any of that bullshit, you call the cops. Immediately. Then me, okay? Understood?" our dad said forcefully, arranging his face in a pose of grave seriousness.

He adjusted the rearview mirror and became uncomfortable in the seat as if he were about to reroute the car to Salt Lake City and settle things this instant. "You don't know what this guy's been through since you've seen him last. He could be a straight-up psychopath, and you have to think of McKenna."

"He lives in Utah, Dad," I said, focusing on a still-life of grazing cows.

"What did the letter say?" Adele asked.

"What does that matter?" he asked, his security guard instincts kicking in.

I pushed on, ignoring my father. "He told me how he enjoys living in Utah."

"Right, as if he recently moved there and not a decade earlier when he made – what did you always call it? 'His mad dash from the Midwest.'"

"Yes," I agreed, surprised she remembered that, and continued, "He mentioned that he was an accountant; in fact, he made some lame joke about how everyone thinks accountants are so dull and that they might be right."

"Gawd," Adele groaned.

"What else?" my dad asked very seriously, like a private investigator collecting pertinent information before proceeding with a case.

"He said he had taken up Karate to drop a few pounds. He mentioned he felt guilty for missing his mother's funeral a few months back without further explanation. Just boring shit really."

Adele nodded, also putting on her best private investigator impression.

"He asked what I did for a living. Did I ever put my hard-earned degree to use? How was Laura? Did I ever make it to Africa?"

"I don't remember you ever entertaining the thought of traveling to the dark continent," Adele said dramatically. "And you haven't talked to Laura since you stole her job at the cheese shop after graduation. I do remember you threatening to run off to southern Spain at some point."

"I didn't steal her job."

"She must have committed some atrocity, real or imagined, that got her exiled, right? What did she do to make it permissible to take her job? Fail to approve of an outfit? Give you a queer look? Forget to return a call?"

"I've always said, if anyone ever did anything to either one of you, I'd be in jail," Dad said to the highway before eyeing us one at a time.

"Yes, we know. Because you'd kill him, whoever he is," Adele said wearily. "You've been saying it from the moment we hit puberty. If anyone ever did anything to either one of us, you'd be in jail because they'd be dead."

"That's right," he said, wishing his response had more gravity than it did.

"And of course, Willow would get up in arms saying it felt like a Cro-Magnon, unenlightened thing to say, you remember?"

"Such a particularly male solution that solved nothing," I said. "You can mock me, but you agree."

"And you stopped saying that once you had McKenna," he said. Adele smirked obnoxiously before my father added, "Things change when you hold your baby for the first time. Or even find out you're pregnant," he added, which emptied all emotion from Adele's face.

"I wouldn't say I condoned your reasoning, but I certainly understood it and took a strange comfort in it," I said.

"All right then," he said, pointing with his index finger hitting the roof of the car.

"No mention of Brayden and your tragic divorce?" Adele inquired, ignoring my father's indirect plea not to give up on having a child.

"Oh wait, Chet. Now I remember. Tall, skinny guy. Always had one piece of hair that was white, I recall. He was nuts about you."

"Who wasn't?" Adele concurred with a deep jealous-filled eyeroll.

"He attempted suicide when you split up, right?"

"Nope," Adele said harshly.

My shoulders dropped. "Wasn't him, Dad."

"You should never take your star player out of the game," he said defiantly. "I hate when people, especially young people, can't see any other way forward." He paused to turn down the radio, which I didn't realize was even on. "It's just a loss of perspective. There's so much more to life—if they could just reach out to someone or find a way to push through."

Anytime the subject of suicide came up, my father would say, "You should never take your star player out of the game," seeming to forget that Adele's husband, Scott, had killed himself without any warning and without leaving a note. He simply left for work, entered a carwash parking lot, pulled out a gun, and shot himself under the chin.

"Of course not," Adele said, following this quickly with, "Not too much farther. It's a gorgeous little church. You could put it in your pocket. It's just charming. Non-denominational, which is nice."

"I've been there, Dell," he said, refusing to be deterred.

"I haven't," I added too eagerly.

"You should never take your star player out of the game," he repeated.

"That wasn't him, Dad. Willow just said," Adele insisted, trying in vain to slide him off the topic.

"Any more beer up there, Dad?" I asked. "Running a little dry back here."

"I remember this one time," he began. "We were up at the cabin: Scott, Adam, Adele, and I. You guys weren't married yet, were you?"

"I don't know what story you're telling, Dad."

"We were at The Depot—"

"Still don't know, Dad. We always went to The Depot."

"Did we ever eat anywhere else? At least fifteen restaurants, and we ate and drank at the same place every time we went up there. Did you have the onion ring tower? Play exactly one hundred and fifty dollars' worth of pull tabs? As if I don't know."

"Who knows about the food? Anyway, we were at our usual table, bullshitting, drinking. When these girls…"

"Girls?" I asked, raising my left eyebrow to the sky, trying to pretend that Scott's life hadn't ended in the worst possible way.

"Women, my feminist daughter. Two women, I think. One for each of us. And before you can say anything, I was a grown man, unattached, with women who had joined us of their own volition, clearly seeking out fun and companionship, which is healthy, I think. Everyone says being alone is good for the soul, and I suppose it is," here he stopped but started again for fear his contemplation would derail his momentum. "Anyway, everyone involved was sober and consenting. At least to *start,* everyone was sober.

Satisfied?"

"Yes, Father," I said. "I have the letter from Chet with me if anyone wants to see it."

"I do," Adele said pathetically.

"The night goes on, with plenty of booze, lots of pulls tabs, darts, you know, the regular routine. Eventually, we invite them back to the cabin and, within twenty minutes, we are in the front yard, around the bonfire, sipping whiskey and chatting. The lake is black as oil, and the shoreline across the lake is even blacker. You can hear the waves whispering. You feel small, but not in a bad way. Protected or part of things maybe." Here he paused. We could all see the picture he was painting. It had been our second home since we were kids. "Suddenly, Scott disappears. We figure he's using the bathroom or refreshing his drink or calling you. But then he's gone a really long time."

This sentence makes Adele visibly uncomfortable.

"And all of a sudden, we hear this howling from the backyard. It's strange. It has that – what is that called – Doppler effect," he said, snapping his fingers. "It's growing closer and closer until it's right on top of us and, low and behold, Scott is running around the cabin, buck naked."

I smile soundlessly at the memory. I can't see Adele's reaction.

"I mean, we are all shocked; what are these girls, women, going to think? Here we bring these women to an isolated spot, ply them with booze, and now one of the men is naked? We look like perverts, especially Scott, and he wasn't even interested in these girls – women – obviously." He gave us both a quick glance. When his eyes met mine, my face lit up but faded again when he directed himself back to the highway and the lonely corridors of time. I shifted my glance out the window at the endless fields. "I play it cool and say to Adam, 'Go take care of that idiot.'" He pointed a thumb over his shoulder as if the memory were happening in real-time. "I try and make small talk with these girls – women, especially Marnie. Maureen? Marnie – who is getting more gorgeous by the second, which they always do, by the way. With every sip," he says with a chuckle. It's not clear who he is talking to: me and Adele, some imagined audience? Sometimes I think my father would have been better served by a couple of sons. "A few moments later, I hear that same crescendo, and around comes Scott and Adam chasing each other around the cabin, both howling, and now they're both naked! Nobody says a word. Well, after a few laps around the cabin, their shortcomings bouncing around, if you know what I mean, Adam tackles Scott into and through the old red fence, you remember that rickety old thing? *(We do.)* Which breaks, and they end up in the dewy grass, rolling around, laughing, like a couple of fairies."

No one in the Datsun is laughing. He doesn't notice. I can see Adele's face in the side mirror again, vacant like an old Victorian doll.

"Come on, Dad. I'd like to get back to my thing here."

"Marnie, the one I was hoping to get to know better—" he said.

"We get it, Dad."

"—locks eyes with me across the fire and says (here he pauses for maximum effect), 'You guys really like to party.'"

Before Scott's suicide, this was the moment when the audience would have erupted with laughter, as much at the punchline as at the expectation of the punchline (as we had all heard this story numerous times). But the reality has caught up with him (as it always does now) that Scott, his son-in-law, last seen in an open casket, eyes closed and blackened, was long gone, having left his eldest daughter a widower before thirty. The smile slips from his face, and we all sit in silence, watching the azure sky, wishing it could take the memories of Scott away.

"Well, did you, you know, get her?" I finally asked my dad to break the agony.

"Of course not. They couldn't get out of there fast enough. Even though they had no idea how to navigate the maze of dirt roads and get back to the highway. Giving them directions was a nightmare. There was no way they didn't get lost. I could have killed Scott."

"Mhmm-hmm," Adele exhaled deep from her lungs.

I needed to act; pat my still-grieving sister on the shoulder, hug her around the seat, say I was sorry for her loss (the worst expression in the English language, but what else was there). Of course, were I to do that, she would shake off my hand like a stinging bee, curse the day I was conceived, consider leaping out of the moving car (most certainly not to join the beloved). What Adele hated, more than losing Scott, was the public fashion in which it had occurred. It gathered up all the shattered pieces of their life and dropped them outside the perpetually humming carwash, the terminus of all his memories. It turned her soul white-hot. There was no doubt in my mind that this wedding was an act of defiance, an attempt at excising Scott (and all his history) off some universal ledger. Her second divorce would cure her of this notion.

After a moment, he adds, "He was a great guy."

"Yeah, he was all right," Adele says, her head propped on her hand like the faded cover of some old romance novel.

My father, spent from telling the story and who hadn't had a drink since he had started, downed and quickly opened a new beer, passing it over to Adele, who took a sip and passed it back to me.

"Anyway, you were saying about this ex-boyfriend of yours," he said, finally breaking the terrible silence, drumming the fingers of his white chapped hands on the steering wheel.

Staring out the tiny window at the large, blue Minnesota sky and endless fields of expiring corn, I found myself again holding my breath, as if I were diving deep into some dark, unforgiving expanse of water whose secret wish was that I never again find the surface.

"I need to ask you a favor."

"On the day of my rehearsal dinner and one day before my wedding?" Adele said, the beer can held an inch away from her large, expectant mouth, her mustache tickling the rim.

"I was talking to Dad."

"I was going to say," she said, with a sneer and exaggerated eyeroll I couldn't see, but which registered an 8.0 on her internal Richter scale.

"What is it, honey?" he said, scooping up my eyes in the rearview mirror. His expression was warm, as if we were alone on the cool summer nights, sitting across from one another in his backyard around the bonfire pit, sweetly buzzed, the fire lighting our faces from the chin up, casting shadows up rather than down. That was a gift of his, his solicitude. Or maybe it was something we just shared. I hoped it was the latter.

"I was wondering if you could watch McKenna for a

couple of days," I said.

"I don't know why not. I'm a free agent," his eyes flashing wild with mischievousness.

Before I could thank him, Adele said, already on the case, "Hold on. Are you going to miss my wedding? You are, aren't you? You're going out there. This fuck wrote you a letter, and now you're dumping your kid on Dad and darting out there? Aren't you? Does Brayden even know?"

Even though she was facing front at the long, uneventful road, her eyes were glaring directly at me, at the little, prettier sister she never asked for, never wanted, and who always got her way. Thinking back to that night in my cinderblock dorm, after too much to drink, a Grand Canyon of guilt hollowing me out, with no one to tell and longing for a connection with my only sister, the Indigo Girls staring down at us from the walls, I regretted telling her about my pregnancy from Chet the second it came out of my mouth.

My father's head shot back a look of shock, panic washing over him, causing us to swerve momentarily towards the ditch before finding the road. "That's not what you're doing, is it?" he asked me through the rearview mirror. "This is your sister's wedding. This is the big event of her life. Tell me your sister's not right?" he asked as if begging me to deny every accusation she had launched against me for decades. It was the same question he asked me when Adele told him I was engaged to Brayden. And then more moderately: "You know I don't care what you do, but this is your sister. Your family. Especially after what happened with Scott."

No mercy. And with nowhere to run. But it had always been that way. I remember the day I took the job at the cheese shop. I was excited. The hours were convenient, and they offered health insurance. It wasn't great, it certainly wasn't a career, but it was steady. My mother would have been thrilled the way she always was at any of my victories, no matter the size. I was not prepared for my father's words. *After all the things I have done for you. Through the depression and the cutting. The sleeping for entire weekends. You have a college education, and this is what you land on.* I sobbed for hours. It took a lot of nerve to mention family from a man who wasn't there the day I entered this world and only ostensibly knew me.

"It's just like when Brayden broke his ankle skiing in Wisconsin, four months after you divorced, and you drove for hours through a blizzard and picked up his sorry ass." She chuckled cruelly.

"He didn't have anyone else."

Adele turned all the way around. "How badly do you need to be needed? How empty are you? You could never make a clean break with him, with any of them. You always wanted to make sure they never got over you, not completely," she said, snatching the can away from me as a form of rebuke.

"You said you had the letter," my father interjected.

"I knew you'd find some reason to bail."

"What else did he say?" he asked.

"Nothing. He just told me about his job, asked about McKenna. Just like I said."

"Ten years later, you're dropping out of your sister's wedding to travel halfway across the country; he must have said something."

"He didn't ask anything, *anything* of me," I offered, my eyes forced quietly downward.

"You're not going to get your money back from your dress. It was a custom design," Adele said, staring ruefully out the window. We had been crammed in this moving mid-life crisis like a lime in the neck of a Corona bottle for most of the afternoon, the shadow of my past shaking me down, and the horrible prospect of Adele's wrath was finally before me.

"I don't understand. Who exactly is this guy?"

"He was just another jerk tied up in knots over her."

"It's more than that," I said.

"Right, you dumped him without warning and got pregnant with Brayden in the blink of an eye. Just another day at the office for you."

"I see," my dad said, his face twisted all up. "That is tough."

"Tough? He was so devastated that he dropped out of school and hopscotched across the country, never to be heard from again. Until now. To ruin my wedding."

The sun dipped briefly behind the clouds and reappeared, stretching its auburn arms.

"You don't remember any of this, Dad?" Adele asked, nearly yelling.

"You girls were into a million things: boys, drama, boys," he said, clearly trying to lighten the mood. "It would have taken an Excel spreadsheet to keep up. I had better things to do. I figured it would work itself out, and it usually did."

"Until now," she said, crossing her arms. "Look at your daughter; she loves it."

I did occasionally fantasize that I annihilated him, made it impossible for him to trust again, dooming all his subsequent relationships, damning him to perpetual bachelorhood and childlessness forever. How couldn't I? He dropped out of school and put a two-thousand-mile stiff arm between us. It may not have been love, but it wasn't nothing. A sense of shame fell over me. My eyes fell into the pleats of my brown corduroy skirt.

"Sorry, did I upset our little hothouse orchid?"

"Hothouse orchid?" my dad asked.

"She means... *you* mean," I said, turning to her, "I'm delicate, right?"

Adele, unable to control herself, sighed dramatically. "Why else would you leave just days after getting this letter? The day before my wedding? That and your ego. This is just like when you hid in Dad's truck when we were kids. I made some crack about living in an apartment, and you bolt. Anything to get away from me. Anything to hurt me."

"What do you think he wants, honey?" Dad asked, holding his hand out to silence Adele.

"He never forgave you," my sister said, answering for me. "He had a whole plan mapped out: marriage, family. Hell, if I know why. The way you walked all over him. From the moment you told him you were pregnant with another man's baby, his dream ended. That baby was supposed to be his, as if he was entitled to the fruits of your uterus."

"You know I can speak for myself, Adele."

"I'm defending you, for God's sake. Me... after what you just did."

"Why did you think he wrote you the letter?" my father offered.

"A decade later? She figures he's still carrying a torch. That he booked it out to Utah, halfway across the country, merely because of you."

"He did," I said, shrugging my shoulders.

"Unbelievable. I'll dispel that little myth for you – he didn't."

"Didn't he?" my dad asked. "It seems like you could draw a pretty straight line from their breakup, her pregnancy, and his leaving, up to and including this letter, which I wasn't aware of and which I do not condone," he said, years too late. "It just seems odd this would all come up again so long after everything happened."

"Really, doing some great parenting there, Dad," Adele said.

"That's enough, Adele," he said, raising his voice.

"The last thing he ever said to me was that he was so brokenhearted—"

"You got knocked up with someone else's baby."

"Could you let me finish?" I paused and waited until I was sure she wouldn't interrupt me, feeling a wave of regret and nausea flush my entire body. "He was furious. The only thing he ever wanted was me, and I had found someone and started a family. I was happy."

The truth was that, at the time, my happiness didn't come from being a newlywed with an infant, but knowing that from over the mountains, across the plains, through one of the tiny poorly-insulated windows of a rented double bungalow, he burned with envy for my life; I savored his jealousy, not only about Brayden and my newborn child, but about my not needing him. Why was his pain so much more potent to me than my new family? Even now, that letter sets loose a sea of storms inside me I hadn't felt since the first taste of freedom after my divorce. The amount of shame that brought me, and continues to bring, is ineffable.

"Romantic nonsense," Adele scoffed, turned, and

stuck out her short, thick tongue at me.

"Anyway, you're not."

"Not what?" I asked.

"Happy. Never have been, never will be," Adele said ruefully.

"That's enough, Adele. Enough. And that was it, until this letter?"

"Yes."

I was lying. He called incessantly after he arrived in Utah. Mostly he just inflamed old wounds, tried to renegotiate how everything went down, as if that would change the outcome somehow. Then, he would accuse me of moving on to Brayden as swiftly as I had because I was unable to be alone. That I didn't exist unless I saw myself reflected in another's eyes. He said that if I learned how to be at peace with myself, I'd be the best friend I ever had. It was nauseating. This naturally led to him trying to convince me to move out there, as if *he* had exiled *me*. He was drunk mostly. When I wouldn't indulge him, he would get furious. "I have my family to raise," I would assert and lower the receiver. Watching Brayden cook dinner and listen to the sound of my child-stranger wail, it certainly didn't feel like I hit any sort of lottery.

"He did ask one odd thing in the letter."

"I knew you were holding out on me," Adele said, with barely suppressed rage and panic.

"At the end of the letter, he asked, how was the child? Not how was my daughter, or McKenna, but how was the child? It reminded me of therapy with Brayden. He would sit on the edge of the couch, bullshitting for forty-five minutes. Then seconds after we confirmed the following week's appointment, he would confess some majorly bad shit and walk directly to the car."

"Like a therapeutic cliffhanger," Adele said with a wry smile.

"Anyway, that's what Chet did in this letter. Spouted a bunch of shit about his job, his mom's funeral, and then threw that in at the end."

I wondered if the word *child* and the memory of this abstract thing-person that barely existed for him, a separate entity from my McKenna, and having taken shape with half my genes and half another's, gave him pause, making him consider how versatile sperm and egg are, how haphazardly they can mingle and mix like partners at a high school prom to create a unique and independent being, negated this supposed originality that he imagined.

"He probably just doesn't know her name," Adele said.

"It's not that surprising," Dad said. "I've heard you two talk about how insensitive men are. As young men, this is probably true, whether it's immaturity or ambition," he said, surrendering a conclusion with a lifting of both hands.

"Immaturity," we said in unison.

"But as a man gets older, grows into himself, lives his life, he softens, becomes sentimental."

"Like Niagara?" Adele said, immediately regretting bringing it up.

"Whereas, in my experience," he said with emphasis, "women seem to get harder."

"He means we turn into bitches," Adele said, cutting through the crap.

"Well, it's because of the world, run by your gender, Dad. Sorry to say, but it's true."

"That's very possible. I'm just saying, it's not out of

the realm of possibility he is grasping something not just about you and what transpired but about that time. Being a young man on the cusp of his life. When everything is possible. Something he thought he lost because of you, or what you symbolize," he said to satisfy Adele before she could object. "He'd be, let's see, in his late thirties, well into his career. Do you know if he has kids now?" Dad asked, settling back in his seat.

I shook my head. "Why?"

"Did you freak out when you turned forty, Dad, and maybe buy some kind of, I don't know, cliched sports car?" Adele joked.

He waved her away, immediately annoyed. It was clear he had something he wanted to say, something he had put serious thought into, maybe without even realizing it.

Regaining himself, he said, "Men get reflective at that age. Actually, forty was no problem. Came and went. I thought, 'Midlife crisis my ass.' Something made up by television or shrinks to line their pockets. I was already grey, had a good-paying job. You guys had turned out nicely. Then I turned forty-one."

"Then you bought the car," Adele interrupted.

"Can you forget about the damn car for a second?" he asked, drilling her down with his eyes. She shrunk in the seat to the size of a mouse. It was satisfying. He took a deep breath. "It's hard to describe. I didn't buy the car," he said slowly, deliberately. "Or chase younger women. I made a list," he paused, peering inside for several seconds as if the list was still there, "of all the things that needed fixing around the house as if I were going to sell it. Closet doors that needed replacing, blinds that needed upgrading, fresh carpeting, that crack in the patio that needed filling in, walls that needed painting."

"Were you going to sell the house?" I asked, troubled by this idea without knowing why. I never cared for my father's house or thought of it as home, but the idea of him selling it sent a wave of panic over me.

"No," he said casually. "But I spent nearly a year fixing all kinds of shit, went through all kinds of cash, exhausting myself, diligently crossing things off this list."

"I remember that," Adele offered cautiously.

"Why did you do that?" I asked.

"I don't know exactly. I think about it now and then. You girls had moved out. I had tried twice and failed twice at marriage. I wasn't exactly setting the world on fire at work. Wasn't management material, I suppose, not that I hadn't tried on a couple of occasions. I didn't have any hobbies. No great aspirations. Something said, 'Your house has served its purpose, sell it, and buy a townhouse.'"

"And?"

"*Wait*," he said quietly.

"Wait?"

"For something to reveal itself, for the finish line to appear on the horizon, for it to be over, to ride things out, a sign, death, maybe, I don't know exactly."

"That's ludicrous. Your life is far from over," Adele objected.

"I know that now. I obviously didn't sell the house."

"That stuff isn't rational, Adele," I said, annoyed at my sister's obtuseness.

"You would know," she said, staring out the window.

"Then what happened?" I asked, sincerely curious.

"Nothing. It passed, I guess."

The sound of his voice, added to what I knew about

his response to his retirement, said otherwise.

"Well, that is not one hundred percent true. I noticed two things. Two small things. One, I began to look forward to spring rather than autumn."

"I don't remember that," Adele said.

"I do," I said, lying.

"I thought you might," he said, although I had no idea why, but it felt significant even if it wasn't – much as I wanted it to be. "The melting of the snow, the blossoming of the flowers. I found myself longing for it the second Christmas was over. As if there was a tree inside of me every winter waiting to reawaken. Having a sense of relief, a real warmth for it when it arrived."

"And the second?" I asked eagerly.

"I found I had become a morning person. After all those years of staying up late, waiting for the sun to go down, drowning in the horizon, to fix a cocktail and feel relaxed, now I was going to bed at 9:30 and getting up at five, five-thirty."

"I don't know if Chet's at that point yet."

"You don't know why he's reaching out. You don't even know him. Couldn't it be that she was just an asshole? That she treated him poorly, and he hasn't gotten over it and wants to tell her she's a fucking horrible person?"

"Willow, how serious were you guys? Before you can get started, Dell, sleeping together does not mean they were serious."

Adele let out a loud, sarcastic cackle. I rolled my eyes.

"He was nuts about her like they all are. She couldn't have cared less, she never did."

"That's not true."

"You cared until you didn't." Before I could object,

she added, "Until you got what you needed. Then you did what you always did. Acted cold and distant until they broke up with you, satisfied it was their imperative, what a great trick... or if they wouldn't take the hint, cheat on them."

"That's not true."

"You cheated on Brayden."

"Christ," our father moaned.

"That was different."

"And how did he find out? Didn't you leave your computer up with the fucking emails on display for him to find and then act dumbfounded when he responded like anyone would?"

"A man's past is very important to him," my dad said with emphasis, diving back inside again, stopping until he had our attention before proceeding. "I would get done with all that work on the house, dog-tired, and just sit on the patio, drinking a cocktail or three, thinking about my life. Places I had been, friends, and especially all the women I had been with."

"I'm not sure I want to hear this," Adele said.

"I may be your father, but I'm also a man."

Adele shrugged with a pout and refused to look at him.

"I had shared my life, my time with these people. Some for only a few months. Others only a night or two. In some cases, things went on for years. Young women, old women. Affairs with married women. Even a couple of hookers. Did they think about me? Did I impact their life in any way? Good or otherwise? I was willing to negotiate. In the end, time is all you have."

"Married women? Hookers, Dad?" Adele asked, grimacing, tossing a look of disgust back to me, which I ignored. "Doesn't seem like the man I now know."

"At the time, these women were so important to me, every decision, every fight, life or death. They seemed epic in the story of my life, and now their significance had been chipped away, eroded by time, a cliff on the ocean battered away by the wind and indifference. Don't worry, I won't say Niagara Falls. Was it a reflection on them? Or me? Maybe. We seem to choose so indiscriminately. Throw our hearts so carelessly. No different than how we choose our careers or where we live," he added parenthetically. "Maybe that's why they seemed to mean so little? Thinking back, most of them seem no more memorable than a newspaper signifying a date, time, and place."

"I'm sure whoever you're referring to would be very flattered," Adele said, still refusing to look at him.

"I don't mean it like that," he said, motioning for the can of beer. She obliged. He took a quick sip of it and handed it back. "For all I went through with these people, the break ups and arguments, the late night rough and tumbles, the passion, the marriages, and divorces, all that was left was a neutral recognition that, yes, this happened. That was the real surprise. I can see you girls don't understand. There was some pain I never thought would heal, pain that was blocking all the joy in my life like the moon blocking the sun during an eclipse, and yet it was gone. Time seems to have excised the pain but, in the process, stole the joy as well. I didn't expect the joy to fade. It was a startling and lonesome realization."

Staring at the side of my father's face, I realized how much I didn't know about his life.

As a child, you assume you are the center of your parent's universe, the origin from which there is no regress, never realizing you joined the novel of their lives, ignorant to their entire history of joys and heartbreaks, triumphs and tragedies, banalities, and that they too – once upon a time – were born bringing joy (and an end and new start) to their parents lives, and that their parents had a life and so on and so on. Much of this is my mother's fault. For her, the moment I was born everything else ceased to matter. I was the project of her life. All was prelude. Of this, I am certain. Who my father was when I made my grand entrance, I did not know. He was married unhappily. And the story of his saving Adele from a terrible upbringing is canon at this point. What did I mean to him when I entered his life? Did I change the trajectory of his journey? Or was his absence at the instant I took my first breath some indication I was unwanted, even unloved? That I was a mere speed bump, a change he resisted? Perhaps that was why I had given so little inquiry to the narrative that came before.

"Anyway, I'm not saying all this to get your sympathy. It just seems like we expend so much energy searching for, getting, and disposing of love. Without thinking of the cost, it takes. Maybe you were really important to this Chet. Maybe he's reappraising his life, and he felt he missed out on something. Perhaps he needs to clarify some things."

"You really think that's what's going on," I asked.

"I don't know the man."

"Please don't say she is the one who got away," Adele moaned.

"Don't minimize your sister's situation. Everyone has their own path to negotiate," he said with a wag of his finger.

My dad's words seemed august, full of fought-for wisdom, and were having an effect even on Adele.

"Did you tell Mark about this letter? Or about this little trip?" she asked, making me wish I could roll the window down and drop her out. "Mark? Your man? Fat, unattractive guy? Worships you?"

I was taken aback. It hadn't even crossed my mind. Christ, in all my ruminations about Chet (and Brayden, and that drama from so long ago), I hadn't given Mark a second thought.

"I didn't think so."

Our father glared back at me, letting me know without uttering a syllable this needed to be remedied, that he was disappointed in me, neutralizing all the goodwill that had been built up over the course of the conversation.

"What business is it of his?" I asked with a toss of my hair.

"Well, he is your boyfriend, isn't he?"

"I suppose," I said.

"Well, you are sleeping with him, aren't you?"

"Yes, we're sleeping together," I said and, after a beat, added, "I wish there was a better word for that particular designation. Boyfriend sounds too juvenile when you're an adult."

"For once, I agree with you. Amazing, right?"

"It's so different when you're young. Men were everywhere, and I was mad about all of them," I said, feeling like a character in an F. Scott Fitzgerald short story, "and never noticed how many of them were losers," feeling very much back in my life.

"Or didn't care."

"Fair enough." Rethinking what she said, I added, "I'm not sure. It's not that I didn't know they weren't up to par.

It was just so easy to whitewash their shortcomings. He's selfish, but he's fun. Or he's too into sports, but he's great in bed. He's ugly but good to me. Anyway, when one disappointed you, another one came floating down the river. There was never a shortage of men back then. And they all adored me."

"That was the real prerequisite."

"Now time has left me with a bunch of overgrown teenagers; men with no careers, middling lovers, with no interest in marriage... not that I'm interested by the way. Never again. I make that crystal clear, and no one objects, which shouldn't bother me but, of course, does."

"Are you forgetting where we are going?" she asked, holding up her gargantuan engagement ring, which twinkled in the mid-afternoon sun, brushing it awkwardly against her cheek.

I was shamed into silence.

"They do seem to enjoy television and beer more than sex, don't they?"

"I *never* saw that coming."

"Seriously, what the fuck?"

I saw my father suppressing a chuckle.

"Not with the doggedness with which they attempted to pry their way into my pants for so long. I could have had my face blown off in a war, but as long as my vagina worked, it was a go."

Adele let out a long, deep belly laugh.

"You ladies don't know what you want," he finally offered.

"How so?" Adele challenged.

"You're either complaining it's all we want, or we don't want it enough. And somehow, we're the ones constantly obsessed with sex?" he said, dismissing us both.

"Still, not telling Mark?" Adele said, comically wincing.

"I can't talk to him about Brayden, much less Chet. The context would be lost on him. Examining the rings of a fallen oak isn't the same as experiencing what that tree lived through."

"The generational shifts of its existence," Dad offered.

Adele shook her head before saying, "You're not that into him, are you?"

"There's just no spark. I mean the sex is serviceable. I've even climaxed a couple of times. Or so I've told him under duress. Sorry, Dad, you have modern women. But he's good to me. Not exactly the version of my life I had envisioned when I got divorced. But I can't be too nasty. I need the guy to watch Tank when I head out to Salt Lake."

"You're terrible."

"I know."

"But not necessarily the worst thing," my dad added.

"No?"

"All the grand passions in my life have been too intense to last. And if they did, they'd kill you."

"I know all about that," Adele said softly.

"Sometimes I think we do it – sex – because that's what you do in relationships. It's written into the contract."

"It's unavoidable," Dad said.

"Just get it over with and move on," Adele added.

"Make sure to say that right before you cross the threshold on your wedding night," I said.

We all laughed.

"You know what I mean."

"Sadly, I do."

"He's just on me all the time. To move things forward.

To get more serious. *We eat together, we share a bed.* As if that means anything. After we had only been dating a month, he wanted to know if I loved him."

"The direct, full-frontal assault," Adele said.

"I didn't even love Brayden."

"You didn't?" Dad asked, sincerely surprised and more than a little disenchanted with his youngest.

"My entire adult life, men have bullied me: into sex, relationships, flattered me into things I didn't want to do, instead of allowing these things to progress naturally. After six months, he suggested that he and his son move into my basement."

"Seriously?" Adele asked.

"His custody shit wasn't going well. I made such a big deal about it he'll never bring it up again," I said with a laugh. "That's why he'll be watching Tank."

"You'll have to tell him about the trip first."

"Do I have to?" I said, taking a long swig from the can of beer.

We passed an island of trees and brush huddling together, rising inexplicably from the earth.

"And this *has* to be done in person?" Adele said, her eyes fixed straight forward on the highway, her left hand fiddling with the radio dial, confessing more hurt than she meant to.

After a few minutes, our speed decreased dramatically as we pulled into a Super America, which appeared like an explosively-lit-consumer-brick Mecca.

"I need to take a squirt, you two need a break?" Dad asked.

We did, and he parked the car.

"Where are you off to?" Adele asked suspiciously, as

I climbed out of the backseat of the car, walking opposite the gas station.

"To call Mark. Isn't that what you want me to do?" I asked. My dad disappeared into the gas station.

Adele looked at me, hard and long.

"Don't think I haven't noticed this entire conversation has been about you even though we're on the way to my wedding rehearsal, a wedding you dropped out of the day before, in a completely unnecessary way. Don't say anything. Just go call your boyfriend and ask him to watch your cat as you go run off to extinguish your guilt. He won't realize how selfish you are until it's too late," she said and walked away, joining my father.

Crossing the parking lot, I sat on the curb opposite the entrance and smoked. I was near tears. I had two cigarettes before calling Mark. He picked up on the first ring.

"Hey, doll, how are things going?" he asked, exhaling hard, no doubt lowering his large frame down into a sitting position.

"Uncomfortable as always. The backseat of my dad's car is not exactly a luxury ride, cool as it appears from the outside. It's like being in a submarine. It's nice to see my dad, though. Although it's hard to have an unguarded conversation with Rasputin monitoring every word from the cockpit."

"Are you there already?"

"No, we're just taking a pit stop," I said. Kicking a shoe off I continued, "It's been what it normally is. Adele clamoring for our dad's attention. It's embarrassing. Like, we've heard the stories, Adele. Oh, but things took a turn when my dad found out she has an IUD."

"What kind of turn?"

"He really wants her to have a baby, and she really doesn't. That was a whole back-and-forth. I think I was the favorite in that exchange. First time for everything, I guess. And then I found out that my dad nearly sold the house after Adele and I had moved out. He started making this list of things that needed fixing: windows, closet doors. Totally weird and unexpected to hear."

"Doesn't seem so weird; the house was probably too big for just him," he offered cautiously.

"That wasn't it, though," I said, popping my other shoe off. "He didn't want to sell it. I mean, he didn't, so… It was like he was worried that his life had stalled, or he was haunted by being alone, death. So, he went about doing all the stuff on this list to distract himself."

"Sounds like he had a lot to say to the both of you. It could be something you could expand on if you took him to lunch."

"I said I'd think about it. You don't have to push so hard, Mark. Sometimes, you can just listen."

His silence was ripe with hurt feelings, no doubt wondering how it was possible that he could love someone so damn difficult when it came so easily for him. If only I knew what was right in front of me, life could be so wonderful. It disgusted me that I knew so accurately what he was thinking (no matter how very misplaced). I stared at my socks, unsure if I was more bitter at how incorrect he was, how easy he was to read (even the stubborn silence over the phone), or at how effortlessly love came for other people. Perhaps, as was usually the case, I was the problem. I took another puff of my cigarette. "It reminded me of my last week of college. Everyone was partying, having their last hurrah before being shoved off into the world.

I had a million invites but zero interest. In fact, I went to exactly none."

"No?"

"Instead, I walked the entire campus. Thinking about all I had been through; classes, boyfriends, the friendships built, what I had been through, and where I was going. I wanted to demarcate that a certain part of my life was over, you know?"

"I do," he said, no doubt marveling at how unpredictable I was, even at that age. It was hard not to be seduced by the soft-focus lens he viewed me through. To him, I was a museum piece, perfect, behind glass, unalterable.

"I even walked to this cemetery a mile or so away that this boy and I used to frequent."

"A cemetery?"

"We'd bring a blanket, a bottle of wine, talk about life, death, our parents, standard sophomore-year bullshit. We'd get a little buzzed and wander through the tombstones, pat the heads of angels. Close as I'm getting to heaven. There were tombs going back to the Civil War."

"Screw."

"If you say so, sure. The French say sex and death are related, so you almost have to. It seemed like the cool, edgy thing to do. You'd have to go to college to get it, I think. Ugh, you're jealous," I said, stubbed the cigarette out on the curb, and lit another.

"How did your dad respond? When you told him all this?"

"Oh, nothing. I mean, I didn't."

"It seems like a way to make a connection, but I wouldn't want to push so..." he said, trailing off resentfully.

"Wait, isn't it your day with Mitch? I totally spaced.

I can let you go," I said, starting to slip my shoes back on and stand up. The tobacco in my throat and lungs was foul and sickening.

"He's outside with friends."

I lowered myself back down and followed Adele through the tall panes of glass of the gas station, from the magazine rack, halfway down the candy aisle, and over to the freezers until I could no longer see her. She reappeared next to my father at the register. I followed their entire exchange, Adele pointing towards the parking lot and me (no doubt complaining that they were nearly finished when I hadn't yet entered), our father counseling her to relax, patting himself down, then turning to Adele to cover what he was short. Exhaling, I pushed my words out like a hard, obstinate shit. "I've got a little favor to ask."

"Anything," he said unconvincingly.

"Do you think you could take care of Tank for a couple of days?"

"Sure, where are you going?" he said, reverting to his lapdog self.

"I'm embarking on a little road trip to Salt Lake City," I said as playfully and dismissively as possible.

"Salt Lake City! Need any company?"

"Then who would take care of Tank? He needs his insulin shot twice a day, and I can't trust his medical needs to just anyone. You know how specific they are," I said, taking a deep, silent breath.

"You're not going to see some guy, are you?"

Perhaps he would discover my selfishness sooner than Adele had predicted. Neither Mark nor I spoke for some time. Closing my eyes tight, Adele's words echoing in my mind, I finally said, "Someone from my past reached out."

"So, it is an ex. If it was a childhood girlfriend or some long-lost family member, you would have said so," he said, more to himself than me. "This person from your past, what does he want?"

"You mean does he want me?"

"That was unnecessary and cruel, even for you," he said and hung up.

Wriggling my feet back into my shoes, I trudged through the parking lot and into the gas station. Not seeing my father or Adele, I ducked into the women's room where I began to reapply my lipstick. Adele loathed makeup: spending money on it, using it, what it represented (especially since it worked so effectively on the opposite sex), and never tired of telling me so. She never learned how to apply it properly or with any nuance (and her features, the too-thin chin, the wide forehead, and sallow eyes seemed to work against her), and she appeared, at best, like a clown and at worst, a fraud – but she could never swallow her pride to ask her younger, prettier sister for help. Dropping the lipstick back into my purse, I considered touching up my eyeliner when I heard the double toot of a car horn. I knew it was Adele.

Exiting the women's room, and before I had made my way through the gas station, I could see her in the car, leaning over, hand hovering over the horn. Before I could react, she pushed down again. Toot-toot. Toot-toot. As I approached the car, Adele pushed the door open with her right foot, her hands placed firmly on the dashboard, refusing to exit the car. She had been taking the pole position since we were legally old enough to sit in the front seat. Had I been a more forward person, I would have stood my ground until she acquiesced, getting out of the car and letting me in first. It was pointless. I wedged my way into the casket of the backseat as she cracked open a new beer, no doubt annoyed she'd have to share that delicious mixture of barley and hops with me, and we pulled back onto the lonely stretched-out highway.

Three years ago, Brayden and I divorced. With nowhere to turn, McKenna and I moved in with my father to regroup, save our resources, and begin a new chapter of our lives. There were no visionary plans. I had no list of suppressed dreams my marriage had kept at arm's length. In fact, I was petrified of my new existence. I couldn't imagine anything outside the circumscribed boundaries of work, meals, and sleep. Adele, on the other hand, appeared to be having a nervous breakdown as a result of this arrangement. "You're having a family without me," she often repeated. It was just like Adele to transform the trauma of my divorce into an existential threat to her life. On top of that, a few weeks after I had moved in with him, without fanfare or notice, he retired from the truck-driving company. This was it for him, as he had ceased working for the security company some years earlier.

I had never thought about my father retiring or the implications of retirement until he came home with that small cardboard box tucked under his arm. "One box can't be all a person has to show for thirty years of service, can it?" he said, leaning against the kitchen doorway and watching me with wild anticipation swimming in his eyes. I stood silently across from him without the capability to respond. It wasn't just that I didn't know what to say, how our back and forth should manifest itself (obviously, there was a myriad of things I *could* say, much like when someone loses a loved one, one could say, *'I'm sorry for your loss,'* but

I wanted to avoid that particular iceberg), but tragically I had no idea what he *needed* to hear in order to comfort him (sympathy is more specific than you'd think).

"I worked there for over a quarter of a century, and do you know all I have to show for it?"

"One box?" I ventured.

"Can you believe that?" he answered, full of sorrow and surprise.

This happened nightly for several weeks. Just he and I. It was the first time I realized what an oversized presence Adele played, not only in his life but in all our lives. It had left me like an atrophied leg, suddenly being called upon to bear the weight of an entire body. Two bodies, really. I was not prepared.

In a certain respect, my lack of an adequate response was irrelevant. He wasn't addressing me. He was addressing time, the retreating hours. It was as if he had suddenly become aware that the sand in the hourglass had shifted heavily downward. In the process of supporting his family, his job had stolen the majority of his life without asking his permission and without his noticing. What's worse, he had an inkling that, if he had given his permission, it was on some contract he hadn't realized he had signed. This shocked him too. All the usual signifiers: grey hair, elbow and back pain, depleting funds, grown children, and divorces had been somehow ignored. It visibly pummeled him. He was like a plane shot out of the sky. One night, when he had had too much to drink, he emerged from his bedroom and stood in the doorframe for a long, lonely time. "The horses are racing toward the horizon, and I can't stop them. I think I'm going crazy." He re-entered his bedroom, shut the door. This frightened McKenna. It frightened me too.

    He never fully recovered. From retiring, or the insight that the majority of his life was behind him, unchangeable, open to interpretation to be sure, but locked up. What was curious was how much didn't change. He didn't develop a severe drinking or gambling problem or become a political radical for the left or right. He didn't dye his hair to its original black or tear off to far east Asia in search of a wife to fill the vacant spot beside him in the car (and bed), to cook his meals and do his laundry, until he crossed the finish line. Conversely, he wasn't inspired to make positive change, either. There were no activist causes or drawing up a cliched bucket list: no sky diving or taking a long put-off trip to Europe. His interest in his granddaughter (and me) remained the same. There was just a kind of melancholic grandeur about him – like he had boarded a one-way train and was content to watch the world pass by until its final stop. In practical terms, he spent most of his time at home, visiting the grocery store every Sunday (and apparently the legion on Wednesdays) and indulging in every sporting event on the three television sets and two radios set strategically in every room (including the bathroom), with no visitors outside of Adele (and me and McKenna once we moved out) and underpaying a neighbor's boy to shovel in the winter and mow in the summer. That and spoiling his dog Coco whom he had adopted without warning one winter day and seemed to genuinely adore. Everyone else, family and friends, had ebbed away once he had brought home the raggedy box from Piper Trucking that he had stuffed next to his closet and had remained a problem for some time.

    "Are you nervous?" he asked Adele playfully.

I took a sip of the beer, wedging it between my legs. It was cold.

Adele shrugged. "I don't know. Not really. We haven't been together long enough for me to be nervous."

"John's a good guy," my dad said. "Has a solid job. Well-mannered. Knows his college ball. Willow, for god's sake, don't Bogart that beer."

"I'm not a Bogart," I said, handing the nearly empty beer to my father, who frowned at the weight of the can, mumbling 'uh-huh,' before finishing it off.

"The hell you're not. With beer, pizza, conversation, time. You've always taken more than your share. An armchair psychologist might say you're trying to make up for a lack you feel in other areas of your life. Eh, don't get all hurt. I'm just teasing," Adele said, reaching her left hand back towards me. I slapped it playfully away.

"Anyway, you stayed with Scott way too long before marrying him. Things never work out when people do that, instead of getting married a year or two in."

"Why's that?" Adele asked.

"I don't know. But it always works out that way. There's a reason couples like that wait so long and why that label dooms them."

I thought about Brayden, Mark, Chet, and men in a generalized way. Every interaction with them resembled what I was taught about history in junior high: that it was predetermined, rocketed with undeterrable momentum, toward a target – with no room for coincidence. And even coincidence folded into the eventual narrative. A banal conversation headed toward that moment of crisis when you were asked out on a date, that date poised towards the bedroom, dating to marriage, marriage to babies, and so forth.

These relationships, once forged, had their own subsets for living arrangements: from spending the night to moving in together, renting to buying, and once you bought, another subset: something affordable, upgrading to something larger (with the onset of a family), and downsizing when the kids leave. Would my relationship with Mark follow this seemingly unbreakable (and pedestrian yet heartbreaking) trajectory? Did I have other options? I knew that I didn't want to marry Mark or anyone ever again. I barely wanted to date him or anyone. If so, what were they? And if not, why did I proceed to see anyone?

"There it is," Adele said, pointing to the pocket-sized church surrounded by nothing but open space and an exhausted-looking cemetery, headstones leaning this way and that. The empty eyes of the angels poised mournfully skyward, wondering why their Lord had forsaken them. It was seemingly plopped down in the middle of Covertown's mellowing cornfields as if it were carried along and abandoned by some sad, shrinking glacier.

"How did you pick this church anyway?" I asked as it approached.

"John's whole family is from here."

"I knew that."

"Uh-huh," she grunted.

In truth, I knew very little about John or anyone she had dated, including Scott. Not that there were that many. I knew that she seemed to have an endless array of complaints about him: that he was uncommunicative, humorless, obsessive about cleanliness, and played with her nipples the incorrect way, whatever the fuck that meant.

Pulling into the Church parking lot, John's mother, Agnes, stood on the front steps of the church, arms crossed, a nun's stern expression on her bone-tight face. She was a staunch Roman Catholic from generations of Covertown farmers (and all Republicans to boot). Her distaste for small talk and her dour attitude hung on her like a pungent body odor and assured you didn't stay in her vicinity for too long.

"Jesus," I let out.

"He'd climb down from the cross and split town if he saw her coming," my dad said with suppressed mirth, for fear she might somehow hear him through the closed windows. "It's starting already, Adele, and you're not even married."

"Just try and get along with her or ignore her completely. Either one is fine with me. I'm not marrying her family."

"Oh, honey. You are," Dad said.

"Can we not talk about this at this very moment?"

As Dad put the car into park, he sat back. "Do you remember Carys and Andy?"

"Of course, they only lived next to us for forever?"

"They giggled their way through their entire wedding ceremony."

"Nerves. End of story."

"That's what the consensus was," my dad whispered.

"I'm not saying it. I refuse," said Adele. "It's stupid superstitious nonsense that you've said at every wedding we've ever been to."

"Willow?"

Nodding gravely, I responded, "When you laugh, you're not in control of yourself. It's spontaneous. It's a sign of the presence of the devil. So stupid," I muttered into my chest.

"It's the first thing I thought of when they divorced."

"Everyone out. Wait, wait, gum, does anyone have any gum? She's going to talk to us about the drinking," she said, doing her best to shove all the beer cans under the seat. Agnes was already moving towards the car like a righteous avenging missile.

"I don't," I said, opening and closing my purse.

"Lecture. She's going to lecture us," he said, reaching past Adele, checking the glove compartment, pulling out a smushed and worn pack of Big Red.

"How old is this?" Adele asked, glaring at us while shoving a stick into his mouth.

"Does it matter? I'm not gonna kiss her," he said, waving the pack away, chuckling to himself, exiting the car. I took a piece as well. Adele got out of the car with that horrible sense of inevitability, walking towards Agnes, who immediately asked, "Do I smell beer on your breath?" It took all my power not to burst into laughter. Chomping loudly, Adele shook her head, "I don't think so." Agnes stared Adele down, unconvinced.

"If the priest sees any drinking, any bottles, or smells any booze on anyone's breath on church premises, he will not perform the ceremony."

We stood across from Agnes in a kind of familial Mexican standoff without saying a word.

"I see you all understand or don't speak a word of God's English."

"We understand," Adele said. "Of course, none of us would ever do anything to jeopardize this beautiful dinner and certainly not the ceremony. Not in a place of worship."

Agnes turned, and we all followed her into the church. My dad gave me a mischievous smile and a shake of his head as we entered.

The wedding rehearsal was short and utterly charmless. I did as I was told, and no mention was made of my being ousted from the grand event. I watched Adele as she nervously memorized where she was to go at every moment of the ceremony. Was this what she wanted? To join her life to this man she seemed only ostensibly to love and this family that seemed, at best, indifferent to her? The moment it ended, my father and I made our way outside the church to the top of the tiny staircase. John and the wedding party made repeated trips to my dad's car to chug beers. Adele was nowhere to be seen. Besides that, there was nothing in any direction. It was silent. The sun was threatening to go down, lending the fields and cemetery an air of autumnal heat. Agnes slipped up next to my father.

"It has come to my attention that you may have beer in your trunk."

"Oh yeah," he said, staring at the horizon.

"Everyone keeps congregating around your car. I would like you to take me there and open it," she said, about to take a first step towards his car.

"There's no beer in my trunk."

"I beg to differ," she said, stepping back.

"Wanna bet?" my dad asked, continuing to stare at the horizon.

"Excuse me?"

"I'll bet you twenty dollars, there's no beer in my trunk. If you agree to that, we can walk over there. If you're right, I'll give you twenty dollars, and you can dump all the beer, cancel the wedding, whatever God commands. If I'm right, you owe me."

Her face puckered up tight as if she had sucked on

one huge, angry demon-infused lemon and turned bright crimson.

"I will not," she said, turned on her heel, and marched back into the church.

I knew he was furious.

"What a dickhead."

I chuckled. This was the gravest insult my father could call you when he was fuming. Dickhead. *What a dickhead.*

"That's gonna cause some problems," I said, shaking my head. "Of course, it's all in the front seat."

"What a dickhead." He smirked. Then his face went blank. "Relax, I'm not mad. I know I pushed her to include you."

"I felt weird about it," I said, lowering my head. "I didn't know anyone in the wedding party and having to tag along to dress fittings, the tastings, the bachelorette party. Everyone knew she didn't really want me there."

"I've always wanted you two to be closer than you are, especially since both your mothers passed. Even before. It's my prerogative and my failure."

I didn't know what to say to that.

"You can't leave any other day?" he asked, tipping back, leaning on the handrail. "Just because you're making this gesture, driving halfway across the country, doesn't mean you're going to get the outcome you're expecting."

"I know."

"Breaking a man's heart, no matter how badly, does not require a lifetime's worth of penance. I don't know what you're hoping to accomplish—"

"I had an abortion once, how about that?" I said. "Didn't even tell the stupid son-of-a-bitch. Deprived a man of his child and got knocked up with McKenna a few months later. That's why I'm going out there to give the man the courtesy of the conversation he never got to have. That we should have had in the first place."

Our conversation ended with the abruptness of a car crash. I glanced up at him, petrified. It was apparent he had not known the true wretchedness of what I did to Chet. Adele had never told him, had never given up the long-held secret that I had disposed of his first grandchild. I was shocked. A warmth, a true warmth that I had never felt for my sister, came over me.

"Come on," he said, motioning towards the car with his head. I stood, fighting back tears. "Nah, come on."

We trudged down the stairs, across the dirt parking lot, and to my father's beautiful yellow 1976 Datsun 280Z. He pulled out two beers and handed me one. We drank them, slowly, silently until they, and the sun, were gone.

"There was something else that happened when I turned forty-one. Something I didn't want to say in front of your sister," he said. Two groomsmen headed towards the car; my dad waved them off. "When I was fixing up the house, I came across one of your art books. I was exhausted and just started flipping through it. It fell to Picasso's *Frugal Repast*. Knocked me right on my ass. I thought, there it is – my first marriage."

I squinted. "You have a copy of that in the hallway."

"All those years," he nodded. "Just a reminder of. I don't know. Of how things were. Of how not to be. Loss. Regret. Not to hold on. To be better," he said, trailing off. "I just wanted you to know that."

"That would kill Adele," I said, looking up at his face.

"I don't know why. She hated her mother."

"Now I feel like creeping through the house to see

what other secret messages I've missed," I said.

He laughed silently.

"Everything we do and say tells people who we are, honey. We just don't pay attention. Yet, somehow, we are always surprised by the person right in front of us."

We opened two more beers and drank them until they were gone.

"Think they're done in there? This place gives me the creeps."

"I'll go find out," I said.

"Just know that should you change your mind and decide not to go, Adele will still want you here, even if you're not in the wedding."

I nodded, fighting back tears once again.

At the top of the stairs, Agnes had appeared. I was still holding my beer. As I was about to enter the church, her eyes narrowed. "Careful with the holy water. Wouldn't want you to get burned before your sister's big day."

I laughed out loud for the first time since I had received Chet's letter. "You're a spiteful bitch, lady. I dig that." Passing through the large wooden church doors and past my sister's fiancé, I shouted over my shoulder, "You would have lost twenty bucks to my dad. Never bet against a Hennings, lady."

Chapter Two
Rushing the Horizon

"Put your life in order."
- Sophocles, Antigone

I watched as the large, unmoving barge of clouds held the sunrise beneath them in an attempt to brand the flat brown earth. The thick marijuana smoke, a scent I associated with youth, depression, and sex on deserted roads in the backseat of cars, consumed the vehicle. Savoring it for a second more, I tucked the lizard-shaped pipe under the driver's seat and cracked the window. The sweet vapor was sucked into the atmosphere along with the years. It was strange how often my thoughts found their way back to that time. Strange, because I was but a hollow-eyed apparition, floating through the hallways, petrified, obsessing over the size of my breasts, sleeves covering the cuts rushing up my arms like dancing water, wanting nothing more than to be consumed by some beefy, awkward boy. Why was that? Why did that time hold such sway over my timid imagination? The only thing I can surmise is that, troubled and alone as I was, my life was circumscribed, filled with less ambiguity. Once the car was properly aired out, I rolled the window back up and tried to ignore my hot, tired eyes.

Before I could decide on the next CD to play, my cell phone began to buzz. Glancing at the dashboard clock, I rolled my eyes. 8:37. It was the third call in as many hours. Again, my dad. Well, to be more accurate, McKenna from my dad's cell phone. At this point, I had resisted her life-or-death pleas for her own phone; Brayden would soon crack. First, she asked permission to have a toaster strudel for breakfast. Then, feigning panic because she had forgotten her piano music at her father's and wouldn't be able to practice. *Then practice your clarinet,* I told her, lowering the phone to my lap.

"What do you need now, McKenna?"

"Coco," she began, dissolving into a mess of tears, incomprehensible yips, and monosyllables.

"Slow down, honey. I can't understand you." I stabbed unsuccessfully at the radio, throwing the blower on high, a full-throated slap of hot air catching me in the face. Her tears and hyperventilating immediately receded into the distance, swallowed up until I couldn't hear her at all. "Coco, what?" I asked, pushing the phone tightly up against my ear until it burned.

There was a shuffling like sandpaper against concrete before it dropped into a chasm of silence. I snapped off the blower and radio, my eyes darting from the highway to the radio and blower, as if McKenna's voice could be located somewhere between the grey pavement, burning sky, and the panel of my car. Eventually, my father's voice filled the emptiness.

"Willow?"

"What's going on, Dad?" I considered exiting at the next off-ramp, turning my heap of a car around, and calling the entire venture off. "Is everything all right?"

"The dog caught a chipmunk."

My eyes widened at the glowering horizon, the only witness to my anticipation. "And?"

"Nothing really."

"Dad?" It was the kind of answer he gave when something was really wrong; when he was nervous and didn't want to answer.

"It wasn't quite dead."

"Lord," I said, raising my foot off the pedal, watching as another off-ramp raised its eyebrows at me before it passed by with a shrug.

"You know Coco. She chomps at it a couple of times and is done with it. I had to get the shovel to put it out of its misery."

"And McKenna saw this," I said soberly. A long, slow drink would have been great right about now.

There was an extended pause.

"You don't understand. That thing was taunting her for hours."

"Who was?"

"The chipmunk. It was the damnedest thing," he said, exhaling and surely shaking his head in that particular way, bemused by the situation, as if he were outside it. I could see him as clearly in my mind as if he was sitting right next to me. I brought the car back up to cruising speed. "It would pop its head out of the end of the drainpipe, cackle, dash back in, and start cackling again. Coco nearly broke her jaw trying to bite through the thing. And you know how obsessive the poor girl is. She sat there for hours, staring and whining. Eventually, I took matters into my own hands."

"What does that mean?" I asked, my right hand pushing through my purse until I found the pack of cigarettes and teased out a cigarette. I cracked the window, the universe letting out an agonizing scream. "And be exact," I said, lighting up, since I already knew the final result, if not the method.

"I got the ladder, shoved the hose into the top of the gutter, cranked the spigot—"

"For real?" I coughed out a large plume of smoke. "You flooded it out?"

"The second she saw it, she snapped it up, and that was that. I don't feel bad," he said, rushing all his words together.

"That's not the issue, Dad," I said, still coughing.

"Of course, I had to scoop it up with the shovel and force her to follow me to the garbage. Otherwise, she would park herself at the drainpipe all day."

"Smart dog," I said, heaving and chortling all at once.

"Hey," he barked sharply, my dad once again.

"Except that wasn't that, Dad. Your granddaughter had to watch you beat what was left of its life out of it with a shovel," I said, lowering my voice as if she were with me in the car. "You should have made her go into the house while you finished the thing off, at least. Christ, she's going to her aunt's wedding today."

For years after McKenna was born, I suffered terrible insomnia. Laying there, night after night, as the darkness crept in, listening to Brayden snore, I would catalog a telephone book's worth of 'what ifs.' What if she doesn't wake up? What if she's snatched out of her room while we sleep? What if she gets struck by a car? Gets on the wrong bus after school? How did any parent get through the day knowing their child was navigating the ice-cold world, unprotected, unaware of the innumerable catastrophic and well-camouflaged traps waiting for them? And it wasn't simply the calamitous life-altering shit splashed across the newspapers and television every day that kept me awake at night. It was the mundane little heartbreaks and humiliations, both as a person and especially as a woman, that wrecked me. *You look heavier, too tall. Not pretty enough. Too smart. Too loud. Too quiet. You know you want to. Do it for me.* One at a time they were manageable, snowflakes in early spring. Melting upon impact. But without a strong sense of self, one I needed to provide, one perhaps I didn't know how to give, they would accumulate until, little by little, they would bury her alive. Or maybe that's how it happened to me. That was another concern. What if I crippled her with my inadequacies?

When I expressed my concerns to Brayden, he would either toss platitudes at me – *the only thing that's truly yours is your mistakes, failure builds character* – or shrug and say nothing at all. Neither was of any comfort. So, there I lay, night after night, fearful for my daughter's fate and that the bargain ceiling fan, which Brayden had hastily installed, would crash down its helicopter blades, slicing open my head and leaving her motherless. If I could have, I would have put an impenetrable bubble around McKenna—fuck failure, screw character.

I heard my father exhale heavily, disappointed in himself.

"Did you hear what I just said, Dad?" I felt horrible pushing him. It did not come naturally.

After a long time, he answered. "Yes."

"Is she there?" I asked, tossing the cigarette and rolling the window back up.

"She's asleep in her bed. The whole thing wore the poor girl out."

"McKenna, Dad."

"Oh, right," he said, coming back to life. He called out to my daughter, adding parenthetically, "I couldn't let Coco suffer."

"Or the squirrel," I added, although he didn't hear me. There was a muffled fragment of a conversation bleeding through the earpiece of the phone. I could hear the sound of my daughter. Not what she was saying, just the soft, gentle puff of syllables and the rise and fall of her breath. Her voice betrayed a hint of lisp like it did when she was two years old. This regression happened when she was upset. That was a magical time when her personality started to emerge from the tail end of her infancy. It was no longer just eating, sleeping, and changing diapers. She discovered something new every day, every hour in some cases. You could almost see her synapses exploding, tripping over one another as they expanded inside her little head. I felt my eyes glaze over as the resurrection of that phantom passed before me on the surging concrete.

That was also when I started taking her to swimming lessons. Every Sunday (and the occasional Saturday) for most of her childhood. I would rise early, wake her, change her diaper, get her a bottle, slip our swimsuits on, a pair of clothes over our suits in the fall and winter, strap her into the car seat, and drive the half mile to the rec center. It was something just the two of us did. Brayden was petrified of the water. Afterward, we would go to McDonald's. I'd have a slow, quiet coffee and a hash brown and watch as she ran, climbed, bounced, and barreled down the slide of the Playland (she never made a companion of fear like I had) and waved at me from behind the hard, plastic mesh before going home, both of us to nap.

I recall the second set of classes with particular fondness. The main objective was to teach the children how to close their mouths and eyes as they were submerged. It's not a natural thing to learn. They always reemerged with a look of bewilderment and betrayal. Many sobbing before and after. It caused me tremendous anxiety. More for me than McKenna, I think. Baby swim class is a den of anxiety for parents. I remember the moment she scrunched up her little face and dipped her head under the water. It was an astonishing thing to witness. It was the first indication that McKenna had a sense of confidence that I lacked; that perhaps her life would hold brighter things than it did for me. Overwhelmed, I plucked her out of the water more joyous, and proud, than I had ever been in my life.

I could hear my father urging her to the phone.

"Coco killed a squirrel," she said, barely audible.

Hearing her wisp of a voice, hundreds of miles behind me, alone and grief-stricken, brought upon me a sense of shame I hadn't felt since I had first said aloud (to my mother, to anyone) that I could no longer be married to Brayden. As if to emphasize the millions of second doubts and memories of wrong choices and sleepless nights, the sun burst through the clouds. It hit me hard, as if I were emerging from deep black water, my heart beating in my eyes and ears. I swiped at the visor, my hands tightening around the steering wheel, and remained still until the yellow lines reappeared, coming at me like bullets, praying the road did not bend.

"Hey, peanut butter, you okay?" I managed to spit out.

"When are you coming home?"

"In a few days," I said more convincingly, as the sun receded behind a wagon train of clouds. "I told you."

"Are you going to bring me something?"

"It's not that kind of trip."

When she didn't immediately respond, my organs turned to ash. What could she understand of the purpose of my journey, the history lurking on the far side of this man whose existence she (and the older sibling she nearly had... did have?) wasn't aware of, and how it covertly intertwined around her (and her father) like a serpent? Especially when these currents, crosscurrents, and murky undertows were a mystery to me as well.

"I'm sure I can find you a little something," I said, easing off the gas as I came into a tangle of traffic. There was a relief to be reminded of existence, of humanity in all its inconsistent, messy beauty, racing towards and away from something and nothing.

"Yea!" she said breathlessly, again two years old.

"Now, be good for your grandpa and have fun today. Maybe I'll find him a little something, too. You think he'd like that?"

"Mm-hmm."

"Now put him back on."

"Sorry about that," he started. "She doesn't understand why you're not coming."

"You're in charge, Dad. Handle things and stop bothering me," I said. "I had hoped to have a quiet drive to put my thoughts together and figure out what the hell I am doing, and I can't do that if you keep calling."

"It's the last you'll hear from us," he said.

* * *

Crossing into Nebraska several hours later, I squinted and attempted to see the opposite border. On the single vacation I had taken with my father, in my junior year of high school, he had joked that the state was so flat you could see all the way to the other side if you looked hard enough. My father was not one to vacation. Especially in those days when work consumed all of his time. But this trip came at a particularly rough period for our family. My aunt Mia left my Uncle Dwight, Adele's mother fell ill, and my father and I had not been on speaking terms for several months. It was also the year my father had been dating Dominic, *Dom,* a tall, flat, curly-haired RN from Duluth.

When my aunt, Mia, announced she had filed for divorce, no one was surprised. Dwight was a remote, casually cruel husband and father, who had come to exactly zero family functions as far back as I could remember. When you visited their apartment, he remained burrowed in the bedroom, a hidden yet foreboding presence. If you dared use the bathroom, you'd see him spread out on the bare mattress, a muted baseball game on the television set, the sports page sprawled out before him like gospel, a bottle of Johnny Walker, and a dirty spotted juice glass beside him on the nightstand.

On one occasion when I stayed the night, Mia, her son Michael, and I were sitting on the living room floor of their apartment, camped around the coffee table playing Monopoly, several popsicles in various states of decomposition in colorful bowls, when Dwight emerged from the darkened hallway, opened the fuse box cover in the entryway and flipped the breaker, killing the power to the entire apartment before disappearing back to the bedroom, slamming the door. Sitting in the dark, no one spoke or moved. I was petrified. I felt Mia's hand reaching for mine. When she found it, she gave it a hard squeeze. "Don't worry, guys," she whispered. Nevertheless, we sat in the darkness for twenty minutes before she dared turn the power back on, and even then, when we returned to our game (drinking the popsicle juice), behind every inadvertent burst of laughter, a silent threat lay hidden down the darkened hallway.

Shortly after Dwight moved out, Mia was visiting our house, her hair thinner and greyer, her eyes taut and red. "Here," she said to my mother, handing over a stack of papers. It was a copy of Dwight's most recent work self-evaluation. "I guess he hasn't forwarded his mail to his new apartment yet."

"What am I looking at?" my mother asked.

"Right here," Mia said.

"What matters most to you?" my mother read aloud. A moment later, her eyes shifted up from the papers to Mia's eager, wrinkle-lined face and inflamed eyes.

"Can you believe that?" she asked. "Not that boat in the garage. Or the damn television."

They took their glasses and moved into the living room. When they were no longer paying attention, I picked the papers off the table, scanning them until I found the damning question and the single-word answer: "Family." I wasn't sophisticated enough to intimate that perhaps he was simply telling his superiors what they wanted to hear. Or to understand that, despite appearances, in the far recesses of his heart, he may have been telling the truth. Either way, the disconnect between the man I had known my entire life and that one word was too much to comprehend. Here was another father, another man, who said one thing and behaved in the opposite manner. I decided to do something about it. Of course, being a teenager, I had limited options and almost no resources. I did what I could. I stopped speaking to my father.

No one noticed. At least not initially. He didn't call that frequently, and when he did, I was often out. When he finally managed to catch me at home, I declined his call. When my birthday came a few weeks later, I claimed to be too sick to accept his dinner invitation. Eventually, several months after my noiseless proclamation, he showed up unannounced at the house. Panicked, I locked my bedroom door and refused to come out. "Give her time," I heard my mother say as he left. I felt vindicated. My mother never pressed me for an explanation. However, when he asked me to dinner a month later, she insisted I accept his invitation. I shrugged and sulked my way through the entire affair, poking at my plate, barely uttering a word. Newly christened with my driver's license shortly after that, I was ordered to his house to take him out for a breakfast of steak and eggs. I had no choice but to do what I was told.

Coming up the driveway, I passed a woman I was later to find out was Dom, making a swift exit from my father's house, disheveled, clothes askew, slinking along the bushes like a rat jumping ship, neither making eye contact nor offering a word. Ducking into her car, she peeled away, rounding the corner with an embarrassed squeal. I nearly left. But not wanting to face my mother, I reluctantly made my way to the kitchen where I found my very hungover father. *What was that?* I asked. *About four vodka cloudys too many*. That prelude was more memorable than our breakfast, which was without incident.

I didn't realize he had started actually seeing her until I arrived at his house a month later to find her relaxing on the couch, feet on the coffee table, pushing for all of us (and her nephew Matt) to drive to a resort town outside of Denver for a family vacation. My father's initial response was a hard no. But she was persistent. It turns out her deceased husband of twenty years had never gifted her with a vacation and, apparently, the onus had fallen on my father like a passed-on debt. Apparently, it didn't matter to her that I had come to drive him to the hospice care facility where Adele's mother, Kimberly, had recently been moved. Ovarian cancer was running off with her life (much to the surprise of the alcoholism ravaging her liver). In the five weeks Kimberly had been there, he had not visited. Adele had called, begging me to take him there. No saint herself, Adele had only visited once. Not only was Dom indifferent to Kimberly's suffering, but she sensed an opportunity, suggesting Matt's friend Franklin could take Adele's place if she were unavailable. The expression on my father's face at this idea was something to behold. Nevertheless, he wouldn't budge.

Family confounds me. A few weeks earlier, I wasn't talking to my father. Now I was driving him to see his ex-wife, a woman he once loved, who was dying, who I imagined he would want to say goodbye to but apparently did not, and I was doing all of this to ostensibly support a half-sister who never did a damn thing for me.

Arriving at Meadow Glen, neither my father nor I said a word. Propped up in the oversized bed, arms at right angles, hands flat, positioned over the perfectly folded blankets, Kimberly appeared dead, as if posed for a post-mortem portrait. She neither spoke nor moved. All that was perceptible was the rising and contracting of her chest like a tide forsaken by the moon. Adele buzzed around like a fly, busying herself with her mother's hair and blankets, barking at the nurses, assuring us (despite appearances) of how well she was doing. Even now, the image of her in that bed waiting for Mr. Bones to take possession leaves me unsettled. My father left the facility like a broken horse. He agreed to the vacation the next day.

It would be a stretch of the imagination to call what we embarked on a vacation. It was poorly planned, sloppily executed, disorganized. We made the fourteen-hour drive with exactly two stops for bathroom breaks and meals, with little conversation. Once we arrived, it was every man for himself. I don't recall *any* planned family outings. We didn't go horseback riding or sit at the pool together. From the moment Matt and Franklin woke (which wasn't early), and after they inhaled every piece of food in the refrigerator, they vanished only to be heard entering the room late into the night. Although my father had shelled out a small fortune to rent them bikes for exploring the surrounding mountains, it only took a rudimentary exploration of the grounds to discover the bikes had been ditched behind a dumpster so they could hole themselves up in an unlocked tool shed to smoke weed the entire day. For their part, my dad and Dom languidly toured the town, shopping, sampling the various restaurants, dabbling at the casino. Once the sun tipped its hat, they sat at the hotel bar drinking mojitos, watching the sky explode over the mountains, finally retiring to their room sometime after eleven. Thinking about it now, I guess everyone enjoyed their very separate vacations. Everyone except me. With no companion, too lazy to do any sort of hiking, and too embarrassed to lay out at the pool by myself, I spent the majority of my time in my room watching local television, ready to throw a fit about my period if anyone tried to get me to leave. No one did.

Four days later, we packed up and headed back towards Elmwood. Stopping the night in Lincoln, we stayed, at Dom's insistence, at a four-star hotel. Or what passed for one in Lincoln, Nebraska. It was in a converted warehouse with poorly lit hallways and smelled what I imagined an 18th-century slaughterhouse smelled like. After dropping my bag off and giving myself a cursory glance in the mirror, I decided I needed some space from our one-room confinement.

Sitting on the curb in front of the hotel, I tossed pebbles in the sewer. A man in a tan jumpsuit swept the sidewalk in front of a hardware store. An elderly couple held hands and disappeared around a corner. A Girl Scout troop clattered by in single file, clinging to an invisible axis. A lone teenager with hair obstructing one side of his face cruised by on a skateboard. The town gave the impression of not wanting to be disturbed, as if its back were perpetually turned on you. Pushing past the center of town, I crossed its one bridge. Beneath was a river that was long, cool, and still like the upturned blade of a knife, across which was nothing but road and an eternity of hills and trees. I made my way to the embankment lined with goldenrod and sat at the water's edge. It would have taken nothing but a nudge to dissolve my bones to tears tumbling into the sluggishly moving water.

Reentering the hotel and exiting the elevator on my

floor, Matt and Franklin were making a hasty escape from our room, suppressing laughter as they pulled the door behind them. I stood motionless. Spotting me in the middle of the hall, Matt shrugged, "Have fun with that." They both disappeared down the stairwell, their feet pounding like wild horses, their voices detonating into cruel laughter. As the hallway fell back into silence, I could hear Dad and Dom arguing. Our room was across from the alcove housing the ice and pop machines. I lowered myself between the two humming warm machines, pulling my knees tight into my chest.

"You're so cheap. You are. There was a nice gourmet pizza shop across from the park, and you came back with Dominos."

There was an extended silence. I did not know if my father was speaking or just taking the abuse like a dilapidated farm being pummeled by a hailstorm. If he was responding, I could not hear him.

"It's the last night of our vacation. Why couldn't you do one special thing for me and the boys?"

There was another extended silence, finally broken by my father's strong, direct voice.

"I'm cheap?"

"Deaf too, apparently. Yes, I said you're cheap. Because you are. Look at this place. It's disgusting."

"Not only did I take you and your nephew on a trip across the country, but I took his friend, neither of whom had any money. I paid for them. Their food, lodging, souvenirs. Bikes they didn't ride. Not you. A trip, incidentally, where no one bothered with Willow."

I knew that tone. Slow and deep and deliberate. My father, boiling.

"I've stayed in four-star, five-star hotels, and they were nothing like this."

"This place you demanded we stay?"

"Ronald would have. God rest his soul, he would have. He wasn't cheap. He knew how to take care of his family."

"Ronald knew how to take care of his family?" he said with a peal of harsh laughter.

"Yes, he did."

"Ronald died fucking that waitress from the *1200*. I know it, you know it. Everyone knew it. I know why you ended up at my door. It didn't work. It didn't punish him. And it sure as hell didn't resurrect him from the ground."

The door burst open. The sound of footsteps came fast and hard. I pulled my knees tight, squeezed my eyes shut. Dom bolted past, sobbing loudly. As she attempted to catch her breath, the ding announcing the arrival of the elevator was followed quickly by the sound of the doors opening and closing. My father soon followed. There was a hesitation when he approached the elevator. He sighed loudly and cursed under his breath. Opening my eyes, I watched as he stood, hands on his hips, head hanging, damning the hotel and the entire trip, before turning back. I closed my eyes. It was only a moment before I could feel his presence.

"Willow?" he said. Opening my eyes, he stood offering a hand. He pulled me up and looked back towards the room. "Those terrible boys probably devoured the pizza."

"I'm not really hungry."

"What I mean..." he said, stopping himself. It felt like his anger was about to land at my feet. "What I mean is, why don't we see what beautiful Lincoln, Nebraska, has to offer," he continued slowly, forcing a smile.

"I was just out there, and it's not very encouraging," I said, brushing the dirt off my butt, then my hands.

"You want to sit in the room?"

"No."

"All right then. I think I saw something in the lobby before." Looking towards the elevator, he exhaled, thinking no doubt about the consequences that would be stubbornly waiting for him in that small room, and directed us towards the stairwell. "Safer this way."

Entering the lobby, an echo of voices rushed up into the high-ceilinged air like doves. It carried that aura of anticipation found at a concert before the lights go down. At the end of a long hallway, a group of well-dressed people were clustered together, talking. There was an easel outside the entrance with an awkwardly staged picture of a smiling couple announcing the wedding of Paul Harris and Amy Lockwood. Peeking into the large room, the majority of the guests were congregated around two bars, forming long lines, extending past the tables onto the dance floor. On the far side of the room, there were two sets of sliding glass doors opening to the outside.

"Back there," my father said, already in motion again, dodging and weaving through the crowd and around the tables like a seasoned wide receiver. I struggled to keep up.

Coming outside, we paused and looked around, our eyes adjusting to the light, both struck by the hard autumn heat. There was a firepit with an already generous fire surrounded by picnic benches, dotted with fat bridesmaids like gumdrops, young boys draped languidly across them like disregarded clothing, girls weaving around them like butterflies, and circles of people, mainly men, standing in several groups, holding drinks, talking gregariously, laughing. Yet even in the warmth and constricting clothing, everyone looked relieved that their duties had been fulfilled and they could finally relax, laugh, get drunk.

"Looks like the entire town is here," he said flatly, scoping out the scene. "They must be waiting to announce the bride and groom. They're probably out hitting the bars. Having their own time before they have to put on a show for the guests. Your mother and I did that."

"You did?"

He didn't bother to answer. Instead, he took three broad steps and found a spot by two bridesmaids, both heavyset, both oozing out of their pink chiffon dresses. He immediately began chatting with them. I marveled at the ease with which he initiated conversation. There was no hesitation or self-doubt. He was able to create a sense of intimacy almost instantaneously. By knowing when to speak and when to stay silent, how to break the tension with a well-placed joke. But above all, by listening. In these moments he wasn't the man I had so much ambivalence about, but someone I was naturally drawn to and could even learn from.

"This is my daughter I was telling you about. My youngest. The oldest, Adele, was recently married. To a salesman. Best of luck," he said with a sarcastic shake of the head.

They both nodded at me.

"But what a long, hot day, huh?" my dad said, leaning towards the bridesmaid he was sitting closest to, who was keeping her arms tight to her side. "Good day, though," he added, smiling, his teeth shining like diamonds plucked from the beams of the sun.

"True on both counts," she said.

"Mandy, right? You guys were great out there. It was a beautiful ceremony," he said, gesturing towards the hotel. "Good choice of music and scripture."

"For sure," the other bridesmaid said. "It wasn't the standard stuff you hear at every wedding."

"Not sure we need the fire yet," he said, fanning his face and sticking his tongue out. They both chuckled. "Somebody was being ambitious. Probably wanted to get to the open bar as fast as possible. Speaking of which, where are my manners?" he added quickly. "Let me get you two a refill."

"Oh no," the other said, waving him away.

"I insist. You worked hard today. Mandy and?"

"Veronica."

"Veronica. Mandy and Veronica," he said, leaning back, taking them both in. "Don't tell me you didn't. You've been in Amy's shadow all day." He held his hands out, motioning for their cups.

Veronica finally capitulated, "Thank you. I couldn't walk another foot in these heels."

"Amen," Mandy said, fanning her face with a napkin.

"I need about fifteen of those."

Mandy handed over her glass.

"Coming right up. Beer?" They both nodded. We both stood up and made our way back inside, through the reception hall and up to the bar, where the lines were now shorter. We were at the front quickly. I wondered if he would get me a drink.

"I need two beers for those lovely bridesmaids out there, a vodka cloudy, lowball, for me and…" turning to me as if on a whim, scrutinizing me briefly, "a beer for you?"

"White wine."

He gave me a questioning look. "Why not?"

"Why not indeed," I said, shrugging.

As the drinks were presented to us by the bartender, my dad pushed a neatly folded twenty-dollar bill into the tip jar. The bartender nodded. As we were walking away, he raised his eyebrows and smiled broadly.

Delivering the drinks to the grateful bridesmaids, he said, "I expect to see you both on the dance floor later. And Mandy, don't drop out of school. I know it's hard, but it will be worth it."

"Thank you."

We ducked back into the reception hall and snagged ourselves an empty table towards the back.

"The trick is to get in and out. Keep it short and general. Not too many details. Talk too much, and you risk giving yourself away. And flattery always works. Always. Now it's free drinks as long as we want," he said, sitting down, exhaling.

"I feel like you've done this before."

"Your mother and I crashed a few weddings in our day. In fact, we crashed a black family reunion once, in..." he said, pulling up the memory out of time, "Stillwater."

"You did? How did you manage that?"

"We were staying at the same hotel. They were on the patio attempting to take a group photo, but they hadn't hired a photographer so they couldn't get everyone in the picture all at once, so I offered. There were a ton of them. Could have started their own football team. I started chatting them up. Even talked my way into a couple of photos. Next thing you know, they asked your mother and me to stay. We had an absolute blast. Said I was the coolest white guy they ever met," he said with a slow nod of the head.

"What were you doing in Stillwater?"

"I was there for a softball tournament. Before you came along your mother used to come to all my games. There was nothing like looking up – I played centerfield, by the way – and seeing her smiling face. Then we'd all head back to Halek's for drinks and ninety-nine cent wings."

"You did?"

"For years," he said. "I must have played for them for fifteen or sixteen years. You knew that."

"I didn't. When did you stop?"

"I guess it's been about nine or ten years," he said, slowing as he finished the sentence. "Jesus."

There was something heartbreaking about the fact I didn't know my father played softball with my mother cheering him on in the stands.

There was a little sign on the table that read, *"We've hired you as our official photographer. Don't let us down,"* and several disposable cameras scattered on the tabletop. Setting my wine glass down, I picked one up. "Smile, Dad."

He lifted his beer glass up and presented his oversized smile with all his beautiful teeth.

"How about this?" he asked, balancing his drink on his bicep. Pointing at himself and back out towards an imaginary body of water, he said, "Which way to the beach?" This was something he had done since Adele and I were children. I had no idea what it meant (since, until now, he had never taken a vacation and never talked about retirement), but it never failed to warm my heart.

"Great," I said.

"All right, your turn," he said, motioning for the camera.

Handing it over, he snapped a series of shots of me.

I gave him a series of well-rehearsed poses: my tongue stuck out, crossed eyes, looking into the distance stoically, pouting (boys went crazy for that one), and one respectable pose for posterity.

"This reminds me of Adele's reception."

"Never thought she'd get to the altar before you."

I chuckled. "Wait, you can't be serious? Are you serious?" I asked, bringing the glass up to my lips and setting it back down again.

"It's a numbers game. Everything's a numbers game. She never dated that much."

"No, no way. Not me, Dad. You're way off. I was thinking about when Mia left without Michael."

"That was the strangest thing. The last thing I expected at my daughter's wedding was for my nephew to need a ride home because his mother went MIA. I was flabbergasted," he said, taking another sip from his glass. "Who forgets their kid? Mia's had her problems. Dwight was no picnic, but she was always a good mother. Well, her heart was always in the right place."

"You looked me in the eye and ordered me to find her."

"I remember."

"I scoured the entire reception hall. The bathrooms. The parking lot. The kitchen. She was gone."

"She left with Joey. She had been seeing him before she and Dwight split."

"Is that why Dwight left her?"

"It's complicated," he said.

"What does that mean?" I asked. I also made a mental note that I did not care for white wine.

"It means Dwight can point to Joey and say *that…*"

he said with emphasis, "is why their marriage ended, ignoring his culpability in what a train wreck their marriage was for the past twenty years. You're going to find that people will grasp at anything that absolves them of responsibility. How's that wine?"

"Huh? Great," I said. "But Mia did cheat?"

"Yes."

"That's horrible."

"Yes. Apropos of nothing, but Joey is a garbage collector, which has got to mean something," he said, letting out a loud guffaw. After a moment, "They did some crazy stupid shit," he said, a sparkle in his eyes, begging me to ask him.

"Like what?"

Easing back into his chair, he grimaced, "I don't know."

"Come on, Dad," I said, sipping my wine.

"All right. Just one. But this is just between—"

"You, me, and the lamppost; I know, I know."

"One night, they went out boozing hard. Ran up huge bills and spilt without paying. Got kicked out of a couple of places. They hit a mailbox with her car, I think. That sort of thing. One night, they got back to his condominium, and she couldn't get him out of the car. He's passed out. He was a really big guy. Tall. She leaves him in the car and goes to bed. Several hours later, he wakes up in the garage, in the pitch black, has no idea where he is, and freaks out. He starts kicking at the car, the windows, punching at shit."

"Jesus," I said, my mouth agape, my hands wrapped around the stem of the glass.

"The next morning, he doesn't remember a thing, but his hands are cut up, two windows are broken out on the car, the insides are ripped to shreds, there's blood going up the stairs. It looks like a massacre took place. Forgetting Michael was low on the offenses they committed during their brief tenure," he said, chuckling quietly.

"Not for Michael," I said, still astonished. "Wasn't Scott freaking out that night too?"

He thought for a moment.

"The second keg was running low. He had someone from the reception hall cornered, threatening that if the place ran out of beer, he would rain hell down on the place, demanding a third keg. He's like that. He's a great guy. But it's always guys who aren't good with money who throw it around."

"What do you mean?"

"He's caused some problems at work. I know Adele's worried he is going to quit, and they just bought that condo," he said, taking a sip of his drink. "In other words, the honeymoon period is over. That's just between you, me, and, well, you know."

A man approached our table. "You mind if I take this chair?"

We both shook our heads no. We watched as he held the chair above his head and took it all the way to the far side of the room, squeezed it around a very full table, and sat down.

"When I was little, Mom would bring this portable black and white television outside on the little concrete patio behind our apartment, and we would watch our shows as the sun went down. I would lay on my stomach constantly fiddling with the knobs and antennae, drinking apple juice, and Mom would sit against the building with a glass of wine, chatting with neighbors."

"What made you think of that?"

"Hunter," I said, suddenly feeling very buzzed.

"Your cat? That thing never liked me. In all the years I came over, I think she let me pet her once. Usually, she took a swipe at my pant leg," he said, finishing his drink, the tension melting away from his face.

"When she died, I cried for days. I started writing down all the things I loved about her. How she wouldn't leave my bed when I had chickenpox. Or how she would crouch in my bedroom door when I got out of the bath, her eyes glowing in the dark, wanting me to sprint down the hall so she could jump at me spreadeagle, all four orange limbs coming at me."

"She was a tough little cat," he said, pointing his glass at me.

Without my having realized it, everyone had migrated from outside, the fires had been extinguished, and nearly all the tables had been filled up. The D.J. was carefully monitoring the entrance.

"One night, Mom and I had a fight. It was the only time I ever said I hated her. Laying in bed, I was petrified she would die in her sleep and the last thing I said to her was that I hated her. I flipped on my light and started writing down all the things she did for me," I said, my eyes welling up.

"What brought this on?"

I shrugged. He tilted his head. "Come on. Give it up. I'm just starting to have a good time."

"Do you think Kimberly is going to die?" I asked.

"Well, that didn't last long," he said, laughing sardonically. He took a long look around the ballroom, his face darkening. "Looks like we're running low." Before heading to the bar, he wandered aimlessly around the reception hall to a table where the two bridesmaids were sitting and chatted with them briefly. When he came back, a drink for each of us, he sat for some time, not speaking. "Kimberly used to say that if she had to do it all over, she wouldn't have gotten married."

His eyes zeroed in on me like an eagle above a stream. I knew what he was asking of me.

"Mom never says anything bad about you."

"I know it's common to think highly of people after they die," he finally said and abruptly stopped. I waited for him to continue a thought that felt unfinished. To say that even when Kimberly was at her worst, selfish, and morally compromised, she was forever her authentic self. It was the only complimentary thing I could think of to say about her. But he didn't say that. It was as if she was already gone.

"It was exciting at first."

"What?" I asked. This was not what I was expecting him to say. My entire life, he had only spoken with derision about his ex-wife.

"Being with her. Like a roller coaster barely staying on the tracks. When I met her, no one talked about alcoholism. She was just fun. Unpredictable. Then your sister was born." I sighed and took down half the glass of wine. Here we go again. The rescue of Adele and canonization of my father. "I was a young man. I wasn't ready to give up my life yet. Becoming a parent is supposed to change you. I never thought Kimberly's drinking would stop. But I thought it would slow down. I never thought it would get worse. But it did. A lot worse. I panicked and jumped ship."

"You bailed?"

"I bailed," he said, looking up. "I only took Adele

when it was obvious Kimberly was incapable of caring for her."

"You mean you didn't want her?"

He stared into his glass for a long time before answering.

"It's not that. I had a new life. I had a one-bedroom apartment, for Christ's sake."

I didn't understand what I was hearing. All I had ever been told was how my father had rescued Adele after the divorce, been her knight in shining armor, not that he had taken her unwillingly. And now he had just confessed that not only was he not a hero but that he had walked out with no intention of ever coming back for my sister. How bad did things have to get to save yourself but abandon your wife and daughter? Why compound your cowardliness by presenting it over and over as a hero narrative to anyone who would listen? Why exalt one daughter to the diminishment of another? Did Adele know this? Did she have any idea you were a fraud? Of course not. The combination of his startling words and the wine was making my head swim.

"All I knew was that I resented the hell out of her for a long time," he said, finishing his drink, a mixture of still unresolved anger and sadness overtaking his face.

"*Ladies and gentlemen, it is my pleasure to welcome, for the first time, Mr. and Mrs. Paul Harris.*"

From the hallway, the bride and groom, holding hands and smiling, eyes glassy, made a leisurely entrance. The bride steered her newly minted groom from table to table for introductions, congratulations, and small talk. She peered at him with loving deference as he bent over with effort to capture what was being said, with little success.

He simply winced and nodded awkwardly, waiting for an opening before laughing broadly. He was quite drunk (more drunk than the bride). After a moment, they moved on to do the routine over again and again, no doubt longing for the respite of the honeymoon suite.

"I saw Ronald once not long before he died," my father said, turning back to me as if he hadn't just shaken the entire foundation of my life (and my sister's too).

"Yeah?" I asked slowly, pulling my glass back.

"Actually, I saw him a few times. Always at *Mr. Mix's*. Never with Dom. He had a reputation as a skirt chaser. Dom's been through some shit," he added by way of tempering my contempt for her, although I sensed it was just for appearances. "I was meeting an old friend for a couple of bumps, and I went to the bathroom, and there in the stall is Ronald with this woman. I was finishing up when the bouncer stormed in, grabbed them both, and started dragging them out. As they are being routed to the exit, the woman – and I'll never forget this – orders Ronald to take his glasses off."

"Why?"

"To prepare to fight. As they are being tossed, the woman breaks free and gets in a fight with two of the waitresses. She grabs the can of beer Ronald is drinking and throws it at them, breaking the mirror behind the bar. The last thing I hear as the door shuts behind them is Ronald saying, 'You cut my lip'." He stopped speaking again.

A large crowd had gathered at the foot of the dance floor. The groom took the microphone and gave a long, meandering, occasionally sentimental speech which the audience begrudgingly tolerated, and the bride seemed pleased with. A smattering of applause greeted him when he was finished.

"We should probably get back upstairs," my father said. Never had such a simple sentence so succinctly summed up the pull obligation has on us, something we so readily agree to and immediately resent. Standing, he emptied his glass, setting it with a thud onto the table. I followed suit.

Outside the reception hall, my father began signing the large, framed photograph of the couple with a felt pen tied gracelessly to it with string.

"Thanks for the very free drinks," he wrote, repeating aloud what he had written. He offered me the pen. Hesitantly, I took it.

"Just sign it," he urged.

"Take it easy, and if you get it easy, take it twice," I wrote, also repeating back what I had written.

"That's much better than what I wrote. I'm going to steal that."

"It's Gaelic. Or so says my boyfriend. He says it all the time."

"That I did not need to know, love."

An older man in a black suit with a large mustache, carrying a tray full of empty glasses, came out of the reception hall. "Excuse me, are you with the bride or groom?"

My dad took my hand, and we high-tailed it down the hall to the stairwell. The last thing we heard as the door shut behind us was, "What room are you in? Sir? Sir?"

Now it was us laughing as we raced through the stairwell. Bursting through the door into the hallway, we stood doubled over, huffing and puffing, stifling our disobedient laughter.

"Well done," he said.

"You think they'll come looking?" I ask, looking back

towards the stairwell.

When he didn't immediately respond, I turned to find him still doubled over. He seemed unable to catch his breath. I didn't know if he was laughing or having a heart attack. I started towards him, "Dad?"

"Nah," he said, waving off my concern. "They won't come for us."

"Are you okay?"

"Yes."

"Good."

"No, I mean to answer your question. From earlier. Yes, I think Kimberly's going to die," he said quietly, straightening himself up.

"Oh."

We looked at one another soundlessly, each with a sadness of our own.

"Is that why we're here?" I asked.

For a moment, my father's eyes were filled with a mournful, pained expression, then he turned away from me.

"When your mother and I were dating," he began, quietly leaning against the wall with one arm, still not facing me, "I would come over to her apartment. While she was cooking, I'd quietly go through the place, turn over the corner of the rug, and tilt several of the pictures when she wasn't looking. She'd be telling me about her day and fix the corner of the rug, stir the spaghetti sauce, straighten one of the pictures, drop in some of the spices, and fix the second. After dinner, I'd take the trash out. Lifting the lid off the garbage can, I'd stare in astonishment – the trash was organized. All the bags were tied and stacked perfectly. The inside of the can, pristine. I guess you could say she got the last laugh. You could put that in your memory book."

Wiping the tears from my eyes, I chuckled softly to myself.

"Sometimes I'll leave something, like a CD or a book, in front of my stereo and go to the bathroom and by the time I get back, Mom has put it back in its proper place on the bookshelf," I said in a near whisper.

He laughed out loud, turning towards me.

"Come on, the warden is waiting," he said, taking my hand and leading us down the hall.

Opening the door, Matt and Franklin were lying next to one another on the bed watching television, and Dom was sitting at the small round table, reading glasses on, going through her checkbook. Peering over her plastic frames, she said, "Classy. Getting your minor daughter drunk," and went back to her numbers. No one said a word for the rest of the evening.

The next morning, we headed back towards Elmwood. Matt and Franklin slept the entire way. Dom and my dad spoke only when necessary. Backing out of Dom's driveway, we never saw Dom (or Matt and Franklin) again. At least she got her vacation.

Creeping through Lincoln an hour later to fill up my tank, I made one pass through the town. It hadn't changed much, although almost nothing looked familiar. The hotel was still there, lifting itself out of the row of three- and four-story buildings like a promise of a future that refused to arrive. That and the one lonely bridge leading passengers out of town. I still don't know where that bridge led and what was beyond those hills.

Growing up, I used to garden with my mother. Every

Sunday after mass, on our hands and knees, we would water, weed, and nurture the small bit of land each tenant was allocated. Inevitably, one of us would come across an entire flower, pedals, stems, and leaves, that was withered and gone. With barely a tug, it would come out in your hands, roots and all. You think it would be easy to spot a dead flower, barely able to hold its head up, so easily able to remain camouflaged just by abutting up next to an abundance of life. I judged my Uncle Dwight harshly when I was a girl. It wouldn't be until I was much older that I would understand how tragically effortless it is just to stop loving another person. There was no doubt he was a reprehensible husband and, at best, a neglectful father. But at some point, he loved my aunt Mia. Whether it hit hard and short like a cloudburst or if, twenty years on, he considered his wife across the breakfast table and no longer recognized who he saw, only he knows. But at some point, it ceased. That's why now, ten years later, making my own mad dash from the Midwest, I have gained a greater sympathy for my Uncle Dwight.

And of my father?

Thinking back to that vacation, there was something heartbreaking about not knowing that my father played softball with my mother in the stands. Not the actual fact of the matter. A lot of men play organized sports with their girlfriends cheering them on. It just wasn't the kind of couple I imagined them to be. Then, who exactly did I envisage them to be? I had never quantified it before. In a non-verbal, purely assumptive way, the narrative I had created in my mind was of two people who came together out of mutual attraction and whose demise was accelerated by the arrival of a pregnancy. Its essence was one of destruction. It had to be that way. What other option did I have? Traveling for sports? Crashing weddings? Intimate dinners and joking around? That was beyond the perimeter of my imagination.

    Why? For one, they couldn't have a relationship happier than any of mine. But on a deeper level, it left open the chance for possibilities. Of success. Of happiness. Pulling out of Lincoln and back onto the highway, my face became hot. *Unhappiness.* My greatest ambition for my parents was unhappiness and failure. That was what I had actively wished for them. I had always held my father in the lowest regard, even when our relationship was in détente. My mother was in every sense, mother earth, the soil from which I sprung, the foundation upon which I was built while my father was a black hole, a swirling drain from which no light escaped, where I could toss all the excrement of my life. Whenever I failed, he was the reason. That was why I had never shown the slightest interest in their relationship, had asked no questions, knew the scantest details about their past (like knowing my father played softball with my mother in the stands), much less the significant particulars. Maybe had I asked more I would have known more, could have been there for him when he retired or as Kimberly lay sick and dying, and he for me when I needed him. Of course, there was no part of me that wanted this. Any disturbance in that equilibrium could rattle the firmaments of my existence, the narrative I had built about my life. What I could not comprehend as a girl of sixteen was the incorruptible bond between a parent and child. Even that night, as he was regaling me about his halcyon softball days, I had been largely ignoring him. I was trying to figure out if some fictional away game had been the reason he had missed my birth and been largely absent during my childhood. And now? Now I was trying to discover if that bond of parents and child was truly incorruptible. If there was a primeval river of the gods connecting my father and me? If it was possible for the waters to surge back to its source?

Lighting a cigarette, I continued my journey.

* * *

In the ensuing hours since I had pulled out of Lincoln, an armada of thick green clouds had rolled in from the west. They were moving swiftly with a single-mindedness towards some unspoken destination. Lowering all four windows, the harsh, cool wind rushed through the car. The temperature had dropped a swift ten or fifteen degrees. With not one vehicle on the highway or bird in the sky, I maneuvered the car to the center of the highway and pushed forward in the midst of this menacing landscape as if I were a single soldier sent to take on an unseen army. After half an hour, the rain gave a few warning shots before hitting hard and fast, like scraps of metal, waking me out of my fugue state. It was deafening. By the time I got the windows up, the seats and my lap were drenched, my windshield wipers only a formality. I threw the defrost on high to fight off the fog threatening to overcome the glass. My heart rate increased, and my chest hollowed out. I felt faint. Like rising too quickly in the morning, sitting motionless on the side of the bed, trying not to black out. Slowing to a crawl, I pulled the car back to the right lane and focused on the unbreaking white line. An overpass appeared on the horizon like a petrified rainbow drained of its color. Saddling the shoulder, I pulled beneath it; the descending rain immediately muffled, the wipers groaning across the windshield. Dabbing the sweat from my forehead, I watched the torrents of water framed by the bridge, the inside of the car silent.

When we had severe weather at home, McKenna and I would place two lawn chairs at the edge of the garage and count the seconds between the lightning and thunder, every interval indicating the storm was a mile away, or so I've been told. Brayden was afraid of thunderstorms as well as water. I saw no lightning and heard no thunder.

Pulling out my phone, I dialed Mark's number. He picked up, as he usually did, on the first ring.

"Hey, honey. Where are you at?" he asked.

"Somewhere in beautiful Nebraska."

"How is everything going so far? Oh, I'm so happy to hear from you." I heard him sit down with a leaden oomph.

"A storm came out of nowhere, so I pulled over under a bridge. Here listen," I said, opening the door, holding out my phone, wiping the moisture from my lap. "Can you hear the rain? It's coming down pretty good."

"I can hear it. Are you okay?"

"I'm fine."

"Anything of note happen yet?"

"Coco killed a squirrel, sending McKenna into hysterics, but nothing else really. I'm sure they are on their way to the wedding. That fucker Brayden keeps trying to call which means he thinks something is up. Otherwise, no. Just driving."

From the opposite side of the highway, a motorcyclist dressed all in black leather came zipping underneath the bridge, coming to an abrupt halt. He sat for some time before getting off the bike. He propped the kickstand and shook the rain from his leather jacket and pants. Without removing his helmet, he glanced at me before walking up the incline of the overpass, taking a seat. The sound of Mark's laughter brought me back to the call.

"What so amusing?"

"You get so mad at Brayden, and you've been divorced, what, three years?"

"I'm never rid of him."

"Well, you had a kid with him; it's not like breaking up with a boyfriend."

"We may be divorced three years, but I've had to put up with his nonsense since I was fourteen?"

"Fair enough."

"What I wouldn't give to be able to just walk away."

Hustling my way out of the car, I began to walk the length of the protected, dry shoulder, a slight chill running the length of my body.

"I don't think that's an option."

I thought for a moment.

"Do you know what always pissed me off about him? I mean really pisses me off?"

"The granny glasses?"

"Seriously, you're a middle-aged man. And that beard, ugh. But no. He was always telling people that he didn't own a suitcase – I mean he was proud of it. He would bring it up. In the middle of the few parties he went to. I think that's one of the reasons I cheated."

"Because Brayden didn't own a suitcase?" he asked.

"I'm half-serious. It was so willfully ignorant, so, I don't know, isolationist," I said, stepping timidly on the painted white line of the highway as if balancing on a highwire. "I know you don't believe me, but I'm telling you the truth.

I convinced myself I needed a man with life experience: a career, a couple of ex-wives, stocks, someone who had seen the world. Maybe I was hoping that the sum of those experiences would equate to some kind of wisdom. Grant him some mercy. Of course, the only difference between him and anyone else I had dated was that he was grayer, fatter, and tired earlier in the night."

"Don't try and convince me you didn't laugh at every word Marco said."

"Naturally," I said flippantly. I knew Mark thought that the ease with which I spoke about my infidelity mirrored the ease with which I sought it out. There was nothing I regret more now than cheating on Brayden. It stole something from me that ensured I would never be whole again.

At the edge of the overpass, I held out my hand, water quickly pooling in my palm. Shaking it loose, I continued, "Adele would have shamed me to no end for becoming a trophy of his lost youth, admonishing me for always being subjected to some man's passion."

"Maybe you wanted someone who could *impart* something of life."

"He didn't impart a thing, but he didn't take anything either. Unlike Brayden, who had only taken things. Still, being with him, even for a few hours a week, in seedy bars, in the backseat of cars, making love in his dirty little townhouse in that dumb little bed, I felt like, well, not me."

"Perhaps it was the thrill of being touched by a different man for the first time in such a long time."

"Let me tell you, he would have slept with me as long as I would have let him. Sue me, I like sex."

"I know."

"Women who complain that all men want is sex, or

who don't enjoy sex, I find absurd, alienated from their own bodies. And liars."

"Sounds like you were disappointed."

"I mean, I was, I guess. I was so far gone I didn't even realize I was disappointed."

I turned and walked back past my car towards the opposite dry edge. It gave the impression of walking into traffic. Or back in time. If only it were that easy.

"When Lori and I were falling apart, I started hanging out with this woman from work. And before anything too serious had been initiated."

"You mean anything physical," I said.

He exhaled loudly. "We did that." I half-expected him to hang up on me, although I knew he wouldn't. Was the model who sat for the Mona Lisa as obnoxious as I was? Maybe that's what her infamous smile really speaks to – I know how badly you want to fuck me despite my being an unbearable twat. Perhaps leaving her beauty and her beauty alone on the canvas was a kind of mercy to eternity.

"I just, I didn't even like her that much. I didn't know that, of course. At the time it seemed – having her seemed so urgent. But something I have learned is the 'who' is never important."

"No?" I finished my cigarette, walked back to my car, popped open the door, and sat sideways, my legs dangling loosely out. It hit me that Mark was speaking about this woman, and by implication his past, in the same way my father had yesterday. "Because the enthusiasm he exhibited when he saw me naked was truly overwhelming."

"When I was with this woman," he said, ignoring me. "I did most of the talking. Not about her or my feelings. I talked almost exclusively about Lori. How she didn't meet my needs, never listened, how she shut me out. I mean, I had ten years' worth of complaints even though we were only together five, and I was determined to tell them all to this woman over happy hour." He laughed indulgently. "I just needed someone to listen to me, someone to be Lori's proxy since she was MIA. I needed Lori. I just didn't realize it."

For the first time since I had met Mark at *Cooper's Pub*, when I was thirty-five minutes late, stoned, indifferent, and walked in to find he hadn't gotten himself a three-beer head start but stood waiting at the door for me, like a gentleman, he was genuinely interesting.

"When it was finally over – not when we were spending nights and entire weekends apart without not realizing it, I assure you this happens..." Here, he paused for effect. He had a point, but I wasn't about to grant it to him. "Not after we had agreed to get divorced, not after I had moved out, signed the perfectly worded – and hotly contested – papers, not even after she had started seeing someone else."

"No?" The motorcyclist sat staring in my direction. At least, it seemed like he was.

"She would call late at night with terrible insomnia, saying that she was going room to room, crying, couldn't sleep in our bed, and was spending every night on the floor."

"And what? She had to see you?" The rain made a sudden shift and was falling diagonally at a harder rate.

"Yes," he said with authority.

"Mark," I said disapprovingly. "Don't tell me you went to her? You did, didn't you?" I asked, lying across both seats of the car and staring at the dome light. Inside, there were several dead flies.

"We'd had the best sex we ever had in those out-of-the-way motels."

"That was just your bodies saying goodbye."

"But two months later, she realized that starting things up again was a mistake."

"You mean when she met someone else."

"I told you she was already seeing someone else."

"That was insurance. She was probably seeing him before you split. He was there to fill the loneliness. Make her feel viable again. Women go through men like that like Kleenex. We need those before we're emotionally available for a good man." Before he could object or defend himself, I sat up, "When Brayden and I were first together, we were young. We were either fighting or fucking, mistaking that rush of adrenaline for love. Then, for years, we were as emotionally distant as the poles." Here I paused for effect. Giving as good as he got, he refused to acknowledge my point. "So, years later, when I had enough, I did the cowardly thing and cheated, making sure to get caught, and we got divorced. My point is, I knew we were wrong long before that, and don't ask me why I stayed with him because for that, I have no answer. Sometimes you just get swept away. And not by a tidal wave but by the mundane everydayness of living."

"Well said." I had said it before.

"The weekend we were going to the hospital to be induced, my mother threw us a barbeque. Everyone was there: Brayden, Adele, Mia, Stan, Butch, my grandma, my father. I sat in a chaise lounge and enjoyed being doted on. My father helmed the grill. Adele sat with her sleeves rolled up over her shoulders, feet in the water, regaling everyone with her recent exploits to Beijing. We put money on trying to guess the time McKenna would be born. Mia ended up winning. Of course, she was the one who took down the times. When it was time to go to the hospital, Brayden was nowhere to be found."

"Where was he?"

"The warming house. Sitting in the dark. Apparently, he was having second thoughts about being a father. That was when I was convinced we were wrong together. First, my father couldn't bother to show up when I was born, and now my husband was trying to jump ship as I was about to become a mother."

"I'm sure it was just nerves."

"That's what I figured. I was about to say something to ease his anxiety when he looked up at me and commented about how tanned I was. That I was supposed to be staying out of the sun. I never listened to what the doctors told me. I was putting the baby at risk."

"That's hard to believe."

"Isn't it?"

"What did you do?"

"Told him we were leaving in five and went to the car."

The motorcyclist shuffled back down the incline, opened the visor to his helmet, looked directly at me, lowered it again, started his motorcycle with a dramatic roar, and was on his way. I watched as he raced up the highway in the dissipating rain until he was just a speck on the horizon. Was it, Mr. Bones? Death incarnate on the side of the highway, giving me a warning of some sort? Telling me to turn back? To continue onward? That my time was short?

"Was that thunder?"

"Can you name the fourth person to walk on the Moon?" I asked, languidly.

"No."

"Of course not. It's a stupid question. But you can certainly name the person who took your virginity. Or the one who first broke your heart."

"For better or worse."

"There is something about crossing a threshold first – the first to the top of Everest, to circumnavigate the globe, to walk on the Moon – that grants that person special distinction. There's a reason it's called breaking new ground. It's why when people open restaurants, they frame their first dollar and not their second. My dad really wants Adele to have a baby. I mean, he really wants her to get pregnant. He was riding her the other day in the car."

"You said."

"I thought she was going to jump out of her skin. You think he'd know better."

"Know better? I don't follow."

"Several years before my grandmother died, she was going in for hip surgery. She was convinced she was going to die. I mean, she was convinced. *Death is perched at the end of my bed.* That's what she kept repeating." I stood up, crossed the two lanes, and sat on the cement divider in the middle of the highway. In the other direction, a few cars made their way towards me.

"For hip surgery?"

"You didn't see her in that bed, those fierce black eyes, her withered hands clutching her rosary. She was convincing, Mark. She made us say our goodbyes. She updated her will. The only way she thought she would survive was if my Uncle Lawrence, her firstborn, who lived in Manitoba, was by her side. He made it just before she went into surgery. Of course, she was fine. But she attributed it to Lawrence."

"That's just coincidence, obviously."

"She didn't attribute it to that," I said.

"Still," Mark said dismissively.

"My dad hates that story, by the way."

"Why?"

"My father did everything for his mother. Yet, when it came to the big stuff, she always asked for Lawrence. She never asked for my dad. For no other reason than he wasn't the firstborn. That's why when my grandmother fell and was rushed to the hospital, everyone was desperate for my uncle Lawrence to fly out, as if she would magically regain consciousness as sure as Jesus awoke Lazarus."

"Did he, fly out?"

"Of course. But she still passed. I think my dad was happy she didn't survive, in a perverse way."

Raising myself on the cement divider, I began walking away from my car.

"I can't believe that."

"You don't know what it's like having siblings, much less being second born. To spend your entire life running into a shadow. My dad does. Yet, he does the same thing with Adele and me. That's why he should know better."

"I don't get why he's so hot for Adele to have a kid. McKenna is the first grandchild, right?"

"Make sure to give Tank his meds tonight," I said, hanging up. Lowering myself from the cement divider I had two more cigarettes, ignored Mark's return call to apologize and another call from Brayden, made my way back to my car, and continued on.

* * *

The sign for Alexandria, Colorado, my mother's birthplace, had appeared along the side of the highway several times in the last fifty miles. I had been there once, during my summer off from college when I was nineteen or twenty. Well, technically to Casey, the tiny township fifteen or twenty miles to the west of Alexandria. The town, small and parochial, primarily existing on one long, thin strip of worn asphalt, was along the route to Salt Lake City. Or the route I had decided on. *No decision in life is accidental.* I just hadn't determined if I was going to stop. *It was obvious I was going to stop.*

Midway through my sophomore year, my mother decided to retire, take her social security early, and move back to Casey. *I've done what I set out to do,* she told me casually, sitting over a plate of nachos at The Hub, the University cafeteria. *I came to the city, had a career of sorts, attempted a marriage, started a family, had a few adventures. Some things worked out better than others,* she offered with a quiet wink, popping a chip drenched in cheese and sour cream in her mouth. *Overall, I'm mostly satisfied. Of course, I'm overjoyed with you. My Melissa girl is in college. How about that? Now, I just want to go somewhere quiet. Live simply. Spend the days reading, have a glass of wine at night, go to church on Sundays. Maybe volunteer. I already found an apartment. There is a guest room for you. Always will be,* she said with another wink, followed by a swallow of water.

Not once in all the years growing up had she mentioned moving back to Casey. I can't even recall her even talking about her hometown, outside saying it would bore the bejesus out of me. And a guest room? In my mother's home? The thought was offensive. Beyond belief. I hadn't given much thought to our parallel futures, but in a vague sense, I had always assumed we'd have neighboring townhomes with matching flower gardens, spending the evenings with a sunset walk followed by a ritual happy hour, after which we'd settle in for a game of cribbage until the drinks got the better of us. *Well, perhaps I had given it some thought.* Needless to say, I was flabbergasted. Not that you would have known by my immediate reaction.

"I'm a sophomore," I said, poking at the cold, flaccid Nachos chips, wiping the excess guacamole on my napkin.

"Halfway done, sweetheart."

We finished our meal, mostly in silence. I trailed her to her car like every other time she visited, waited until she rounded the corner and shuffled out to the wooded area just beyond the parking lot, sat cross-legged on a little circle of dirt and smoked a half a pack of cigarettes. When the time came to help her pack a few weeks later, I avoided her calls until the number reached fever pitch, but when I finally did answer I begged off, claiming exams that did not exist and which she had no choice but to accept.

I did make an appearance the day she left. As she set the final bags in her rusted blue Chevette, the windows blacked out by her belongings, I stood at the end of the street, cloaked by a hefty old oak, ignoring my buzzing phone and hardening my heart to the long, disappointing looks she kept casting over her shoulder. I watched as she said the tearful goodbyes to a few of her closest friends and drove off to a future that, for the first time didn't revolve around me. Driving in the opposite direction once she was gone, I sobbed, knowing it was something she would never have done to me.

My life didn't change the first few months she was gone. Being in school, I didn't find myself at my childhood home that often anyway. But like an anchor burrowed beneath the deep ocean green, it kept me tethered and ultimately stopped me if I drifted too far. It was easy to distract myself with the necessities of classes, studies, parties, and the couple of boys I was juggling. I rarely called my mother. When I did, I ignored her frequent pleas to visit, neither visiting over Thanksgiving or Christmas, even though she was desperate for me to come. By the time the semester was winding down, I hadn't seen my mother in seven months, the longest stretch of my entire life. What kind of daughter was I?

It wasn't simply that she was ten hours away, living in a place I had never been, forcing me to stay in an unfamiliar environment (raising in me an irrational belief that she would somehow be stranger, freer, less a mother) that filled me with nervous terror. She had met a man at church bingo. As she told it, he was sitting at the table behind hers when he leaned back in his chair and pointed to her card with his dauber. She screamed 'bingo' so loud the woman next to her clutched at her heart. She had offered to split her winnings with him, but he had refused. *Buy me a drink sometime. The name's Nestor.*

The story wasn't out of the ordinary. My mother, with her thin figure, wide blue eyes, and generous spirit, frequently drew the attention of men. In fact, I don't remember a time in a grocery store or gas station when she wasn't granted some favor by a member of the opposite sex.

After divorcing my father, she hired babysitters, offered herself to the double mirrors fastened to the brown dresser, went out, and came home long after I went to sleep. This wasn't simply to find somebody to share her life with. Since my father was out of the picture, she knew my future relationships with men would largely be determined by the men she chose to date. As such, until things were serious, these men were denied access to me. However, I don't recall meeting a single one of these men. Was the entire population of Elmwood and its surrounding suburbs bereft of eligible, worthy men? It wasn't until I was older and divorced that I realized she had sacrificed her womanhood for me. It had never occurred to me how lonely she must have been. Especially since I had made no such sacrifice for my daughter. Now that I was a grown woman, she was free to pick up where she left off so long ago. Nestor was inevitable. After winning money at bingo, she didn't mention Nestor for some time. But once his name reappeared, it did so with startling regularity. Nestor had been my greatest fear in coming to visit my mother.

One morning, still drunk from the night before, I awoke panicking that my mother would die before I saw her again. I had to see her. But before I could call her, before I could act on this impulse, I needed to get to the bathroom. I needed to vomit. Yanking my dorm room open, I was greeted by a crimson pile of someone else's vomit. Jumping over it, I fast stepped to the water fountain down the perpendicular hallway, only to find it covered in a green and yellow pile of vomit. Sprinting down the hallway to the bathroom, I burst through the door, pushed open the first stall door, only to be welcomed by the largest pile of partially disintegrated shit, barely camouflaged by half a roll of toilet paper. Dashing into the next stall, I dropped to my knees and vomited. Sitting on the bathroom floor, back against the partition, legs shooting into the neighboring stall, my panic soon returned. I would never see my mother again. Back in my room forty-five minutes later, I called her and agreed to visit the following weekend. The relief and joy in her voice was palpable. But even after accepting, I wasn't 100% certain I was going. Especially as the hours lengthened, I sobered up, and Mr. Bones refused to recede into the folds of the curtains. Nevertheless, the following weekend, I headed to her new home.

When the exit for Alexandria finally presented itself, fourteen hours had passed, and I still hadn't arrived. The first several hours were uneventful enough; just me, the road, and the low-hanging sun. As I grew closer, my heart began to pound so fiercely that it blocked out all sound to my ears. By the time I reached the Colorado border, my hands were trembling so wildly I could barely keep them wrapped around the steering wheel. I dropped the car to twenty miles an hour, and there it stayed. I stopped just short of the Casey city limits at a gas station, exhausted. Staggering into the women's room, I sat draped over the toilet, head between my legs, my skin slick, the smell of shit and Tampax keeping me conscious. Sitting cross-legged on the hood of the car, the setting sun warmed my face and dried my sweat-drenched clothes. I would have turned around if I thought I wouldn't pass out.

Approaching the apartment complex, I could see the man I knew was Nestor. He was short and stocky with wide shoulders, hunched slightly, slowly raking three smaller piles of red, orange, and yellow leaves into one larger one. He paused, extracting a grey-white handkerchief from his back pocket with effort, and shook it briefly before swiping at his brow.

Turning towards my car, his face contracted when he saw me.

Before I had time to react, my mother was bounding out the front door and at my window before the car was in park.

"Where in heaven's name have you been? I was getting frantic. Let me see you?" she asked, pulling me from the driver's seat, taking me by the shoulders. "Beautiful. Just beautiful. What took you so long?"

"I got a late start. Stopped for gas and food. There was some construction."

"It doesn't matter. You're here now."

Nestor wandered begrudgingly over, lighting a short, hand-rolled cigarette, the tips of his fingertips thick, calloused, and black.

"How is Adele?"

Nestor looked over at my mother, "The sister?"

She nodded.

"As okay as Adele can be, I guess. Very dramatic about the surgery and what not."

My mother looked at Nestor, saying, "She had her wisdom teeth taken out," by way of explanation.

"She wouldn't be put under," I said to both of them. "She was afraid she wouldn't wake up. As if anything could kill her," I said, pulling my purse strap over my shoulder.

"You talk about your sister that way?" he asked, taking a puff of the cigarette, exhaling immediately, gazing off into the distance. His eyes were rounded by a thick gelatinous pink. His breath smelled of whiskey. I looked at him, then at my mother, who frowned.

"And your father? School?" she asked, still frowning at Nestor.

"Fine. Everyone, everything is fine."

"My brother hasn't visited in years."

"You have a brother?" I asked, stuttering slightly.

"He was a bum." I furrowed my brow. "He used to visit. Usually when he needed money or one of his girlfriend's gave him the boot. Those were the only things he gave a damn about – women and booze. He was a real juiceball," he said dropping the cigarette.

"Juiceball?" I asked. Gazing down, the cigarette was still smoking.

He looked up from the ground and directly into my eyes. "Drunk. He was a drunk. Huh, was. He died."

I shook my head, no, even though he hadn't asked me a question.

He sighed disapprovingly, leaning the rake against my car, pulling out his handkerchief, and wiping his nose. "You know how they found him?"

"Ness," my mother interrupted, shaking her head.

"In the middle of a public park, leaning against a trash can, three empty bottles of vodka next to him, vultures circling over his head."

"There weren't vultures, Ness."

"Like hell there weren't," he said, pointing at her, his voice growing loud.

"In the city? All right, I'll stop," she said, raising her hands in surrender. "Ness lived in Chicago before he moved here."

"You sure took your time getting here. By my tabulation, Elmwood is nine, nine and a half hours way. What took you so long to get here?"

When I didn't respond immediately, my mother came to my rescue. "She said there was construction."

"If you say so," he said, grunting. He wandered back to the pile of leaves, pushing them this way and that, before a loud, wet, coughing fit forced him to stop almost immediately.

"Ness, Ness," my mother beckoned. "Why don't you

go lie down?"

"I'm fine," he said, then proceeded to march directly into the house. Were they living together already? It was a routine with a kind of sensitivity. I was too afraid to ask and honestly didn't want to know the answer. I didn't like him at all.

"I'm so glad to see you."

The general tenor of Nestor's mood remained consistent throughout what was a rather pedestrian two-day visit. The three of us ate our meals together at Nestor's favorite restaurant, *Little Brooklyn*, where I soon discovered his preferred meal was a steak sandwich with lightly toasted bread and one pat of butter, which he had for both lunch and dinner. If it were served with margarine or no butter, he would send it back. *I imagined he ate at this establishment every day for years and had never once been served a steak sandwich with margarine or no butter.* At night, we sat around the kitchen table, drinking wine and playing cribbage, never staying up much past eleven. If Nestor did indeed live with her, neither of them gave any indication, as he retired to his own place every night with a dry kiss on the cheek. He had enough begrudging common sense to allow my mother and I time alone together. The two of us spent the afternoon strolling the long, lonely dirt roads about the perimeter of the town under the unblinking sun. I updated her about my studies, the boys I was seeing, Adele, Dad, the usual. She walked me through the activities and adjustments of her days in such a small town. She had a group of women friends she played cribbage with, she volunteered at the church with many of the same ladies, she had Nestor. I tried to discern in the spaces between her words any hint of dissatisfaction she wouldn't allow herself to say. I couldn't sense one.

She seemed genuinely satisfied with her life. The only particularity I discovered was that she was petrified of a local wild turkey which was, according to her, the size of a small Volkswagen Beetle and that she mentioned frequently. To avoid running into him, she would make us take circuitous routes to and from the restaurant, church, and the center of town to her apartment. Nestor had offered to take care of it, but she had demurred. In all my life, I had never seen her hurt any living creature. In fact, when I was fourteen, and after a little too much wine, I had seen her take a glass paperweight with a butterfly ensconced inside and smash it to pieces to set it free.

After mass on Sunday, it was time for me to head home. The turkey was seen milling around the apartment entrance, so my mother and I said our goodbyes inside. Nestor insisted he carry my single bag to my car. As I was about to back out, he leaned in the window. Glancing at the apartment complex, he lowered his voice. "Why did you finally grace us with your presence?" he asked, a section of his dirty grey hair flopping forward like a wing of a falcon. "Because that one's been trying to get you down here for months. Been going on about it. How she asked and asked. How you're too busy with school to visit your own mother."

Shifting in my seat, I glanced at the dashboard clock and at her apartment window which remained empty. The smell of whiskey on his breath was strong.

"I had finals," I said.

"Mmm-hmm," he said, swiping the hair away from his eyes. "Don't come back," he said, straightening himself up, stepping away from my car.

That was the last time I visited Casey while my mother

was alive. She died shortly before I graduated from college. Looking out as I crossed the stage to see my father and Adele clapping, I burst into tears when I noticed the empty seat between them that they kept for her. We went out and got good and drunk after that. Mercifully, it wasn't the last time I saw her. She made it back to Elmwood a couple of times a year, always alone, to visit McKenna and me and some close friends. It should have made me feel like an adult, hosting her in my apartment, preparing her breakfast, taking her in, but as much as I tried, I just felt like an imposter. It wasn't, however, my last encounter with Nestor. When she died, the funeral was in Casey. None of our extended family made the trip. My father offered. I told him not to bother. Although we were not yet married, Brayden wouldn't allow me to take McKenna. As such, I made the trip alone.

Opening the door to the funeral home, Nestor was firmly entrenched in one of the wood chairs with floral pink and purple prints, staring me down. The moment he saw me, he placed his hands firmly on his thighs, lifted himself up, and marched into the receiving room. He took a front seat where he stayed for the entirety of the service, without uttering a word. When everything was finished, and everyone had said their goodbyes to one another and my mother and had begun dispersing, I found Nestor, like the previous time I had been leaving, at the window of my car.

"You always seemed soft to me." He was revved up and plenty drunk. From behind me, the sun washed out his face. The last bits of his grey, blond hair clinging to the front of his massive forehead like newly sprouted grass. He wanted to tangle, to brawl like a couple of old lions. I just stared at the dashboard clock of my car.

"We built a nice life here. One we both wanted," he said. "She died thinking you were ashamed of her. Now she can stop looking over her shoulder, up that long highway back at Elmwood, waiting for you. I'm sure you have to get going."

He took a few steps back. I never saw him again. Whenever I think of him and my mother, I feel a tremendous amount of guilt, as if I am the one responsible for their being together. If only my mother hadn't given up everything to raise me, if she had been even a little bit selfish, maybe she wouldn't have jumped at the first man who came along. A man who, by all appearances, was petty, brutish, and mean. She had to have known that all I wanted for her was happiness.

When the final sign for Alexandria appeared on the side of the road, I drifted begrudgingly onto the exit ramp. There were few signs of life. Just long grey stretches of paved road and a single blue sign with the words 'ALEXANDRIA, 4 miles,' 'CASEY, 12 miles,' and a single white arrow pointing to the right.

Entering the Alexandria city limits, there were two gas stations on opposing corners, like salesmen hawking for your business. After several minutes, I came to Casey township. On my immediate right, an oversized and empty auto repair shop. Further down, a church, its white and brown steeple, serene and formal. On the left, an antique shop, two abandoned storefronts, a religious book and gift shop, and Little Brooklyn, boasting the best breakfast in Goodwin County, and at its very end, that very same gas station I had stopped at so many years ago. It was as if the town had crawled behind a couch to die.

I pulled in and filled the tank. A rusty blue pickup truck pulled in next to me. The driver, a comically thin man with long red hair and a beard disappearing out of view, turned to the woman in the passenger seat and started speaking desperately, motioning wildly with his hands, his head and beard shaking back and forth, his face blooming a red hot. It wasn't clear if they had been arguing or if he was attempting to instigate a fight; either way, she sat, looking down at her phone, her feet up on the dash, without reacting. He jumped out of the truck and slammed the door, hoping she would race out after him. She remained motionless.

Following him into the station, I wandered the aisles. I leafed through a gossip magazine and spun a rack filled with magnets and magnetic bottle openers. Through the tiny round ceiling speakers, I heard what I thought was the faint beginnings of "California Dreamin'" by the Mamas and the Papas. I stood in the middle of the aisle waiting for the moment the guitar riff would cease and those voices, mellow and wan, like the invocation to my Mountain West tragedy, would begin. The guitar would build, raising and overturning its hand, offering up a space for those sublime harmonies, then nothing. The riff would simply repeat. I tilted my head towards the ceiling in anticipation. I might have stood in this aisle for all eternity. The cycle repeated. Perhaps I was dead? In some supernatural weigh station awaiting my judgment before being sent to my destination. Eventually, some non-descript jazz took its place.

I noticed I was being leered at by the obese, acne-riddled man behind the counter, who, in turn, was being silently scolded by a short, blunt woman at his side. Her eyes roiled, jealous and hateful. He devoured me without shame.

My mouth puckered wryly as I turned my attention back to the magazine, exposing the curves of my ass and breasts to him. I began to rock back and forth. This was not the response a modern woman was supposed to have. It certainly wasn't how Adele would react. How would Adele, in fact, react? With outrage, sure. At least in the privacy of her house or in the car with Dad and me. But what would she actually do? She was full of shit, pissed that she wasn't pretty and desired.

Abandoning the magazine, I approached the counter. "Do you have any beer?"

"Last cooler on the right," he said.

I wandered languidly to the large transparent coolers lining the entire far wall, letting my hips sway, playing with a long strand of my hair the way I thought Michelle Phillips would have. Pulling open one of the glass doors, I let the cool air overtake me, briefly closing my eyes. Taking a forty-ounce beer back to the counter, I stood as he inspected my ID for an obscenely long time.

"You're a long way from home," he said, finally handing it back to me.

"Is that the best you could do," I said and paid for the beer and the gas. I was about to exit when I turned back. "Where is the Lockwood Cemetery?"

"The Lockwood Cemetery? That's back towards Alexandria. You'll see a sign."

Exiting with the bottle in the plain brown bag, I took a seat on the wooden picnic table to the right of the gas station.

The truck was nowhere to be seen, leaving the entire area empty and silent. Across the street was a barn, a large fading American flag painted across the entirety of one side, gargantuan pieces of machinery strewn randomly in the grass and the gravel driveway. Along the perimeter were several iron cutouts of trotting coyotes. Half a mile or so toward Casey, civilization gave up on this place, and the pavement gave way to dirt. Other than that, there was nothing but fields of green and fading yellow corn held to the ground by telephone poles, the occasional barn, and their satellite silos in the distance. The sun was high and severe. There was little shade. The beer was cold and tasted good, the perspiration from the bottle making circles on the wooden tabletop. I lifted and set down the bottle several times and made the Olympic symbol. I took a deep breath of the crisp autumn air and, even though I was only a quarter way through the beer, considered getting another. Perhaps two more.

The smell of burning leaves came from far off. I always felt most at ease in autumn, like settling into a big soft chair. Nothing conjured up autumn more than that smell – that and the sound of Ella Fitzgerald's voice. Especially after summer, the season of heat and activity, sitting around a pool or Little Blue Lake, watching birds take wing or hearing the covert cry of a loon as the sun retired. Despite the changing leaves and onset of winter, autumn didn't simply signal disintegration and hibernation. It was also the beginning of school – routine, crushes, the opportunity to reinvent oneself. I recall one sharply chilly evening at a high school football game when I was fifteen, my friends and I crammed into the bleachers, wrapped in jackets and scarves, gossiping and laughing. After the game, as the crowd dispersed, I suddenly found myself alone, in complete darkness, parallel to Blake Behr. He was staring at me, clasping his saxophone. For a moment, we locked eyes. Not knowing what else to do, I started to run towards the school, which was lit up in the distance like the Aurora Borealis. He followed suit. I could hear his footfalls on the unforgiving ground, his breathing heavy as if he were trying to consume me. I started to laugh. He began laughing, too. Before long, we were hysterical. In the black, running and laughing with beautiful Blake Behr. Approaching the lamplights and the school, we slowed and fell silent, and like a river around a rock, broke in separate directions, me towards my friends, him towards the band room. For a moment, I was despondent. Once I married Brayden, so many years later, everything about autumn and my feelings toward it changed.

Brayden always became disconsolate towards the end of August. His father drowned a year after we got married at the beginning of October. And thus, a yearly ritual was initiated. Every September, as the wind began to exert a bite and the days grew shorter, Brayden's mood darkened, his patience brittle. He became irritable and withdrawn – our house, sullen. This all led up to the anniversary of his father's passing, a day Brayden always took off from work to woefully pore over photo albums and watch the few home movies he had. After that, he would go on a long, cathartic bike ride. Then, off to *Mr. Mix's* to drink gin and tonic (his father's favorite drink). Brayden didn't much care for gin and tonic, but there we would sit, across from one another. I was the obligatory witness to his agony as he got drunk. The trajectory, always the same. He began with the memories, enshrining the man. These were as meager as the home movies. After a few more drinks, the resentments came red hot and sharp: his failings as a husband, father, and man. Culminating in abject silence. At that point, I'd call it, ask for the bill, and drive us home, where he'd lock himself in the bathroom and try to muffle the sounds of his sobbing. It was a strain our young marriage barely withstood. I believed since I suffered the loss of my mother, I knew how to be there for a bereft son. I managed alone, and so could he. I offered him no solace and went about our lives as if nothing had happened. I'm embarrassed at how self-satisfied I was as my husband cracked up inside.

As if on cue, my phone began to ring. I glanced down at my phone on the table, although I needn't. It was Brayden. I took a large swig of the beer, setting it back down on the very top right Olympic circle. I would definitely need another. Even if his name wasn't popping up on the screen, I knew it was him. Nearly everything about this nervous, petulant man was seared into my brain: his phone number, his birthday, height, weight, social security number (his shirt and pants size, amazingly), even his mother's birthday. It was like those large communication cables buried deep beneath the ocean floor – you don't know how they got there or who laid them but, nevertheless, there they sit, connecting continents thousands of miles apart. When we divorced, the state declared all that once-pertinent information irrelevant with the stroke of a pen. But no matter how innocuous and useless, it kept us permanently, if unwilfully, connected.

The phone stopped ringing.

But you got McKenna. So goes a chorus of well-wishers from every part of my life, familiar and strangers alike. A bit of commonly received knowledge in the annuls of divorce if there ever was one. It's bullshit. *At least in one manner of speaking.* It's the equivalent of saying a war, with all its carnage and death, was acceptable because it ended with a peace treaty. Of course, I adore McKenna. And yes, she is, without a doubt, the best thing to ever happen in my life. Already she is a better person than me. But it's perfectly acceptable for me to say my marriage was a pile of floating filth. Period.

My phone rang again. This time, I answered. What choice did I have? We created a person (a truly profound miracle I try to never lose sight of), and until the day one of us died, we were two continents forever connected.

"It's me, Brayden."

I had known the man for over half of my life, met at fourteen, dated in college, soon after bearing our only child, and, somehow in his brain, he never thought I could recognize his goddamn voice. It was difficult not to hang up on him, much less share the responsibilities of raising a child with him.

"I thought you were leaving for your mysterious journey today."

"What do you need?" I asked, taking a long sip from the beer, exhaling loudly into the phone.

"I didn't want to bring this up. Especially since you're on your mysterious journey."

"Quit calling it that," I said, setting the beer down on the bottom left circle, grinding it hard into the wood, yet the table refused to give.

"We have an issue." He paused, waiting for me to ask what it was. I refused to do so.

"When I came to pick up McKenna last – let's see – Wednesday, Mark was still there."

"He stays over occasionally. You know that."

"He had just finished taking a shower," he said with effort. Here he paused. I wasn't sure if he wanted me to comment. Again, I didn't. I could hear him pacing in his kitchen, decorated in nearly the exact same way our house was when we were married, only on a smaller scale. "He came out into the living room with a towel wrapped around his waist and nothing else." I stared at the horizon, the blank landscape, and brought the oversized bottle up to my lips and took a slug, again exhaling loudly into the mouthpiece. "It's not something I'm comfortable with."

"I shower every morning, don't you?" I asked, sticking my tongue out at the horizon, at him, at this moronic conversation, and the day we reconnected in that dorm room through our shared weed connection, where we subsequently met every day behind the heavily curtained windows, a rolled-up towel at the foot of the door, spending long afternoons getting high, listening to avant-garde jazz and the Buzzcocks (neither of which I could stand but the weed was just so good). He would go on about politics and video games. It meant nothing. Don't get me wrong. He was obsessed with those subjects. But he was brandishing his feathers. He was peacocking. He had zeroed in on me, and it was only a matter of time before he forced the moment into crisis and asked me out. He did. I accepted. I still can't tell you why. *I had a boyfriend.* The moment I acquiesced, he transformed into a snowplow. He insisted we be exclusive. He pressured me to move in with him before I was ready (but in my lazy-ass rationalizations, I thought, 'half the rent,' right?) He proposed, we got married on a limited budget and purchased a house before we were financially stable. And somewhere in there, I got pregnant, too.

"Of course, Willow."

"At least I hope you do. I know how badly you sweat

at night."

"It's completely inappropriate, Willow."

"Was he naked?"

"It's the implication."

"You don't know that, and neither would McKenna," I said.

"Nevertheless, it's not something I'm comfortable with. I'm just trying to look out for the best interest of our child."

"And somehow I'm not?"

After a lengthy pause, he answered, "No."

"So, you're saying you want to fight? I'm in the middle of nowhere, and you called to fight."

"If it was the other way around, you wouldn't be so dismissive," he said, his voice softer and full of resentment.

He was dead wrong. Our lives would be so much easier if he had someone in his life. Not only to spend time with, to stick his stupid little dick into (and make sure I knew about) but to place his wiry anxieties onto. Why he didn't was a bit of a mystery. He was (if I was forced to admit) mildly attractive (even if the jet-black ponytail, scruffy beard, and John Lennon glasses were a bit much for a man his age, but they weren't going anywhere), intelligent, had a steady job, was a good (if overindulgent and selfish) conversationalist and father. I know he wasn't carrying a torch for me. The long and short of it was he was a starving man, and I was the last meal he enjoyed. There was no other explanation I could come up with.

"We have sex, Brayden. Sex. Sexual intercourse. We have sex. Did you think we don't?"

"You can go out to any bar, anytime, and go home with someone; the chances of that happening to me are, what one in twenty? Thirty? Fifty?"

Men always believe that the ability of a woman to find a lover made everything simpler. As if getting laid was the answer to everything. However, I'd be lying if I didn't admit having someone trip all over you and artificially inflating your self-esteem wasn't occasionally the tonic you needed when you felt like shit.

"Lord."

I lay down on the top of the picnic table. Above me, a battalion of clouds were lumbering by. They wandered on like so many disregarded lives. Directly above me was a large hand, its forefinger and thumb clasped together as if to convince me everything was okay. I closed my eyes. Opening them back up again, its grip was already drifting apart, like a mouth, wider and wider, a snake unhooking its jaw until it was positioned at 180 degrees, finally splitting in two. The two white whisps, thin and long, a wake behind an unseen boat that had ripped the translucent blue in half. I turned and shot a glance at the mostly empty beer bottle and back to the sky. The long, thin wisps had grown too insubstantial to sustain themselves and disappeared, sinking into the blue water of the blue sky above me. Fingers and Thumb. Jaw. Snake's Jaw. Boat's Wake. Sky and water and sky once more.

"Anyway, I agree with you," I said, sitting back up with effort.

"You do?"

"I don't know why Mark did that." Actually, I did. He was a big dumb jungle cat marking his territory, pissing all over my house and Brayden and me. Before he could respond, I added, "It won't happen again."

"Well, thank you. I appreciate that. Truly." He paused,

clearly taken aback. "Do you remember the night I proposed?"

I had gone home for Spring Break of my senior year, and the combination of distance and lack of communication was driving him to the brink. He appeared at the sandwich shop at the end of my shift, insisting I meet him at the Chanhassen Inn. I was not excited. I just found out I was pregnant that morning, was deadly hungover, and did my best to feign enthusiasm about his presence. I thought he was either going to threaten suicide or propose. Either way, I knew I was going to be stuck with him, in some fashion, forever. After slogging through my closing routine, I dragged my feet to the Chanhassen Inn, where he proposed. I was only slightly relieved. Then I told him about our baby. He was over the moon and called it fate. Why had I set my precious stone of a life in a band with him, I could not tell you.

"I remember telling you it felt like I had finally found my home when I met you."

"I remember."

His words were not filled with nostalgia or regret but with a sunset melancholy, as if the best years were behind him.

"I was a little surprised you didn't tell me that you were going across the country leaving our daughter with your father until all the plans were made."

The pacing had begun in earnest again.

"It's my weekend to have her, so what's the difference? You trust my dad. You'll have her on your scheduled day."

"For one, I'm her father. More importantly, we have always agreed upon transparent communication when it comes to decisions regarding McKenna. You've always made a big deal about your weekends, and now you're just splitting town."

"I'm in Nebraska. Not exactly a singles hotspot."

"What the fuck does that even mean? Why are you there? Can I get the contact number of a hotel? Or with whoever you're staying with?"

"No. No. No. Nope. No."

"What if something happens? I am McKenna's father."

All this talk about our marriage, Brayden being McKenna's father. It wasn't just about familial ties and responsibilities. The joy Brayden showed when I told him I was pregnant wasn't only about our child and creating a family. Brayden always feared I'd replace him with another man and prayed that my pregnancy could forge a bond that neither time, distance, infidelity, divorce, or, perversely, death could fracture. It was a vain attempt to firm up the existential bonds between us that he never truly believed in. This was only exasperated when I cheated and then when we got divorced.

"I apologize. For what Mark did. For not giving you a heads-up. I'm heading to Salt Lake City. To talk to Chet."

There was a nervous silence. It went on.

"You're allowed to say something, Brayden."

"I'm just surprised. I haven't thought of him for a long time. Adele couldn't have been happy."

"No. Especially since I'm missing her wedding to do so."

"Shit. That's right. I guess my invite got lost in the mail."

I laughed despite myself.

"What made you decide to do this?"

"Brayden, I don't want to talk about it. Seriously."

"Does he know you're coming?"

"You think I would drive across the county and just show up out of the blue?"

"Yes."

"All right, Brayden. I need to get moving. Would you, on the off chance, be willing to do me a favor?" He waited a long time before he answered, no doubt cataloging all the ways I had wronged him during and after our marriage. "Coco, my dad's dog, mauled a chipmunk – my dad had to finish it off with a shovel and, unfortunately, McKenna witnessed it all."

"What the hell, Willow? Doesn't your dad have any common sense?"

"I already talked to him. Everything can't be my fault."

"Can't it?" he said with a chuckle. "It would make my life a helluva lot easier."

"I was hoping you could stop over later – at your convenience – and make sure she's all right."

"I kind of had plans for the day," he began, still chuckling. "Nothing you would like or approve of, no doubt."

Standing up, I walked over to the trash can, tossed the empty bottle, made my way to my car, and leaned on the bumper.

"What would you think about my visiting Nestor?"

"Jesus, why?"

"He calls me a couple of times a year. All fucked up and lonely."

"Since when?"

"Since my mom died."

"Jesus, I didn't know that."

"Why would you?" I asked.

"Even when we were married? You really never told me anything," he began. Then, catching himself, asked, "What does he want when he calls? To tell you what a great daughter you were."

"Something like that. I thought that maybe I should check up on him."

"Screw him. He was never nice to us. Never visited. Kept your mother away from you and McKenna. Let him rot."

"So, one vote for no."

Brayden laughed. A tractor lurched into the parking lot to a large, empty space to the side of the gas station.

"You sure have an effect on people."

"You think that would be a good thing. I appreciate your honesty. I couldn't ask Adele or my dad."

"No. That you could not do. I'll head over to your dad's."

"You know, they have left for the wedding already. I don't know where my head is," I said, thinking I probably should get some food in my stomach.

"Willow?"

"Yeah?"

"There's not that many people that would do that. Visit Nestor after all he put you through. You're still the most unpredictable person I know."

"I gotta get moving."

"Drive safe."

Pulling out of the gas station parking lot, I saluted the fading American flag on the barn's side and headed back through Alexandria. When I saw the sign for the Lockwood Cemetery, I pulled onto the gravel road and stopped in front of the gates. The road split into two and wound around the cemetery. Tombstones fanned out to either side and in the middle island, large mausoleums topped by obelisks and angels dominated the view. Sycamores and weeping willows dotted the grounds, keeping most of it shaded, and several wretched spigots gracelessly poked out of the earth. At the very far edge, a groundskeeper sat on the headstone eating a sandwich. Somewhere beyond these wrought iron gates lay my very dead mother. I thought about Aaron, who I had made love to in that graveyard by my college. It felt so freeing at the time. I remember afterward in that post-coitus glow, still drunk, thinking, quite majestically, that we had juxtaposed the essence of life against the decisiveness of death. Some victory. I didn't even like Aaron. Putting the car in reverse, I eased myself back onto the road and made my way to the highway. I wasn't ten miles further when my phone began to ring again. It was my father.

"You seem to be calling again when you said I wouldn't hear from you anymore today," I said curtly, my mother firmly behind me.

"McKenna wants to give a funeral for the squirrel."

"Haven't you left yet?" I asked, my blood pressure skyrocketing. The last thing I needed was to be blamed for my father and daughter being late for Adele's wedding.

"It's about to start, but she insisted I call. She wants to do it tomorrow morning, and she's adamant about asking you herself."

"This is absolutely ridiculous. Put her on."

"Mom," she began hesitantly. "Is it okay if we have a funeral for the squirrel?"

"Of course, honey. But you don't need to worry about it right now. Just enjoy Aunt Adele's wedding and take a lot of pictures for Mommy, okay?"

"Is it all right if I put it in your blue shoe?"

Jesus Christ.

"That I wore to prom? I guess, yes. Shit…." I said as the phone bounced off my shoulder to the floor, disappearing from view. "Hold on, honey. Mommy dropped the phone," I said, my eyes toggling from the road down to the floor and back again. Squinting down at the gas and brake pedals, the phone was nowhere to be seen. My left foot brushed around spasmodically in an attempt to locate it. In the background, as if from a blackened room, the muffled sound of my daughter's voice could be heard. A white Jetta raced by on my right, followed by a blue pick-up truck, the driver staring down at me until he was well past.

Dropping my shoulder, I swept my hand under the seat. It was a landfill of lost and forgotten items: two lighters, a pen, countless balled-up napkins, and an empty pack of cigarettes. It was like delving into the dark, long-forgotten memory of the car itself. I tossed them on the passenger seat, my fingertips blackened. These were articles that wanted to be forgotten and had no interest in being written in the pages of history, anyone's history. I grew bitter. My life was cluttered with people and places I wished erased: Mark and his demands for a love I didn't have to give, the heat of Brayden's resentment for divorcing him, Adele and the wedding I was currently missing, and the wrath I would bear for as long as she remained married – alive even – and, despite appearances, my father's secret shame that I was not the daughter he wanted: married, successful, happy and, above all, loyal. Not to mention Chet. That fucking asshole. Screw him for the decades-long hooks he managed to keep burrowed in my skin and the ghost of the child that kept us connected. I even felt a whispering abhorrence for my daughter. Without her, I would not be fastened to this wretched, agonizing existence. There was no sun shining on me from any of them. Only a black suffocating disappointment that so often forced me to the ground. They could be someone else's history for a change. But everywhere I went, around every corner, there they were. I lifted my feet and took another fruitless pass under the seat. Sweat swarmed my brow and behind my ears like stinging black flies. A long, slow curve in the road halted my search. I called out to reassure my daughter, my voice hoarse. "Hold on, honey. Mommy's all right." If she responded, I could no longer hear. All I wanted to do was crawl into a dark, cavernous bed somewhere and sleep. But before I could commit to this enormous resentment, the road straightened out.

Sliding my shoes off, I tucked my feet beneath the seat. Miraculously, I came upon the phone. Freezing both feet in place, my toes clung to it like a bird on a mouse. I slowly maneuvered it out from beneath the seat and snatched it. Straightening myself back up, I found myself barreling towards a brown and yellow station wagon.

"Oh my god."

Slamming on the brakes with both feet, the tires let out a dry squeal, loud, long and sustained, like the screaming of pigs at the slaughter. It was the invocation of death itself. The car came to an immediate halt that defied the laws of physics. I winced, anticipating shattering glass and collapsing metal before being hammered into the steering wheel. Then silence. A gripping cavernous silence.

Opening my eyes, I was astonished to find I was hugging the steering wheel. Easing myself back into the seat,

I reached for the rearview mirror and found the Chevy logo imprinted onto my cheek. The highway behind me was empty, ahead of me nothing but pavement, above me sky. The station wagon was gone, dissipated into thin air as if snatched up into the heavens in my place. My head and back ached. I wriggled my toes, raised my shoulders, and made fists of my hands, listening for the sound of cracking bones. To the left and right of me, there was nothing but green and blue and brown. Eventually, I found my purse, lit a cigarette, sat still in the middle of the highway, and smoked, not once witnessing a passing car or truck in either direction. My lungs filled and emptied. Smoke poured from my mouth and nose. It felt like some giant primordial creature had shoved its arm into my chest cavity. Lifting my shirt, the bruising had already begun. Stubbing the butt out in the middle of the steering wheel, the horn briefly voiced its dissatisfaction like a disturbed sleeping cat.

Opening the door, the sound of chirping cicadas overwhelmed me as if the fates were arguing over my destiny. Leaving it ajar behind me, I marched, still in socks, around the front of the car, whose grill and shielded motor growled at me like a cougar ready to devour me. To my left, a bird soared and disappeared, sucked into the horizon. Shuffling to the gravel shoulder, I took another twenty paces up the highway and made a ninety-degree turn. I dropped the cigarette at my feet. Down past the ditch stood several feet of brush withering before an eternity of decaying corn. In the far distance, a smattering of trees stood, molting their leaves. The last of the summer heat was burning itself off like a fever that had just broken. By evening, it would be as crisp as seltzer water. Tilting my head, I took the still furious sun straight on like a raging bull. It stung the back of my skull. Pulling my hands to my face, everything was scarlet and black. Blinking through the molten swirling light, I lowered my head, squatted, and felt the beast on my neck and back. I picked up the cigarette from the ground and took a puff. Nothing... its end, cold and spent. I lowered myself to the ground and lay on the side of the highway. The rocks burrowed into my back. The sun turned the inside of my eyelids red. The cicadas descended, cackling, buzzing, mocking, a Greek chorus. I wrapped myself in my own arms and tried not to sob.

I was raised in a liberal family, surrounded by liberal friends with progressive values. When I revealed I was pregnant, no one congratulated me. I was told in resolute tones that it was my body. When I confessed my decision, the silent nods I was greeted with confirmed the predetermined verdict that had been placed before me. Even Adele was in communion. At the time, I felt no remorse. None. In my mind, I was emulating my grandmother as she lay on that matted, worn, smoke-saturated carpet – taking the appropriate action, staunch, on my terms, clear-headed. I thought I was making another bold decision when I went forward with McKenna with Brayden not long after Dead Girl Grey.

And now?

Mostly, I try not to think about it. On the rare occasions my mind passes over Dead Girl Grey, I can't figure out why I did it, especially without telling Chet. I do know that day never goes by unnoticed or sober. January 8th. That's the day, birthday, death day. I had learned to live with it like an undiagnosed tumor. But Chet's letter ripped through me like an earthquake beneath a graveyard. It tossed up tombstones, partially decomposed corpses, the not-quite-dead scratching at my insides: that incident in the parking lot with Sarah and her boyfriend, that blowout with my mother in middle school after which I attempted suicide, cheating on Brayden, my-never-to-be-born first child. Once I saw the return address on the outside of the envelope from Chet, I knew I had to go to Salt Lake City. I had to put a pillow over those wet, hungry mouths.

I slept. It was the blackest, hardest of sleeps, untroubled by dreams, my idling car, the hissing cicadas, or fingernails on the insides of coffins. It was not unlike the night in my junior year of college I drank half a bottle of Jack Daniels and was found under a bush in the middle of the campus. I was rushed to the hospital by that hysterical ambulance to get my stomach pumped. I woke up in much the same manner by the sound of a man's voice I did not recognize.

"Ma'am, are you all right?"

I hesitated to open my eyes. Was this to be another decision made on someone else's terms? To ease another's burden? The rising sound of panic in his voice forced my hand. Bent over me, nose to nose, was a curly-haired man with a baseball hat on, his face flush. As I blinked, relief washed over his face. I arched my back. The ache had not gone. The dread only intensified. Sitting up, my breathing was labored. My entire body was wrapped in a sweet sweat, like thin cellophane.

"Ma'am?"

My car had been moved to the side of the road, some distance in front of us. He looked over his shoulder.

"It's a miracle it wasn't hit," he said, turning back to me.

I stared at it a bit longer, wiped my moist forehead,

and glanced at the highway. The cicadas were still going strong; angry, no doubt, my life had been spared. Several cars whizzed by on the opposite side of the highway.

"When I was a child, I didn't know what cicadas were. I just thought it was the sound of the sun when it was very hot. I nearly became a permanent addition to the station wagon in front of me."

He waited for more details. He looked out at the field, listened for a moment, but said nothing.

"What time is it?" I asked, the sweat turning my body cold. I began to shiver.

"Quarter after six."

"Jesus." I was behind schedule. "I dropped my phone. My daughter. She's probably worried sick." I attempted to stand but tipped back to the ground immediately.

"Why don't you wait a moment?" he asked, placing his arm across my back.

"I need to talk to my daughter."

"Give me your phone, and I can—"

"Help me up!" I thought I was screaming at the man, but my voice was nothing but a whisper, a suggestion of panic.

With effort, he got me to my feet. I stood motionless. Glancing at him and smirking, we looped arms and made our way back to my car. The sun was high and far and hot and kept its unblinking mustard eye on me. I plopped into the driver's seat. The heat was suffocating. I felt mildly nauseous. A car whizzed by, laying on its horn.

"There really was no need to stop," I said out the window.

He took off his hat with one hand and wiped a line of sweat with the same hand.

"I just really had to go the bathroom, and there wasn't a rest stop. I must have dozed off."

"And the car?" he asked, placing the hat back on his head, a hint of a smile appearing at the corner of his mouth. Now that he knew I wasn't hurt, it began. He could attempt to alchemize our meeting, first by reducing the uniqueness of the situation into a mere damsel-in-distress archetype and then transforming it (he hoped) into sexual potency. Men never stop. *Maybe we never stop, either.*

"That one is harder to explain," I said, starting the engine and cranking the air conditioning, which sputtered out torrid and resentful. Taking a deep, painful breath, I looked directly at the logo on the man's cap and said, "I'm not going to give you my number if that's what you're waiting for. You're just a guy that found me," I said, my eyes diving immediately into my lap.

After a few awkward moments, he made his way back to his car. He focused on my image in my rearview mirror. I could see him working up the courage to come back. In the end, he pulled onto the highway, his eyes forced stubbornly forward as he passed.

Relieved, I reached under the front seat and, after some digging, found my pipe. Before I could take a hit, my phone, which had somehow cruelly ended up on the passenger seat along with my purse, began to buzz. It was Brayden. I yanked open the glove compartment, threw it as hard as I could into its shallow belly, and slammed it shut. The door popped back open, flapping comically like a python's disconnected lower jaw, rejecting and mocking my fury. I slammed it shut again. I needed a moment before my life came clamoring back for me. After a momentary silence, the desperate ringing began again. Leaning forward,

I opened the glove compartment. Before we were fully connected, the sounds were already scuttling.

"Willow? Are you alright?"

It was my father. The sound of music and a chorus of voices were in the background.

"Yes, everything is fine. I just dropped the phone. It was wedged under my seat."

"I don't need another body on my hands."

Rubbing my hands over my eyes and squeezing the bridge of my nose. "No, I suppose you don't."

"I need to go for fucks sake."

The line went dead.

I put the car into gear and crept slowly along the shoulder, daring a state trooper or avenging angel to end my mission before it went any further. When none did, I merged onto the highway and pressed forward, taking the first exit that presented itself several miles down. Turning right, I continued to drive. Eventually, I came across a large, unpaved parking lot at the end of which stood a low, plain white building with a small black sign that read: *Stand Up*. I needed a goddamn drink. The hours of driving and the constant barrage of calls from my daughter, father, and ex-husband had nearly wiped me out, and I wasn't even halfway to my destination and the main event.

Leaning against the back of my car, I took several deep breaths. The air was heavy. The rain was far from finished. Off in the distance, a family of silos and three silver-roofed buildings were backed up by a line of trees of deep amber. A slow-moving tractor could be heard in the distance. Adele was married by now, the reception in full swing. No use calling to wish her congratulations. Our relationship had gone through another seismic shift, one it may never recover from, and I was in the middle of the country chasing ghosts. I made my way to the entrance.

Opening the door, I was blinded by the darkness. Blinking hard several times, the surroundings slowly emerged. There was a U-shaped bar dominating the left side of the space, each end anchored by large oversized wooden posts, populated by an assortment of older men. Against the far wall opposite me, there were three black leather booths, empty, and two tables standing between them and the bar. I ordered a whiskey coke and took a seat at one of the tables.

A conversation was going on at the bar between the bartender and a customer who, by the familiar manner, was clearly a regular.

"Have you ever been on a city bus, Ritchie?"

"Of course, I've been on a bus," the bartender said, wiping the inside of a glass with a washrag.

"Then you know why I had to have a beer to get on that son-of-a-bitchin' thing."

"At eight in the morning?" he asked, still fiddling with the glass.

"Yes. Yes. Yep. Yes," he said, pounding the bar with every affirmation.

"Then they kicked you off?" he asked.

"Can you believe that shit?" he said, taking his drink, leaning back into the chair.

The bartender laughed easily into his chest. Three of the other five men at the bar laughed too. Even a cursory glance told you they were also regulars. The confines of these four walls delineated the entirety of their social lives. These were power drinkers, professional imbibers. The only reason these men worked was to pay rent, sit on these cheap bar stools, and eat (the last being optional on most days). Every ambition they ever had – in their profession, as fathers, husbands, friends, and as men – had been sacrificed, swallowed up by their addiction, this disease, this grand passion, whatever you wanted to call it.

Next to Ritchie sat a man in a sweater vest, quietly keeping vigil over his drink. His shirt and pants were pressed and crisp, his hair freshly cut, his brown-but-mostly-grey goatee was neat if a little long, his belly large but not obscenely so. His loafers rested easy on the crossbar of his chair. He was single. Of this, I had no doubt. He had been hurt by one or two women whose memory he vigilantly kept watch over in the deepest recesses of his heart. There was an ache for convalescence from a profound pain in the way he cradled his glass with only his fingertips and thumb, in his careful manners, but also a deep knowledge that he could not live with a woman again. Or one could not live with him, more likely the case. He was too stubborn, too set in his ways. So, he retired from some large city to be alone. To drink. After a bit, he never touched his drink again, and he left several bills on the bar and left.

"Post to post?" the bartender inquired to the bar at large, finally setting the clean glass down.

"Wanna see something hilarious?" a voice asked me. I turned to find a short, brunette woman, thick in the hips, glassy-eyed, with endless streams of hair at my table, who had appeared from out of nowhere. "Mind if I join you?" she asked, already pulling a chair out.

"Sure, I'm—"

"Hold on," she said, pointing to the bar.

I watched as the bartender set up five glasses and asked again, "Post-to-post?" while reaching for a bottle of whiskey.

"For everyone except him," Richie, the man who had been kicked off the bus said, pointing harshly at a decrepit old man sitting just to the right of one of the posts. The man, huddled over his drink, and who had one eye missing, grimaced into his chest but did not object. Unless you made a point of seeking him out, he seemed nothing but a shadow, a ghost slipping out from a break in the faux wood paneling.

"What the hell, Ritchie?" the bartender said, setting the bottle of whiskey down hard, taking inventory of the responses from the rest of the men who sat in stubborn silence.

"You think everyone doesn't know your game," he said, speaking directly to the ancient form who remained silent, only motioning his jaw as if adjusting a set of ill-fitting dentures, "sitting there as everyone buys round after round and then suddenly when it's your turn, poof, you're nowhere to be found, so no. I'll buy for everyone except him."

"He lives in his car," the bartender said, leaning in and whispering, although everyone could hear him.

"Jimmy, the barkeep, hates when Ritchie does this," this woman said. I had forgotten she was sitting with me. I side-eyed her but kept my attention on the bar. "He's a Catholic, a near Saint. Doesn't believe in credit cards, divorce, or premarital sex, and believe me, a few women have tried. He's mixed on the Jews."

"Really? That guy?" I asked. That was hard to believe anyone would want to bed the bartender or anyone in this dark, forgotten place.

"Everyone except him," Ritchie insisted more forcefully than before.

"It's true," the woman whispered. "Dead Eye, that's what people call him, you know, being the case that he only has one eye."

"Why?"

"Because he has one eye," she said, scowling at me.

"No, not why do they call him Dead Eye, how did he lose an eye?"

She bellowed loudly. "Of course. You're not stupid. Are you? No, of course not. He's a vet from some war or another. Or maybe it was a manufacturing accident. No one really knows. The story seems to change depending on how badly he wants a drink. Hell, it's probably just a story. Maybe he has both of his eyes, but we've been told so many times one is missing we don't see it!" she said, laughing again. "His wife is dead or gone. Ditto his daughter."

"Does he really live in his car?"

"That's what everyone says."

"That's terrible," I said, giving him the once over. The man was short, his beard unkempt, and he seemed to be bent in a perpetual hunch like a chicken pecking at the ground.

"Maybe he mooched off his wife, too," she said with a barely contained guffaw. "Anyway, he's a cheap screw, and Ritchie hates it."

We watched as all the regulars except Dead Eye were served a fresh round.

"Take it you've been here before."

"Live up the road in the Tranter trailer park. For about six years. My husband and I decided the two of us needed a little break. He decided. I didn't decide nothing."

"I'm sorry."

"Don't be it was my own doing. Well, aren't you going

to ask?" she asked, leaning in close to me.

"I didn't want to pry."

"Happened a couple or ten days ago."

"What happened?"

"For that, we will need another set," she said, rising. "Whiskey Coke, I think you were drinking?"

Setting the drinks down, she began.

"Brian, my estranged husband," she said sarcastically, "Can you believe I married a man named Brian? Anyway, we were going to his best friend's wedding. Who, for the record I don't even like? Anyway, I put on this tight little red dress. One I know drives him crazy. Brian, not the groom. Probably him, too," she said, her eyes flashing. "But the thing is, I'm running late. I'm always running late. So, he goes on ahead of me. It was just up the road at the VFW. Anyway, time gets away from me. I have a couple of bumps, and I end up busting into the church right as Annie—"

"The bride?"

"The fucking bride," she said, dropping her head. She stared at the floor in remembered shame. Lifting it back up, she continued, "I burst in like a Roman candle right as she is walking up the aisle. After that, I zigzagged around the reception like a pinball," here she paused and downed half her drink, "demanding to know why Brian wouldn't have sex with me. Why won't Brian fuck me? I need to be fucked. I need my husband to fuck me. Over and over. To the bride, the groom, their parents, Brian's parents."

Two of the men at the bar turned our way as this woman went on about needing to get fucked.

"Why were you saying that?" I asked, bringing my glass to my lips without taking my eyes off her.

"We had been having a hard time as of late. In the bedroom," she said, dropping her voice dramatically, annunciating every syllable, making a twisted-up face.

"Those are the worst," I said.

"I don't know what changed. It just snuck up on me. Out of nowhere, we hadn't fucked in three, four weeks. The strange thing is I hadn't even noticed. Now I'm reading books, putting on outfits, looking up porn. Says he's tired. Tired. One thing I know for sure is that if a man says he's too tired for sex, it's a big juicy lie."

"No doubt about that," I said.

We both chuckled, shaking our heads.

"I'm not a bad-looking woman," she said, running her hands up and down her sides, from her overripe breasts all the way along her wide sumptuous hips.

"Not at all," I said reflexively. But giving her a good hard look, years of hard living emerged: ashen skin, yellowed teeth, deep wrinkles around the eyes and mouth. There was no way she was older than thirty-two (and without a doubt a knockout at eighteen), but she looked on the far side of forty. Clearly, that was why she felt comfortable in the dark confines of a bar, where the years were hidden in the shadows and plenty of alcohol.

"What happened?" I asked.

"Carl, the groom, had to take me aside at his own wedding. He did his best to shut me up. He tried to assure me that Brian would fuck me, that I was beautiful, it was a phase, but I wouldn't let it go. Thankfully, he got me away from the dance floor. And the bar, for that matter."

"That's right, leave without your free drink and without picking up a round," Ritchie was growling contemptuously as Dead Eye skulked towards the door. Exiting, a burst of light lit up every surface like the first instant of a nuclear explosion. We all winced until the door slammed shut, and darkness and artificial light subsumed the bar.

"Like clockwork."

"Anyway, what did Brian do?"

"He didn't say a word. He left me twisting in the wind in front of everyone. Eventually, a girlfriend took me home. I've never felt so betrayed in my life. I didn't even remember much the next day. I only had that feeling, you know, that heavy, sick feeling, that I did some bad shit."

I nodded. I knew that feeling.

"When I tried to bring it up, he just changed the subject. Then, after days of radio silence, before he went to work one morning, he tells me we need some time apart. Thus, our little break. But the trailer is in his name, so I ended up at a girlfriend's place. Men and money. Even when they barely have any," she said. "I did tell him to stay the hell out of this place."

"He got the trailer, and you got the bar."

"Could be the name of my autobiography. Life never gives you a fair shake. Why don't you get us a couple more drinks?"

As I rose, she took both of my hands, the veneer of bravado suddenly dropping like a curtain exposing the hidden workings behind the stage. "I don't know what I'd do without him."

"What do you drink?" I asked, coming back from the bar.

"Beer and orange juice." When I paused, she added, "Just ask for the ghetto cocktail. I invented it. I'm Melissa, by the way."

"Willow."

Before I had even set the drinks down, Melissa was already talking. "Enough about me. I want to know about you. I know I've never seen around here before." It seems that in the short interval it took me to order and procure the drinks, she had moved on from the subject of her crumbling marriage.

"I'm on my way to Salt Lake City."

"And what exactly is in Salt Lake City."

"A very ex ex-boyfriend."

"On a break from your man, too?" she asked, shaking her head in solidarity with my situation, which she assumed (and hoped) was the same as hers.

"No. Well, yes, a permanent one. We divorced three years ago."

"Now we're talking. Long-lost love?" she asked, her eyebrows arching excitedly.

"No," I said with emphasis. "The thought that I dated him to begin with is beyond comprehension."

"Isn't this little journey going to give him the impression you might, I don't know, want to jump his bones? Oh, that's much better," she said after taking a long pull from her drink.

"What a comically horrible idea."

"He's a man, honey. It doesn't matter what you've told him. They are immune to words. He's going to come to that conclusion. Imagine the anticipation he's feeling as you barrel thousands of miles across deserts and rivers just to see him. I know I'd be ready to go the minute you pulled into the driveway. *It's great to see ya. How was the drive? Get your pants off.*"

"I hadn't thought of that."

"You hadn't thought of that?" she said incredulously. "Back when Brian and I were engaged, we were on a camping trip with a bunch of people. The place was lousy with bugs. And it was as hot as Hades. Anyway, I made the mistake of being nice, nice, to his friend Ryan. I was raised with manners. That night at the bonfire, when Brian went to get us a couple more beers, Ryan made a clumsy pass at me. Not only was I with Brian, I had a ring. So, if you're not aching to jump this guy, then why are you going to see him?"

"When we were in college," I said, taking a sip of my drink, "I broke up with him only to get knocked up by another man."

"That," she said, pointing assuredly at me, "is an excellent country-western song. You are a country song."

"That's not the worst of it. Before I dumped him, I got pregnant and got rid of it without ever telling him."

Squinting at me, she set her glass down and asked, "Are you an alcoholic or something?"

Setting my drink down, I said, "What? No. I don't think so. Although there have been times when I felt things, alcoholism or drug addiction threatening, like on the horizon if you know what I mean? But why, why are you asking me that?"

Perhaps it was time to settle up and get back on the road.

"I was just wondering why the need to make amends. No need to freak out, landmine," she said, relaxing back into her chair. "Easily set off," she explained before I could ask. "How long ago did this happen?"

"Nine years ago."

Her eyebrows arched so high on her forehead I thought they were going to take wing.

"Right," I said, feeling lonely and judged, wanting more than anything to make a good friend of the drink in front of me which now seemed off-limits.

"Don't pout," she said, pushing my drink towards me. "I'm just curious what would make you tell him after so much time. Isn't it in the wind, honey?"

"That seems to be the consensus," I said. She waited for me to continue, her eyes narrowing again, her two eyebrows landing easily about her eyes once again. "It's not just the pregnancy and abortion."

She signaled the bartender for another round and for me to resume.

"I was going home for Christmas break my senior year, and Chet, that's his name, had offered me a ride every break of college, since we lived in the same town. I didn't really know him. He was on the periphery of my group of friends. I knew he liked me. But that wasn't unusual. It was college. People swapped partners like baseball cards. You get the picture."

"I went to Bartending School, but yeah I get it."

"I said no thanks, end of story. Then that one time, that one God-awful time, I agreed."

"Why that time?"

I shrugged, no longer able to resist my drink.

"Come on. I just told you I ping-ponged through my husband's best friend's wedding asking everyone why my husband wouldn't fuck me, for God's sake. Don't bullshit me here. It's the key to the whole puzzle."

"It's so stupid," I said, exhaling loudly. "This guy I had been seeing. We had gotten into a fight and broken up. No big deal, right?"

"Happens all the time."

"He was pissed and being an asshole. The last thing he said to me as he stormed out of my dorm room was that I should grow a pair of tits." She gave me the once over.

"Everything seems fine to me."

I grimaced. The bartender set down our glasses. I handed him our empties.

"It sent me into a tailspin. I was either high or drunk for a week. When Chet asked if I needed a ride like he always did, I accepted. I was so hungover. Maybe still messed up. He was going on about his classes and who knows what else. But as I watched him steer the truck, I decided that I was going to make him fall in love with me. Not get him to fuck me, see."

"That's easy."

"I didn't flirt with him or get him to screw the hurt out of me. I set out to make him fall in love with me, and I did. I made him fall in love with me."

"We've all done that, honey," she said, twirling the ice in her drink, pulling a cube out and sucking on it before letting it slide back into the glass.

"I've never told anyone that before."

"Feel better?"

"Not really. It was cold and calculating and selfish and terrible. I never had any feelings for him. He fell hard, and there were so many unintended consequences. I was such an asshole to him. Mistreated him every chance I got. He just took it. Just ate my shit with a smile."

"How can you respect someone who just rolls, right?"

"And afterward, even without knowing about Dead Girl Grey—"

"Dead Girl what?"

"It's what I named it, the baby."

"Mm."

"Even without that knowledge, he flipped out after I dumped him. He stuck around for a while, but eventually, it was too much for him. He dropped out of school and—"

"—booked it out to Salt Lake City. Men are so dramatic. They say it's us, but the evidence proves the contrary," she said with a shake of her head. "What a puss."

I sat back and took a deep breath.

"You alright? You're not gonna drop dead, are ya?"

"I'm dying for a cigarette. You mind if we continue this outside?" I asked.

"Let's go," she said, rising. I grabbed my purse and followed her out of the bar. To the right of the entrance was a white plastic table surrounded by an odd number of white, warped plastic chairs. We both lit cigarettes and sat smoking. The air was still thick and damp, but the clouds had lifted, a somber, gauzy light drifting westward. It reminded me of waking up early on camping trips in college to have a cigarette by the glow of the grey of the previous night's fire. Those were easy times, just me and my girlfriends, without concern about makeup, or the judgments of mirrors, or the anticipation when some drunk man would make claim to my body. For the first time, I noticed the mountains looming in the background.

"What does he look like?" she said, exhaling a cloud of smoke.

"He wasn't ugly," I said, pulling my phone out of my back pocket, finding a picture of him from his Facebook profile, thrusting it towards her by way of justification.

"He was definitely driving outside his lane," she said, scrutinizing the photo, the cigarette stuck stiffly between her lips, her words murmured together. "Especially for someone who looks so shy."

"And overeager," I said, chuckling, taking back the phone. "He'd leave gifts outside my apartment door, drop food off anonymously at my work. That kind of nonsense. Even after I moved in with Brayden. If there was a snowstorm, I'd wake up, and our driveway would be shoveled. He would show up at the bar I hid out at."

"How did you keep that from your man?"

"Brayden? I didn't have to. He was never suspicious. As far as the driveway, we paid a neighborhood kid to do it. When Chet did it, the kid just skipped our apartment. And Brayden hated bars. In his opinion, anyone that would spend time at a bar was beneath contempt."

"Not even on his radar."

"He couldn't wrap his mind around the fact that one of those degenerates might actually be a decent person. I just needed a sympathetic ear. About being a new mother and wife. I got pregnant by Brayden shortly afterward."

"Sympathetic, my ass. You're cute – I know, and you know, what they wanted. Without the possibility of pussy, they aren't really interested. No matter how sincerely they claim to want to get to know you," she said, waving her hand. "Shit," she barked as the ash fell off the end of her cigarette into her lap. She hit it vigorously with her free hand until it was extinguished.

"It is the price of admission."

"Price of admission, I like that," she said, nodding ardently. "You gotta fuck them. Otherwise, why bother?"

"That was years later when everything was a mess. But that's a different story. What's that?" I asked, pointing to the far side of the parking lot where sandwiched between a pickup truck and a dirty Honda, someone sat in their car, hands on the steering wheel, unmoving.

"That's just Dead Eye waiting for Ritchie to leave. He doesn't have anywhere else to go. There's not that many options here. He'll be waiting a long time. You're not pouting again, are you? Not about Dead Eye?"

"Before my daughter was born, I got fired for repeatedly showing up late to work. I couldn't get myself to tell Brayden. He watched every penny."

"Men and money."

"I got up every day and left as if I were going to work and sat outside of a McDonald's until six o'clock stoned out of my gourd."

"You never went in?"

"Nope. One day, he had a craving for a McRib, and there I sat. It's not funny."

"It's really funny. I mean you're unemployed, sitting at McDonald's stoned but not going in, and then your man shows up to eat and finds you. It's hilarious. I mean, what did you think was going to happen when he noticed you didn't get paid?"

"A McRib almost ruined my life."

"That's cute, but no, it didn't. I mean, come on." She eyed me. "Anyway, can I continue with my story? One night before the wedding incident, I was determined to end our dry spell. When Brian got home, I played the doting wife. I handed him a freshly poured beer. I asked about his day. His favorite meal was waiting for him, and not on paper plates. I even gave him a backrub."

"All good things," I said, one eye still on the Honda and Dead Eye.

"The second the sun went down, I asked if he wanted to move things into the bedroom. Much to my surprise, he told me to get myself ready. It was lucky I kept a few miniature bottles of vodka under the bathroom sink."

"Why?"

"I didn't think he would say yes," she said, stubbing out her cigarette on the tabletop, immediately lighting another. "You don't know how much anxiety this lack of sex caused me. I was afraid of my goddamn husband. I took a couple of hits, put on a sexy little outfit, perfumed all the pertinent spots, and took my place on the bed. I'm in there for fifteen, maybe twenty minutes. No Brian. Another ten minutes pass. Nothing. Finally, I stomp into the living room. By this time, I'm only in my underwear. My beautiful tits popping. He's on the couch slurping a beer and watching a football game."

"What did he say?" I asked, shifting my glance back to Melissa.

"Nada," she said incredulously. "Not a word about teeing me up and leaving me stranded. I'm standing there half-naked, for Christ's sake. Well, fuck that and fuck him. I crashed through the kitchen, slammed cabinet doors, broke a couple of glasses. Again, nada. Eventually, I went back to bed, locked the bedroom door, and forced myself to go to sleep, expecting a repentant knock in the middle of the night. Jesus, I would have even blown him. By the time I got up, the broken glass was cleaned up, and he was gone. When he came home, it was like the entire incident never happened."

"And you don't think there's another woman?" I asked, checking on Dead Eye's still unmoving form.

"I checked our phone records. Yes, I've become that woman now. But nothing. He never smells like another woman or a shower. God knows I can be a lot. I just don't know why he won't touch me, why we can't get past this. I made an ass of myself at a wedding. Who hasn't? In any case, we are falling apart—obviously," she said, raising both hands, reaching for the solace of her drink.

My grandmother outlived my grandfather by over twenty years. At that point, they had already been married for fifty years. Not only are fifty-year marriages a rarity in our high-speed society, but you are just as likely to receive a grimace of disgust as you are a plaudit of admiration at the mention of one. It wasn't until I was a wife years into my own marriage that I realized what a miracle half a century of matrimony was. Setting aside all the complex cultural and economic reasons for the shortened lifespans of marriages, I am convinced that, just as lightbulbs and laptops and automobiles have a planned obsolescence built into their designs, modern marriages are no longer constructed for rough roads, for the delayed gratification of being with the same person forever (not to mention the multiple incarnations each person cycles through) but, like fast food containers and watches and televisions, are purely disposable. Were Brayden and I truly incompatible, or did we pack up and split at the first sign of rain?

"Hey, I skipped my sister's wedding to go on this wild goose chase."

"You bailed on your sister's wedding?" Melissa asked.

"Dropped out the day before," I said with a rueful guffaw. "Not that she much cared."

"I don't know you from Adam, but I have a brother... and I very seriously doubt that."

"It's not like I was her maid of honor or anything. Honestly, I think she was relieved. I mean she put on a big show of how angry she was, but believe me, she's glad I'm not there. Now our dad can walk her up the aisle and dance with her without having to worry about equal time. For as long as I can remember, it's like I crashed a party I wasn't invited to."

The sound of a motorcycle could be heard zipping away in the distance.

"When I was nine or ten, my dad had this VW bug. I became obsessed with riding in the trunk, which, you may or may not know, is in the front of the car. It was all I thought about for months. I bugged him constantly, but he would just brush me off. Finally, one night after a few beers, I convinced him. Next thing you know, I'm loaded in the trunk of the car."

"You're shitting me? Just like that?"

"Just like that. Anyway, we started up the street, but I couldn't keep hold of the handle on the inside of the trunk; I mean, I was a little girl. Next thing you know, up goes the lid, he has to pull over, and my adventure comes to an end. It didn't dawn on me until years later. But imagine if you were a car coming in the other direction and, in the trunk, sits this little girl. You'd think I was being kidnapped."

"I'm jealous."

"Jealous?"

"You had your dad wrapped around your finger," I said.

"I can't imagine you didn't with that face."

"Maybe if Adele hadn't been in the picture," I said.

"Well, she can't be prettier than you."

"Absolutely not," I said wickedly. "Boys used to befriend her just to meet me."

"That must have killed her."

"I still hear about it. No matter which way I go, forward, backward, there she is, as far as I can see."

"That's my point. I never gave a second thought about my brother. I never realized what a hard-ass my dad was on him. Especially after the divorce. He said it was like we grew up on opposite sides of the Berlin Wall. I dismissed his complaints my entire life until he got tired of not being heard, I guess. Well, I haven't even seen him in seven years. You don't want that to happen with your sister. Believe me."

"I guess."

A blue pickup truck had pulled into the parking lot, rolled slowly past, stuffed with eyes, made its way to the end of the gravel lot, made a wide U-turn, and was on its way to passing us again.

"You seeing this?" I asked, pointing my cigarette in its direction.

Without missing a beat, Melissa stood up and sauntered out to the curb. The truck came to an easy stop in front of her. Leaning forward, the driver began talking out the open window past the passenger. I was too far away to hear what they were saying. It wasn't long before the truck had parked, and the two of them were heading towards us. There was nothing distinct about either man. They were in worn jeans, baseball hats, and old sneakers. One was tall and muscular with a bandage on his forearm. The other, the driver, was thicker, shorter, and strutted as he walked, his wallet attached to his pants with a chain. They soon joined Melissa and, after a moment, me.

"Mind if I bum a smoke?" the driver, who introduced himself as Hewitt, asked Melissa.

"Do you even smoke?"

"I do when I drink," he said, accepting a cigarette from

her. She held onto the smoke for a long time before letting go. She lit it for him, never breaking eye contact. "This is Robert," he said, nodding at his friend.

"You feel like joining us inside?" Melissa asked.

"As long as you're buying the first round," Hewett said, stepping curtly past Melissa.

"I think you have that backward, Hew?" Melissa said.

"I don't think I do, Mel."

"No?"

"Women love to flirt their way to free drinks and then disappear," he said, taking a puff of his cigarette.

"Is that so?"

"I work hard for my money. I'm not going to just piss it away on a stranger. Even if she is pleasing to the eye."

"Well," Melissa said, smiling.

"Not to mention it's vulgar. And you're not vulgar," he said, walking toward the entrance, flicking the cigarette back towards the parking lot. We all followed.

"Honey, you don't know the half of it," she said.

"I can already see you're more than a little familiar with the power of your sex," he said, opening the front door, ushering everyone in. Melissa and I entered. As she dropped her cigarette, she took me by the arm, led me to one of the booths along the far wall, and said to me, "Let the games begin."

"Four beers?" Hewitt asked, still standing, reaching for his wallet. Robert and I agreed. Melissa immediately objected. Hewett waved her off over his shoulder and headed for the bar. "I got it." Robert and I sat down.

"Oh no, I insist," Melissa said, shimmying awkwardly out of the booth, darting up behind him, seemingly prepared to drive her already-damaged marriage past the point of no return.

Robert and I observed the two of them going back and forth without exchanging a word. It was difficult to watch. Not only because Melissa was married but because I had subjected so many of my friends to the same infantile display a million times before, whether I was single, attached, or married. *It's funny how malleable lust is and can masquerade as, well, anything but lust.*

"I had been dating this divorcee for a brief spell," Robert suddenly began. "She was on the phone having a rather heated conversation with an ex, and we were about to run out of beer, so I called an Uber and figured I'd go and be back before she noticed. I get to the gas station, and I tell the driver, this Asian man, to wait, I'll use him for the ride back. I go grab a twelve-pack and come back out. In the meantime, the driver has moved to the other side of the parking lot. I cross over, open the door, get in, and tell him to high tail it back. He just stares at me like he didn't hear me."

"Don't tell me."

"It's not my Uber. It's just some random Asian man's car. He's just staring at me in the rearview mirror."

"What did you do?"

"Got out of the car before he called the police. I ordered another Uber. Forty-five minutes and three beers later, I got back only to be greeted by a completely darkened house. No love for Rob that night."

"You're lucky he didn't pull a gun."

When Hewitt and Melissa returned, they didn't divulge who paid for the beers, and neither Robert nor I asked. Setting the four glasses down, Hewett slid into the booth first, across from me, Melissa next to him. Like I said before, we never stop.

"Are you two just enjoying a girl's night out, or is there a purpose to your little party?" Hewett asked, sliding a glass over to me and then one to Robert.

"Let's see," Melissa began, "I'm in the middle of a divorce, and this one is on the way to Salt Lake City. Salt Lake, right?"

"You two don't know each other?"

"Just met," Melissa said confidently. "But we've become fast friends. What about you two?"

"We just got done working."

"And what do you do?"

"Try to avoid getting picked up by the police," Hewett said.

"Clever," Melissa said.

"We have a small landscaping company," Robert added diplomatically.

"Is that where you got this bandage?" Melissa asked, stroking Robert's forearm, which he promptly pulled away.

Hewett let out a loud guffaw. "That would be a no."

"I've been told I have impulse control problems," Robert said, smiling softly and taking a sip of his beer.

"That true?" I asked Hewett.

"Let's just say Rob here has a habit of ruining my good time. If you had any idea how many times I've been chatting with some lovely lady only to find myself out on my ass because this hothead instigated a fight, you'd shit yourself."

Robert let out a loud, bear-like yawn, stretching both of his hands over his head.

"I apologize. I've just heard this horseshit so often it puts me to sleep. What would absolutely knock me on my ass is if this jerk ever had my back," Robert said. Melissa and I laughed. "You never did, never do, and never will."

"Not a fighter?" Melissa asked.

At this point, there was a pause. It was clear this was a sore spot for Hewitt. For Robert, too.

"It doesn't matter who wins," he said, leaning forward, spilling some of his beer. "You're fucked up, bleeding. Your clothes are torn. You're sore. And the asshole you pummeled feels exactly the same. What's the point of coming to blows if you can't tell the difference between the winner and loser?"

With his swagger, I hadn't pegged Hewitt for a coward. I should have. Brayden, with his big mouth and oversized opinions, had often veered dangerously close to fighting: in restaurants, baseball fields huddled around home plate, the zoo, and even once at daycare, only to back down. He was a coward too. Their swagger was nothing more than colorful feathers used to lure members of the opposite sex.

"You sound like my dad, and that's the last thing I need right now," Robert said directly to Hewett. "My dad, the Pastor, did not approve of fighting. Ego, it's just ego, he would bellow at me," he said to Melissa and me with more confidence than before.

"Well, somehow your shirt always manages to come off during these scuffles, so he might be on to something," Hewett said.

"I think I'm with the wrong guy," Melissa said, her eyes lighting up.

Hewitt and Robert exchanged conspiratorial glances, no doubt assuming they had hit the jackpot.

"One time, he caught me fighting this kid down the street. He was furious. He didn't even bother asking me what the fight was about. I tried to explain, but he'd have none of it. He just sent the other boy away. Told me I was a narcissist," he said, sounding the word out slowly. "That I knew nothing about right and wrong and needed a lesson in humility."

"And what did he do?" Hewitt asked.

"The bastard stood me in front of the full-length mirror in our entryway and made me look at my reflection for three hours to learn it."

"Holy shit," Melissa said.

"My ex-husband's dad was a Pastor too. Same temperament. Used to go all Old Testament on his ass all the time. That's how he put it," I said. "Explains a lot about him now that I think about it."

"Why were you fighting?" Melissa asked.

"The kid was bullying a retarded girl," he said matter-of-factly.

"Seems like a good reason to kick someone's ass," Melissa said.

"It never mattered what Rob's intentions were."

"Come on," Robert said, wincing, wiping up Hewitt's spilled beer. "Not this again."

"His dad never liked him. Not from the minute he was born," he said, pointing into the air with his glass, a small tidal wave of beer again cascading over the side. "Rob got into a car accident a couple of years ago. When the hospital called his dad, he asked if his injuries were life-threatening," he said, pointing at us with his glass before lowering it carefully to the table.

"What a son-of-a-bitch," Melissa said.

"It was his yearly hunting trip. Do you have any idea how much planning and money goes into that?" Robert said, his eyes darting at me and shamefully away.

"I don't understand," I said, looking from Robert to Hewitt.

"He didn't want to interrupt his trip," Melissa said, pulling a napkin from the napkin dispenser, dabbing up the beer Hewitt had again spilled.

"Rob sat in the hospital without his dad, without anyone, for three days," Hewitt said.

"Oh," I muttered quietly. I felt a stone in the pit of my stomach.

"Got a 7-point buck, though," Robert said, patting my forearm several times.

"When the Pastor died a few months ago, we were at Rob's trailer taking the dish off his roof. Cable has just gotten too expensive," he said parenthetically, "when he gets a call from his brother's lawyer. He stops what he is doing and goes white."

"Just stop, Hew," Robert said.

"What did he say?" I asked, leaning forward.

"He wouldn't tell me. He just sat on the roof, hugging his knees."

"I wasn't," Rob snapped loudly, then lowered his voice dramatically, "hugging my knees."

"You're not set to inherit," Hewitt said. "Not his old man's house, fishing boat, baseball cards, car."

"That's fucking rotten," Melissa barked.

"He dropped the dish to the ground and got a bottle of vodka out of the trailer. He takes a couple of long slugs, hands me the bottle, and smashes the dish into the ground, over and over until it looks like some kind of car wreck."

"I fucked that thing up," Robert said with a little boy's smile, his eyes full of hurt.

"Then he sat on the ground and sobbed," he said.

"All right," Rob said.

"I thought we were here to have a good time – forget our troubles."

"That's terrible," I whispered.

Robert waved off my sympathies.

"Best thing that could have happened to the both of us. I just think I'm allergic to my family," he said with a grin, rubbing his bandage.

 "I know all about that," I said.

"Since we are confessing troubles with our old men, which many of us have, I might as well tell you mine. My dad and I had fallen apart over the years, and, in that time, he had gotten addicted to prescription meds. My brother had taken him in and was taking care of him. I hadn't seen them, my dad or my brother, in many years and thought it was time to make amends and help if I could. But when I reached out, my brother wasn't interested in any help or letting me see him."

"He wouldn't let you see your own father?" Robert asked.

"Absolutely would not hear of it."

"I thought you were your dad's favorite?" I asked.

"When I was younger," Melissa said. "When he finally relented for a very short visit, he said the strangest thing. I'll never forget it. *You won't be too impressed.* It was like he thought I was going to blame him for Dad's condition. Or if by some miracle he improved after I was there, he wasn't going to let me claim any credit for it."

"He'd put in the time," Hewitt said.

"Exactly."

"My sister would react the same way. Except she'd be

too selfish to take our dad in and have too much pride to allow me to. It would be assisted living all the way. That way, she could have her life and still retain her advantage by visiting more than me," I said.

"She sounds like a peach," Robert said.

"Oh yeah," I said.

"The last time I ever spoke to him was a few months later. My brother and I had, surprise, gotten into a fight."

"About what?" Hewitt asked.

"I don't remember. When we got done, I immediately dialed my dad's number in a panic."

"Why?" asked Robert.

"I'll tell you why," I said. "She was afraid her brother was calling to tattle on her."

"My love hung in the balance."

"I got a sister, the sister to end all sisters," I said, shrugging my shoulders sadly.

"Anyway, the phone rang and rang. I was about to hang up when he answered. He was very drunk. I'm not even sure he knew it was me. I felt like such an asshole. *It's me, Dad.* We talked for a bit if you want to call it that. He was barely coherent. Finally, he just said, 'fuck it' and the line went dead. It was the last thing he said to me or anyone. He had a stroke taking a dump later that night."

"Your dad is dead?"

Nodding and looking right at me, she wrapped up by saying, "His funeral was the last time I saw my dad *and* my brother. He didn't want me there either. He'd taken ownership of him, and that included his death and everything that came with that, including every ounce of grief. But he didn't really have a choice."

The parallels to my own life were unmistakable. My

mother's funeral was the last time I saw my mother and Nestor. It made my inability to stop and check in on Nestor more egregious, my selfishness more glaring. No matter what I told myself, it was clear that not only was I not stopping in Casey on my way back from Salt Lake City but ever again. I was a coward then as I am now. He would live and die without my knowing a thing about him.

"And you have a sister like this?" Robert asked.

I didn't feel like telling the story of my father and sister, which was the story of how I came to be, but I never had a choice. I had only ever known myself in juxtaposition to my father and sister.

"They broke the mold when they made her. Let me tell you. Things might have been fine for her had I not entered the universe. Since then, she's continued trying to live her life under the impression she's an only child."

"Not happy you came along?" Robert asked.

"Cried when she was told. Fucking drama queen. Acts like my father is a piece of land she owns and that I've been trespassing on."

"Ah-ha," Melissa said.

"They're close? Your dad and sister?"

"White on rice," I said with barely concealed disgust.

"A lot of parents are close with their kids," Melissa said.

"And sadly, parents have favorites," Robert added.

"All true," I said. "I could live with either of those options. This goes beyond that. It's almost pathological. I'm telling you – Adele has tried to squeeze me out of my relationship with my father for as long as I can remember. Once, when I was little, I hid in the back of my dad's delivery truck. He didn't discover me until he got to work. By then, he didn't have time to bring me home, so he sent me back in a cab."

"Couldn't do that now," Robert said.

"Couldn't do that then," Melissa added with a smirk.

"The official story is that Adele was hysterical combing the neighborhood trying to find me."

"And?" Robert asked.

"There's no way it happened that way. Running through the neighborhood looking for me? She was probably throwing my belongings in the alley."

"That seems unlikely," Hewitt said.

"All I remember is pulling up to the house with no one there to greet me. Nevertheless, it's sick. I didn't even know my father or Adele until I was five. Totally indifferent to me. But Adele. When she was a little girl, my father rescued her, literally rescued her. He was her knight in shining armor. Talk about fucking up your worldview. For both of us."

"Like from a burning building?" Hewitt asked with mock sarcasm.

"Might as well have. But no. Not long after Adele was born, my dad's marriage to her mother, Kimberly, fell apart on account of her monumental drinking. He would always say that he left with a suitcase and his bowling ball and was lucky to get that. No, it's okay to laugh. He was funny. Still is, actually. That's what makes hating him so difficult. Anyway, he agreed to weekends, rented a dumpy apartment, and started a new life. Before the divorce papers were even filed, Kimberly had shacked up with a barrel-chested drunk named Sam and his toe-headed daughter, Tina, and that was that."

"Why do women do that, immediately hook up with

another man?" Melissa wondered aloud. No one responded.

"He couldn't have cared less. He was just grateful that she was someone else's problem. Now he could bowl and play softball to his heart's content."

"That's when you know things are bad — when you don't care who your ex is screwing," Hewitt said.

"Exactly," Melissa agreed.

"You don't know the half of it. My dad was a jealous man in his youth. After he and my mother split, he would show up after hitting the bars, ready to pulverize the phantom boyfriend he had concocted in his imagination."

"Yeah?" Robert asked.

"It was a nightmare. But that's a different story. Picking Adele up after work on Fridays, Kimberly and Sam would be parked on the couch with a bottle of Jim Beam on the coffee table, and when he dropped her back off on Sunday night, they would still be sitting there, television off, bleary-eyed and incoherent, the bottle empty."

"That's bleak."

"And he wasn't concerned?" Robert asked.

"You'd have to ask him," I said.

"Meaning you haven't," Hewitt said.

Hewitt's comments and general demeanor were meant to both provoke and minimize, to dismiss the damage the relationship with my father and sister had on me. I had a roof over my head, I had food, was educated. I lived in the goddamn United States of America. In other words, be grateful and get on with things. I had heard this bullshit before. I wasn't about to traffic in comparative suffering.

"No." Continuing on, "One Friday evening, my dad arrived to pick up Adele when a neighbor called him over to the chain link fence. Kimberly and Sam had been gone since Wednesday."

"You're shitting me," Melissa said, leaning forward.

"This neighbor took the kids in, fed them, kept them safe. Apparently, this had been going on for several weeks."

"Where had they been going?" Melissa asked.

"To this day, no one knows. There were no cell phones. If I were to hazard a guess, I would bet a motel to hole up and get fucked up in. Any bar that would have them. A casino. I'm not sure."

"He didn't call social services?" Hewitt asked.

"People weren't like that back then. No matter how bad things got, you didn't mess with a person's livelihood, much less their kids. But my dad did wait until they returned, which they eventually did, drunk and exhausted, remorseless."

"I can't imagine how mad he was," Melissa said.

"Mad enough that Sam refused to come into the house. He crawled into the flatbed of his pickup and fell asleep. Kimberly, never afraid of anything, shuffled into the kitchen and made a pot of coffee."

"Then what?"

"*I'm taking Adele.*" I paused for effect as I always did. All eyes were on me. "That's all my dad said."

"Shit," Melissa gasped.

"He was braced for a fight, but none came. She said nothing, gave no reaction. She just sat at the kitchen table and sipped her coffee. Smoked a cigarette. To this day, he says he was surprised. He said he just kept on waiting, but nothing. Eventually, he packed up Adele's belongings, took her by the hand, and made their way out the door and down the narrow sidewalk to his car. She never called, never asked how he was doing. Nothing."

"So, she never saw her again?" Robert asked.

"Years later."

"That's not quite right. Before he left, he stormed back in to give Kimberly one more chance to fight for her daughter, a chance she didn't take. *Don't forget her blue blankey.* He retrieved it before leaving her house for the last time. And that's why Adele came to live with my father."

I sat back and exhaled. Finishing the story always left me with a sense of relief and dread.

"You said she passed," Robert said. "Was it alcohol? It had to be alcohol, right?"

"She gave it a valiant effort, but cancer beat her to the finish line."

"You sure know the story well," Robert said, making eye contact with me, holding it as long as I would allow.

"I've heard it a million times. At family events, Christmases, weddings, for new boyfriends. There's even a nauseating coda to it, tales of early morning gymnastics practices, softball games, honor roll, and so on. My dad and Adele made, make perfect sense," I said, correcting myself. "From the moment he led her to the car, they were in perfect harmony. They built this life together, one without room for me or my mother."

"Where were you during your sister's rescue?" Robert asked.

"I hadn't been born. Or, as my dad would say, I wasn't even a twinkle in his eye yet. Told you he was funny."

"That explains a lot," Hewitt said.

"Does it?" I asked.

"Sure. Everything was put into place before you had even arrived on the scene. How could you ever have a chance?"

"I guess you have it all figured out," I said.

"Is that why you're off to Salt Lake?"

I didn't answer.

"I think we need a round of tequila shots," Hewett said. Rising, he made his way to the bar and came back with four full shot glasses and set them one by one in front of us. "Drink 'em down to the clown that made you frown!"

Robert shook his head. "Why do you always say the same stupid toast?"

We all drank. The tequila was warm and bitter and collected at the bottom of my stomach.

"Okay, I am dying to know," Melissa asked in a self-consciously jaunty style, breaking the maudlin shadow these deadbeat dad stories had cast over the table. "Why do you take your shirt off when you get into a fight?"

Hewitt shook his head with a smile.

"You always have to bring that up." Robert sighed, curling one of his arms, the fabric of his shirt tightening around his not-insignificant bicep; Melissa's eyes swam with hunger.

"You can't give your opponent anything loose to grab onto," he said with a wink.

"Uh-huh," Hewitt said, tossing back the rest of his beer. "See, when you were off proving that you weren't a fag, I was left alone with all the women. What would you rather have – the thrill of victory, all bruised and sore, or the affections of a good woman?"

"I see, and how long exactly have you been divorced?" Melissa asked.

"What makes you think I'm divorced?"

Melissa refused to speak, letting Hewitt's internal gears

do the work for her.

"Just a couple of years," Hewitt said.

"Five," Robert said, correcting him.

"What happened?" I asked.

"The same thing that always happens," Hewett said. "Someone decides they want something different."

"If you're the one saying it, then she's the one that decided," Melissa said cackling.

"Cheers," Hewitt said, lifting his beer glass and promptly setting it back down. "You know what really pissed me off about the whole thing? She didn't even have the courage to tell me to my face. She up and packed while I was working. I came home to a half-empty house and a note. Not even an eloquent note. I'm moving to Cincinnati with John. Doesn't that just seem, I don't know, too banal a tornado to destroy your house?"

Everyone chuckled.

"I was thinking about her the other day. I was thinking how every Spring we would trim the branches over the house, well, my old house, when I had a house, and Cyn would walk out, waving our life insurance policy. You better watch yourself – one slip, Mr. Karels, and I'm collecting. There's no 911 calls on my watch."

"She didn't?" laughed Melissa, licking the inside of one of the empty shot glasses.

"You remember that?" he asked Robert, an autumnal shadow falling across his face.

"I do."

"That's made me feel really alone. I mean Cincinnati, how abysmal."

"Since we are confessing bullshit, and I'm never going to see you losers again," Melissa said with a chuckle. "I saw my lost love, who moved away right after high school, in the grocery store not a week and a half ago, if you can believe that bullshit, so I know about alone."

"You have a lost love?" I asked, sincerely surprised.

"Don't act so surprised, princess," she barked. "Can we get another round please?" she barked again, this time towards the bartender.

"At the grocery store?" Hewitt said with a sarcastic drawl.

"I was sweaty and covered in dirt from doing yard work, and there was James getting a coffee like he had never left. His hair was thinning and grey, but otherwise, he looked exactly the same. All through high school, I was head over heels in love with this person standing across from me. It stopped me in my tracks," she said, her eyes growing wistful. "He was the sweetest man you would ever meet. Gentle, kind, soft-spoken."

"What happened?"

"He took me home for dinner with his parents, that's what happened. I'd met them a few times. But this was my first formal sit down. Anyway, I ended up in their living room by myself. They were getting us dessert, I think. James had ducked into his room. So, I started paging through this coffee table book. I can't believe what I am seeing. It's filled with boudoir pictures of his mother that she had done for his dad. For their twentieth anniversary."

"On the coffee table?" I asked. The bartender set down four fresh beers making it clear that he was none too happy being yelled at for drinks.

"No bullshit. She's in these provocative positions, draped across furniture, on her knees, her middle-aged tits drooping about. It was horrifying. When she came into the room, it was all I could see."

"And?"

"And? And? And, what?" she shot back at me, sarcastically. "I dumped him and started working at a temporary service."

"No, I mean what happened when he saw you."

"He didn't see me."

"So, you didn't talk to him?" I asked, astonished.

"No." She stopped talking and seemed to contemplate her life for a moment before saying, "I'm married. To a man who provides and puts up with my ass. For that, he should get the Nobel, right? And he's a good man. Last year, during that blizzard, he insisted on helping our neighbors dig their cars out, making grocery runs for people whose cars were dead. He was out there all day, freezing his ass off. I mean, I wasn't going out there. On the way back from one of these runs, he and his best friend Carl stopped to help a woman and two kids stranded on the side of the road – noble, right? But there's not enough room for them all in the car, so Brian gets out to walk home. That's a good man."

She looked around the table for affirmation of what she was saying. That her husband was a good man and that she was good by proxy for being married to him. It wasn't enough for her to know this; she needed to see it reflected back in our eyes, to hear it from our lips. Most people did not have the inner resources to find this within themselves, including me. I was always astonished at the people who did.

"Of course, Carl promises to come back but never does."

"His best friend didn't come back?"

"Apparently his battery was fried."

"Hold on, this is starting to sound familiar," Hewitt said, sitting up. "Did he eventually get picked up by a different car? And dropped off?"

"How did you know that?"

"That was me. I was the second car," Hewitt said triumphantly, holding up his glass as if it were a trophy.

"There is no way," I said, assuming this was a cheap ploy to get laid and that he would get discovered easily.

"Fuck you," Melissa said, casually.

Robert gave me a secret conspiratorial glance, which I ignored.

"I was coming back from the liquor store, and I nearly hit this guy walking down the middle of the road. Swerving to miss him, I nearly took out a stop sign and ended up in a snowbank. He was nearly frozen to death. After he helped get me out, I offered him a ride."

"Are you kidding me?" Melissa said, deadly serious.

"Kindness of strangers," Hewitt said, somewhat distracted, his words slowing. "It was a long ride, but I assure you he told me all about you and how he had to get back to you."

"You're full of shit."

"It happened," he said, glancing over his shoulder towards the bar, where it had gotten incrementally louder. "I dropped him off at your place. He insisted I meet you, but my heat wasn't working, and I was freezing my nuts off."

"That's insane," I said. Robert nodded in agreement. Despite myself, I was beginning to believe him.

"I'm just so taken by this entire thing," she said, eyeballing an upturned shot glass like a crystal ball as if she were witnessing the raging blizzard and Brian struggling to get back to her. "I just can't believe it."

"Hey, do me a favor, switch seats with me," Hewitt said to Melissa.

"What?" she asked, smiling fraily as if he were telling some incomprehensible joke.

"Switch seats with me," he repeated, this time with more urgency. "Right now."

"What's going on?" I asked.

"Let go of me."

"Leave her alone," I said. "You're not being funny."

Before she could object again, Melissa found herself lifted from her spot and shoved over Hewett's lap. There was a rapid crescendo of voices. We all turned towards the bar in time to see Ritchie lunge at one of the regulars. The bartender sprung over the bar, slipped on a coaster, and fell flat on his face. Robert set himself (along with three other men) on the fighters, who continued to thrash at one another as they were being pulled apart. Once separated, Ritchie was tossed out. Robert and the bartender helped the hapless victim up and onto his bar stool. He had a cut above his right eye, and his shirt pocket dangled limply over his chest. The bartender delivered him a fresh drink. The other three men returned to their seats. The entire commotion lasted two minutes at best. Within five minutes, you wouldn't have known anything had happened.

"Are you alright?" Hewitt asked Melissa, then me.

We both nodded.

"How did you know that those two were about to fight?" I asked.

"It was their voices. They got too loud too fast. It's like a plane suddenly lifting off. When you hear that, it's only a matter of seconds before the shit hits the fan."

"As you can see, Hew was helpful as ever?" Robert said to me as he approached the table, breathing heavily.

"Yes, he was," Melissa said, rubbing his cheek.

"You feel like stepping out?" Robert asked me.

"I would love that."

"I think we'll stay here," Melissa said.

"You sure?" I asked. Hewitt nodded for her, his breathing still labored.

Standing up, Robert took my hand, led me outside and around to the side of the building, backed me up against the brick wall, and kissed me. It was awkward, rough, and wet, as if he had never kissed a woman before. As he moved in again, our teeth gnashed together. It stung. I winced. His breath smelled like beer. I closed my mouth and forced his tongue out.

"That was nice," he said.

We kissed a third time, this time with a more relaxed rhythm. It was incrementally better. We did this for some time. His hands climbed the front of my body. I pushed them down. He stopped and looked at me in a curious manner. For the first time, I noticed that one of his front teeth was chipped. Why were nice guys so often terrible at the physical aspects of love? He continued to look at me. Behind him, the sky was cloudy, black, and starless, the mountains rising out of the earth like silent co-conspirators of some crime. We kissed some more.

"You wanna come back to my place? It's that spot right over there?"

I lifted my eyes up over his shoulder. In the distance was a trailer park, the trailers lined up like shoe boxes. I wondered if it was the same one where Melissa and Brian lived.

"Sure."

Taking my hand again, we headed across the parking lot. It was uneven and strewn with rocks, low-growing weeds, and discarded beer bottles and trash. We walked in silence. It crossed my mind to ask why he and Hewett had driven to this place if they lived so close.

"Hew is full of shit."

"Well, I know that," I said.

"I was in the car with him when we picked up Melissa's husband," he said.

"That actually happened?"

"He wasn't helping people shovel out or do grocery runs."

"No?"

"Well, maybe he was. But it wasn't out of the goodness of his heart. His battery was fried, and he was trying to hitch a ride to the liquor store."

"Really?" I asked, looking up at him.

"*I can't be stuck at home with her for days with less than three bottles of Jack* were his exact words."

"What about the rest of it, the woman and her kid?"

"All bullshit," he said. "He got a ride to the liquor store but didn't have one back, so he just started walking."

After wading through a field of waist-high grass, we entered the trailer park. We navigated a long, twisty gravel road. I had a strong premonition that we would run into Brian. There was no reason to believe this, the chances being slim to none. I didn't know if he lived in this trailer park, what trailer he occupied, if he was home, or what he looked like, for that matter. Nevertheless, I diligently scanned my surroundings. About a quarter mile up the road, we arrived at Robert's trailer. It had a set of homemade, unstained wooden stairs pushed up to the front door. He struggled with the lock. This made him visibly agitated. As if the act of opening the door reflected on his abilities in bed. Men thought any act of physical exertion reflected on their abilities with their cocks. Maybe there was truth to it. I made a mental note to keep track of that going forward. As he turned and tugged at the door (and apologized far out of proportion to the event), I did reconnaissance around the small yard for the disfigured dish, as if Robert had gotten the call from his brother's lawyer today. I dismissed his concern with a shake of my head, still trying to locate the dish (and Brian for that matter).

The door finally gave way. We entered the trailer.

"You're going to Salt Lake City?" he asked, turning on the lights, rushing to gather up clothes that were strewn about the floor and tossing them into the bathroom, yanking the door shut.

"Mm-hmm."

"I've been to Lincoln a couple of times. That's about it. Never saw a reason to leave. I have everything I need right here."

That was the stupidest, least self-aware thing I had ever heard. It was hard to imagine any woman anywhere (no matter how desperate or stupid) being impressed by him. It was also easy to imagine his father hating him. I wouldn't leave him any of my meager possessions, either. I looked up into his red, drooping eyes, smiled, and nodded.

"Think you might swing this way on the way back?" he asked.

"Maybe."

He pulled two beers from the refrigerator and handed me one. Before I had barely taken a sip, he pulled me onto his lap on the dilapidated couch. Kissing furiously, he rubbed my back and neck. I could feel him getting an erection.

"Hewitt's not the only one full of shit."

"No?"

"My dad didn't rescue Adele," I said. He stared at me. He couldn't have cared less, but he needed to pretend to. "On this vacation I took with my dad in high school, one without Adele—"

"How did that happen?" he asked, rubbing my back.

"Her mom was dying. It's funny. I know she was praying for her own mother to die so she could come with him. Just so I wouldn't have time alone with him. That's how fucked up my family is. On the last night of the trip, my dad confessed to me that the only reason he took in Adele was because her mom was incapable of taking care of her. There was no agreeing to weekends. He just left with no intention of coming back. He would have never looked back had Kimberly been competent."

I could see him trying to process the gravity of my words, but with all the blood currently residing in his penis, it was a near-impossible task.

"I never told anyone."

We continued kissing. Putting his right hand beneath my shirt, I let him unhook my bra and fumble around with my breasts. His stubble was rough. My face would be red and sore. He attempted to remove my shirt. Excusing myself to the bathroom, beer still in hand, I sat on the toilet, my feet burrowed in a nest of his dirty laundry. It appeared to me that my life was one of those math worksheets you're given in grade school with dozens of equations dotting the page. In my case, it was filled exclusively with problems of subtraction, of things being taken away: motivations, dreams, relationships, money, and people, until I arrived at that very lonely, final zero. Mr. Bones recalling everything that was his. I couldn't identify one solitary thing that he did not possess. If God owned the lease of my existence at the beginning of my life, somewhere along the way it got transferred to Mr. Bones without my knowledge. Flushing the toilet, I opened the door. The kitchen lights were on, and two unopened beers were sitting on the counter.

I told him I needed to get back to Melissa. But he already knew this. I headed for the front door. He made no effort to stop me.

"I wasn't that mad about the house or the car, or any of that stuff."

"No?" I said, stroking his arm. "That dish you destroyed would say otherwise."

"What? Oh yeah. No, I mean, his house was falling apart. Does it look like I have the money to fix it up?"

"No."

He grimaced as if I had sucker punched him, and he was attempting with limited success to restrain a flood of tears (and not just at the immediate pain but as some larger existential injustice).

"Hey," he called as I stepped outside.

"Yeah?" The air was considerably colder, harsher, and somehow more unkind. Mr. Bones letting me know that he had possession of the night, too.

"You need me to walk you back?" he asked, holding the door open wide enough to reveal his face but hide his still prevalent erection.

"I can find my way."

"I wasn't going to anyway," he said and attempted to

stare me down. I had a deep urge to laugh in his face but instead flashed a sardonic smile at him, which he immediately misinterpreted.

"You sure you don't want to come back in? Finish what we started?"

The door was shut, and the front porch light was off before I had finished declining.

Reentering the bar, Melissa and Hewitt had moved to one of the tables, where she sat on his lap furiously making out. When she saw me, she pushed her way off him, screaming, "Landmine!" and dragged me outside by the hand for a cigarette like an over-stimulated high school girl who had kissed her crush.

"You're going to regret that," I said.

"I thought you had ditched me," she said, nearly hyperventilating.

"Nope," I said with a flick of my right hand. "I stopped him before my shirt came off."

"Why's that?"

"It's the point of no return, and there's no sex for this girl for a while."

"No?" she said, plopping down in one of the plastic chairs, which threatened to give. "Was he pissed?"

"Oh, yeah," I said darkly, laughing out the syllables.

When Robert jumped into the fight, the words of my father sprung into my head. *People tell you who they are.* I had wanted Robert to remain motionless, like a hawk over a tumultuous river. I wished for him to prove my father wrong. When he didn't, I was disappointed. Then why did I end up back at his trailer? Especially when there was nothing about him I found appealing. Maybe that's exactly why.

"I don't really like this guy either," she said, tipping her head towards the bar. She reached her hand out toward me, wriggling her fingers.

"I think he got the message by the way you were mauling him," I said and handed her a cigarette, lighting it for her.

"Brian will never forgive me for that," she said.

"He doesn't need to know. To this day, Brayden doesn't know the half of what I did to him."

"But you're divorced, idiot," she said, her head snapping at me.

"Fair enough."

My cell phone began to ring.

"Who's in the world could that be?" Melissa asked, pulling the glass away from her mouth.

"Mark," I said, already exasperated.

"I don't remember you mentioning a Mark."

"My current boyfriend."

"You seem thrilled."

"It's over, he just hasn't been given notice," I said. When it was clear she was hungry for more details: "Right before I left, I came across his tennis shoes. It was the first time I noticed how huge they were. They were canoes. I could cruise down the Mississippi in one of those monstrosities. How would I date someone with such large feet? How could I share my life with someone so physically big? Who put so little value on health and wellness?"

"Much less risk your own life letting some whale lay on top of you once a week?"

"You joke, but there's truth there. It's just what I need, to walk in and find him sprawled out on the living room floor from a heart attack. It seemed a metaphor for his outsized mediocrity. There's nothing wrong with him, exactly.

He's a good, attentive boyfriend. He listens. And all it does is infuriate me. Why is kindness so irritating?"

"I don't know, but it is," she responded. "We can take of that."

Before I could ask her what she meant, Hewitt sauntered out.

"I guess you've had enough of old Hew?" he said, pulling the brim of his baseball cap far over his eyes.

"I'm married," Melissa said matter-of-factly.

"You don't seem that wild about it," he said before making his way to his truck and driving away. We both started laughing.

"That was pretty good," Melissa said.

"Not what I thought he was going to say."

"Not at all."

We continued to laugh into the empty night.

"You wanna get out of here?" she asked as if she had been thinking about it for some time, perhaps since she first approached my table.

"You know somewhere to go?"

Surveying the parking lot, she said, "What about Salt Lake City?"

"Salt Lake City," I repeated softly.

I was intimately acquainted with the impulse she was indulging in. To burn every bridge. To turn a weapon of mass destruction on your own life. It was easy to confuse the holocaust with the cycle of the phoenix. I had done the former enough times to know that, despite outward appearance, they were not identical. Perhaps that's what drew me to Melissa. A hint of who I used to be, who I longed to be, that shadow self that was always threatening to rise to the surface at the slightest provocation. I'll admit, after a day of traversing endless stretches of highway alone, trapped in my head with ghosts and anxieties, the thought of having someone at my side was appealing. I didn't respond. She wasn't looking for debate or a critical eye. Nevertheless, the point was probably moot. More than likely, when morning peeked over the mountain tops, she would be shaken to her senses, and I would be stuck driving her back, putting me further behind schedule.

"I've been staying with a friend not far from here, so I'm basically packed. I don't even have to see King Brian. I couldn't stand to, anyway. We could just go." There were so many consequences to Melissa leaving with me, none of which she seemed to have thought out (willful ignorance is one of the keys to torching your own life). She was already playing fast and loose with her marriage vows. Not to mention her job. *Did she have a job? Could it be in anything other than in the service industry?* Kids? That seemed like a long shot. Or did she say she had none? There was never a plan to repair the damage you were ready and willing to inflict upon the people and things in your life. You were simply a tornado in the blocks, ready to blow everything to hell the moment you gave yourself the go. Which, by the look in her eye, was any second.

"What about your car?" was the only thing I could think of saying.

"I walked here."

Before I could respond, my cell rang again.

"Hey, honey," I said, making a sour face at Melissa. "I didn't see the calls until today. There's almost no cell service all through Nebraska. God's country indeed. Everything is fine. No, I'm not there yet. Yes, I'm running behind. I stopped a few times. Just places."

Melissa snatched the phone away from me. "Is this Mark? I'm a friend of hers. You're her steady, right? Here's the thing: she's not that into you. She met a guy. Went back to his place. She would have signed the contract except for her respect for you. You get what I am saying? Stop calling. It's over," she said and dropped the phone on the table. "Wait, he wasn't good in bed, was he?"

"Not particularly."

"Then, that takes care of that," she said, brushing her hands together.

"He's watching my cat."

"Let's get outta here. I've already spent too many lifetimes in this dump bar."

After retrieving her bag from the trailer park (I didn't see Brian or Robert's damaged dish), we hit a McDonald's drive-thru, ordering more food than two people could eat in three lifetimes, and left *Stand Up* and our two temporary friends (and never lovers) behind.

"What's wrong?" she asked, leaning her head against the window.

"I think I'm too drunk to drive," I said. "How are you?"

When I looked back over, Melissa was already fast asleep. I rolled all the windows down and let the fresh mountain air help keep me awake.

What's wrong, I repeated back aloud. That's what Chet asked me the day before I aborted his child with a clairvoyance that ripped across my face had he been looking at me. But luckily for me, I guess, we were positioned on the different levels of the bunkbeds in my dorm. Instead, I took a breath and closed my eyes. *Nothing*. And then added as a form of verbal alibi: *I'm just tired,* rather than revealing the truth. Not only the truth of what momentous decision awaited at that clinic the next day but that I had cut him out of the decision-making process, had circumvented him completely, substituting his judgment for that of my girlfriends, planned parenthood, and even my sister, even if most of my self-reflection had been in some form of drunkenness.

Just tired, I again repeated.

At the time, I felt I had no other choice. Everyone who knew Chet was aware that he opposed abortion. Not on religious grounds necessarily. Certainly not political. He often told the story (when this subject arose, not as often then as now, I suppose) that when his father was in his twenties, he and his girlfriend, Rosie, a gifted guitarist and eventual truck driver, had a pregnancy scare. It passed. His father didn't much like the girl and under no circumstance wanted to start a family with her. But something changed inside of him when he was presented with the fact that he could be a father, that a child of his might be growing inside of this woman. She got pregnant again. He begged her to keep it. Chet was that child.

"Hey wake up. I found a motel without killing us."

Melissa lifted her head with a slight smile on her face and looked around groggily.

"Salt Lake City?"

"Not quite."

We trudged into the room where we both changed into more comfortable clothes and flipped on the television, the sound muted. Melissa sat on the toilet and went to the bathroom with the door open. Before she was finished, there was a knock at the door. No doubt King Brian. How he had found us so quickly, I had no idea. Although, in my experience, men are remarkably adept at finding women gone AWOL. Especially if they think another man has coveted their property. Melissa sat at attention on the toilet and nervously motioned for me to answer it. Struggling to get off the bed, I shuffled to the door and cautiously opened the door. It was not King Brian. It was a woman of indeterminate age, barefoot, in shorts and a mesh t-shirt.

"Can I help you?"

"You called?" she said with a sneer.

"Most definitely not."

She snorted in the most embarrassed way, pulled her shirt and bra up over her face, flashed us her very worn-out tits, and marched defiantly away. Once the door shut, the two of us burst out laughing. I fell backward on the bed, rolling back and forth, while Melissa danced up and down the narrow runway from the bathroom to the door as she pulled up her pants.

Taking a seat at the foot of the bed to catch my breath, Melissa looked at me. "And somebody, somebody's gonna be pissed she didn't show up."

"Can you imagine?"

"Yes."

Pulling the covers back, I crawled into the bed and switched off the lamp on the nightstand. Melissa went to the door, opened it, stepped out, and took a long look to the left and right before shutting it, locking it, and flipping the metal bar.

"Well, I guess that's a wrap," she said, laying on her bed on top of the comforter, falling immediately asleep. I soon followed.

***

I woke to the sound of cascading water. For an instant, I was transported to my childhood bedroom, listening to the freight trains that ran every dawn behind my house. Pulling the comforter up to my chin, I luxuriated in the memory that I already knew was false. Unable to drift back to sleep, I turned on my side and lay stubbornly with my eyes closed. More memories came. The morning of my scheduled abortion, the day I received the letter informing me I had been accepted to the University of Minnesota, the afternoon Nestor called informing me of my mother's death, telling Brayden about our impending child (and the resentment when he got wasted while I took prenatal vitamins). These and so many more. My life was defined by moments of catastrophe, every option a new discovery in doubt and pain. Life demands, despite every instinct, that I do the impossible and choose (or, in reality, do nothing until someone else does it for me).

Sitting up, my head ached, and my mouth was dry. Melissa was in the shower, humming softly to herself. Pulling my phone off the nightstand, there was a text from Chet – a single question mark. Outside the window, a large mountain appeared to me like the back of a sleeping brontosaurus. I waited for it to lift its head and let me know I, too, would soon be extinct.

Melissa emerged from the bathroom in a pair of jeans and a green bra.

"I have a cousin in Seattle who is thrilled I am leaving the King. Says she is more than willing to put me up until I get on my feet. Has a small guest room. Maybe even a lead on a waitressing job." She ducked back into the bathroom. I was barely processing what she was saying. The sound of the faucet and the furious brushing of teeth could be heard. Popping back out, her toothbrush protruding from her mouth, she added, "I looked up some shit on the internet on how to file for divorce yourself." Then she disappeared again.

Melissa had no choice but to move forward. She had shot past the point of no return. Tilting my head, I could see her watching herself in the bathroom mirror, carefully outlining her lips in a subtle grey lipstick. She was smug about the new life she had just committed to. She dropped the tube into her toiletry bag. Little did she realize that decisions made quickly and under duress were like atrophied dynamite and could blow at any minute.

"Those drinks were obscenely strong," I said, digging through my purse for an aspirin.

"That's why the place is called *Stand Up*. If you sit down, you'll never get up again. Do you mind if we get a little chow before we get moving?"

"I told Chet I was going to be there late last night."

There was a Perkins a couple of miles up the road bordering the highway. The parking lot was surprisingly full, and there was a long wait to get seated. It was twenty minutes before we were attended to and, once we ordered, another forty-five minutes for the food to be delivered to our table. During this entire time, Melissa didn't say a word.

"Can you pass the syrup?"

"This took way too long," I said, handing it to her. "I need to get on the road. I need to get to Salt Lake City and get this over with."

"I'm going back to Brian."

"What?" I asked, stunned. Of all the words that Melissa could have said, this was the least expected and the most obvious. I lowered my coffee cup and looked up into her expectant, nervous eyes.

"You don't have to drive me back. I asked him to come and get me. He's already on his way. You'll never have to see that dump town again. Not if you're lucky, at least," she said with a forced laugh.

"When did all this happen?"

"When I saw James. I don't know, something happened to me. There I stood, exactly zero miles from the last time he saw me. I didn't go to college, and James did. He went off and became a lawyer, just like I knew he could. I started at a temporary service, met Brian at a cornfield party; after a time, we got engaged, then married. End of story, end of life. Seeing him was like seeing the exit ramp to a destiny I missed." I thought this stupid little speech was finished when she took a breath and went on. "Why didn't I go? He begged me to. I'll tell you why. College was not something our family ever talked about. We had no money. I wasn't a good student. Boston might as well have been the moon."

This little soliloquy, about how one bad choice snowballed into a series of even worse choices whose end result was a lifetime of sadness and regret, was something Melissa had clearly rehearsed, probably this morning, if not her entire adult life. I just happened to be the lucky recipient. But I wasn't the intended audience. That would be Brian or James, or maybe even her parents or, better yet, existence itself.

"There's no aunt in Seattle or guest room or bullshit waitressing job?"

"I do have an aunt there."

"Yeah, I bet," I said. "I meant when did all this, with your husband coming to get you, get set in motion?"

"Oh," she said, embarrassed. This was not the response she was hoping for or expecting. "Four or five this morning. It'll be a while before he gets here. You don't have to wait."

"You think?"

However, she did. In a completely guileless manner, she believed not only that I was going to sit patiently waiting for her estranged husband to show up and be the witness to their reconciliation. But that I would celebrate his arrival as if the fates had deemed it so. That's the thing about trauma and pain and grief; it cannot see beyond its own borders. It's willfully and blindly selfish, attending to its own self-abnegating needs. Not unlike a strikingly beautiful maiden who dropped out of her sister's wedding to drop a bomb on an unsuspecting man who never did anything to her but adore her. You'd think it would be impossible for me to get mad at this creature I had so much in common with at this juncture. And yet, here I sat, furious.

"And you're sure he's coming."

"Yes," she said, raising her chin up defiantly.

"I don't have a boyfriend because of you."

"Seems like it's a good thing we're parting when we are then."

"And what about all your problems? The wedding? Your separation? The stupid ghetto cocktail? Your husband who doesn't want to fuck you?" I said, pulling a pack of cigarettes out from my purse.

"He asked if there were any motels around."

"You don't think he's just drunk?"

"Maybe, probably. Who knows? You make do. I don't want to be divorced," she said pointedly.

"Who does?"

With that, I excused myself and went outside for a cigarette. Standing in front of the restaurant, my first instinct was to call Mark. Then I remembered Robert and the call Melissa so casually made ending my relationship and thought better. Instead, I smoked my cigarette and waited for the brontosaurus on the horizon to awake from his slumber. Stubbing the cigarette out against the restaurant, I reentered the restaurant. Melissa avoided making eye contact with me as I approached the booth.

"Maybe you could do me the courtesy of paying for breakfast?" I said, standing before her.

"Sure."

Crossing her fork and knife neatly on the empty side of her plate, Melissa rose and said, "I just need to use the restroom before you leave."

Reluctantly sitting back down, I tossed my cigarettes back into my purse and waited. After some time, the waitress approached the table with a half-filled coffee pot and lifted it languidly. "Refill?"

I pushed my cup towards her.

Sipping silently on the lukewarm coffee, I waited impatiently for Melissa to return. On the waitress' next visit, I handed her the plates and coffee cup and took a glance at the bill she had set upside down on the table. More time passed. I was anxious to get back on the road. Salt Lake City waited.

Shortly after separating from Brayden, I began dating a bartender named Kevin. A one-night stand that transformed effortlessly into a serious relationship, we did dopey things like putt-putt golf and rent tandem bicycles around Little Blue Lake. Once, we even binge-watched the entire first season of The West Wing over a weekend with pizza, buffalo chicken wings, and margaritas without once changing out of our pajamas. Things Brayden would never have done. It was a fortuitous development after the trauma of my impending divorce. Six months into the relationship, Kevin introduced me to Stuart and Kiki. Stuart ran an unsuccessful pottery business out of his basement, and Kiki was a hot yoga instructor at the local YMCA. Stuart had no family to speak of except a distant uncle in Cork that he visited every summer, and Kiki spent all of her free time with her autistic nine-year-old daughter and battling her ex-husband, a stockbroker and baseball card enthusiast. After having such a limited social circle in my years with Brayden, it was nice to have a group of friends to call my own. The three of them went out for brunch on Sundays. Occasionally Kiki needed to see Kevin alone and commune with him about her divorce (her words). I didn't give it much thought. I should have. Two months later, out of the blue, Kevin dumped me via text with no explanation. I refused to mourn. A few nights later, I came home – well, my dad's home – very drunk and fell asleep watching television. I woke up shortly after falling asleep with a sick feeling in the pit of my stomach. Reaching for my phone, I opened Kiki's Facebook profile. There was a picture of Kiki and Kevin, her daughter draped across both of them, with the caption: *My guy*. I never saw any of them again. I had that same sick feeling now.

    I made my way to the front counter and paid the bill. I burst into the women's room and peered beneath the stalls. They were all empty. Investigating the men's room (much to the consternation of the hosting staff and the lone man at the urinal), Melissa was nowhere to be found.

    "Your friend left," I was told by the young woman at

the podium as I reentered the lobby.

I wondered if Brian was already here, back at the very hotel we had stayed at last night, ordering a pay-per-view adult film for the two of them.

"What?"

"When you went out to smoke, she got a call. She looked really upset. After you came back, she left."

"Left? Like picked up by someone or drove away?"

Rushing outside, I scanned the parking lot, only to find that Melissa had stolen my car. When I had stepped out to smoke, livid at her for returning to Brian, he had either called or texted and told her he was no longer coming. That's when she panicked and took the keys. I felt like the stupidest person alive. I wanted to scream. I lowered myself to the curb. The sun was hidden behind a hazy fog of autumn heat. I pulled out my phone and dialed Mark's number. It was a cruel thing to do. But I did it anyway. He was the only person I could count on to answer.

He let it ring several times before picking it up.

"Yep."

"It's me."

"I know," he said. His voice was firm and confident. He wasn't about to take any bullshit from me, not anymore. "I'm still feeding Tank if that's what you're worried about."

"I wasn't worried."

"Why are you calling then? Something your friend forgot to say?"

"She stole my car this morning."

There was an abstract, confused silence.

"Well, I can't... I won't leave Tank unattended."

I hadn't asked him to rescue me, to drive or fly out to this Perkins in the middle of nowhere to save me, but I needn't. This was his unequivocal way of letting me know that would never happen, not now, not ever.

"It's over. We're over, right? Because what the horrible sad girl said was true?" he asked, in a moment of weakness. Despite all the hurtful things that Melissa had said, and were, in all likelihood, true, perhaps there was a glimmer of hope – that I had refused to have sex with this mystery man because of my feelings for him. It was a long shot, a Hail Mary pass, but one he had to take. "Willow?"

"Yes." Our relationship was technically over, blown to bits by the woman who had just stolen my car. But the real answer, the existential truth of the matter, is that we were never really together. Mark was a placeholder between Brayden and the future. Just as Brayden was a placeholder between the young, confused, depressed adolescent and the adult I didn't know how to be. It had become clear to me that, unless I finally found the courage to be alone, this pattern would go on in perpetuity, my life a waste. The problem was not only that I didn't know what I wanted, I didn't even feel any desire. Before he could push me: "Yes, it's over."

It was the first truthful lie I ever told. I shut the phone, knowing I would never see Mark again. There would be no more surprise visits, cleared driveways, surprise meals, or any of the other shit I always pretended to be shocked by and took no responsibility for. It was, all things considered, a good thing. It was then I noticed something in the spot where my car had been parked. I walked to the vacuous spot where my car had been parked. It was my bag. She left me my bag. Throwing it over my shoulder, I took a seat on the white iron-wrought bench bolted outside the door to the restaurant and lit a cigarette.

"Bitch."

After finishing the pack of cigarettes, I did a little detective work. I discovered there was a bus station ten miles from the Perkins. It was a slow, hot, steady walk along the shoulder of the highway. Once at the station, I lay on the metal mesh bench and immediately fell asleep. It wasn't long until the attendant banged on the counter with a stapler and informed me there was no sleeping in the terminal and that all customers were to remain seated upright. The bus for Salt Lake City pulled into the depot a couple of hours later. I felt dirty and exhausted before I boarded. It was sporadically filled. My penchant for motion sickness dictated that I sit near the front.

The bus was preparing to leave; in fact, the door had been closed when an Asian family, a father, mother, and two young children, approached the bus and rapped on the glass. The driver stared at them for an uncomfortable amount of time before he reopened the door. They spoke in their mother tongue, quickly and loudly like rounds from a machine gun. They carried an inordinate amount of luggage. At their father's instruction, they moved towards the back of the beast, their suitcases and plastic bags banging on every seat. The bus driver watched them suspiciously in the large mirror. Once they were seated, he let out a large, disgusted sigh.

"Jesus," he said and sighed again, making eye contact with me in the large rectangular mirror overhead. "I can't stand Orientals. They ching-chong-chang all day and all night."

I looked hesitantly to my right. A heavy-set man buried his face in his phone, and behind him, a thin blonde woman in an orange floral-print dress turned away from me.

He continued to eyeball me. I gestured with both hands at him in the oversized mirror to lower his voice, but this just seemed to embolden him. Turning around with effort, he asked, "You know what you do to quiet their asses down?" He waited and seemed poised to wait until I answered.

I shook my head, no.

"You crank up the heat full blast, and they sleep the entire ride." At this, he let out a huge laugh and turned back around.

"Is that right?" I said, staring out the window.

He pulled the lever, shut the door, put the behemoth in gear, and the bus lurched spontaneously forward.

Within twenty minutes, the bus was uncomfortably hot, and the noise from the back of the bus had ceased. I arrived in Salt Lake City two hours later. Twenty-five minutes later, a taxi dropped me off in front of Chet's house. I stood at the end of the sidewalk and tried to pick up any clues about him or his life. Eventually, I approached the front door and knocked.

A woman in jeans and a loose brown sweater with a large collar opened the door.

"The famous Willow."

She pushed open the screen door. It let out a long, slow creak. I entered. The smell of dirty kitty litter and jasmine overwhelmed me.

DAVID HAIGHT

Chapter Three
Saturday Sun

*We hear you're leavin', that's okay,
I thought our little wild time had just begun.*

Rikki Don't Lose That Number
Steely Dan

CHET rolled languidly onto his back. Placing his hands behind his head, he couldn't help but feel despondent. How could this be? The day had finally arrived. The moment he had been anticipating since he had left Minnesota nine years ago. He would once again lay eyes on Willow; and what's more, *she was coming to him*. Although he had always fervently believed he and Willow would meet again, until she had responded to his letter, he feared their reunion would have to wait until the next life. And even though the phone conversation was brief, it filled him with resounding joy, a happiness he hadn't felt in years. Reflecting less on the words spoken (which were cryptic and minimal) and more on the voice, which was still a thing of mellifluous beauty, not at all changed since they used to get high in those cinderblock dorms, seemingly floating above the ether, it struck him; he had been bereft of authentic happiness since leaving Minneapolis.

Darlene, on the other hand, who always suspected that Chet still harbored feelings for Willow, was furious when she discovered he had written to her; panicked that she had decided to drive to Salt Lake City. Although she was aware of the carnage Willow had inflicted upon Chet's life, she was grateful to play the role of salve and savior and not be reminded (that after all these years) that she was a mere detour, a bit player in the narrative of his romantic life. With that fateful phone call and the announcement that she would be at their doorstep in two days, Willow, who had always been more an idea than a real person, had inserted herself into their living, corporeal world, causing an immediate and dramatic escalation into an already tense situation.

Darlene, who was approaching forty, desperately wanted a family. After trying off and on for several years to get pregnant without success, she had begun to pressure Chet to go to a fertility clinic to get tested. But whenever the subject was broached, she was met with stony silence. When pushed, he denied the possibility of being infertile. His only line of defense – a pregnancy scare a college girlfriend, Becky, experienced. Darlene was not persuaded and continued to insist. If there was anything Chet had learned in their years together, it was that Darlene never let up. When Chet foolishly confessed one night, after drinking half a bottle of wine, that he had rarely, if ever, used protection with any of the women he had slept with, all without incident, Darlene simply made an appointment. Chet was completely blindsided. He shouldn't have been, but he was.

Chet spoke little in the ensuing weeks. On the day

of the appointment, he avoided Darlene completely. He mowed the lawn, did some grocery shopping, stopped in the office, hid in the garage toying with a completely functional toaster, and so on. When the allotted time arrived, he dutifully got into the car and refused to look at Darlene for the entire twenty-five-minute drive to the Center for Reproductive Medicine and Advanced Reproductive Technologies. A couple of miles from the clinic, Chet was still putting on the same meager defense.

"She was pregnant," he offered, staring out the car window.

"I thought it was a pregnancy scare," she said deliberately.

"She was scared when I got her pregnant. And rightly so. We were so damn young. Our sophomore year. She was devastated when she lost it."

"You're being purposely obtuse. That's not what that means. You know that."

Chet did know that. But he refused to relent.

"I've slept with my share of women."

"But none of them got pregnant. Not one. And you never used protection."

"I'm Catholic, you know?"

"When this subject comes up," she said.

"We don't look too kindly on masturbation, either. Waste of life and so forth."

"Uh-huh."

Over the course of time, he had convinced himself not only that Becky had missed her period but that she had actually been pregnant and had lost the child through miscarriage. He had concocted an entire episode in his imagination: of a frantic phone call, rushing over to her dorm, where he found her in the communal bathroom on the floor, in a pool of blood and tears. So desperate was he to maintain this illusion (along with his manhood) that the week before the appointment, through the wonders of social media, he was able to track Becky down (who was living in Ohio and was married with two kids) and called her. After the initial awkwardness and ostensible catching up (wisely avoiding the entire and illusory episode in the bathroom that he had recounted in such vivid detail to Darlene), Chet simply asked her if she remembered having been pregnant with his child. After a long, painful silence, she told him she had not, in fact, been pregnant. She barely recalled the incident. She then requested that he never contact her again and hung up, promptly blocking him on all social media platforms. Embarrassed and humiliated, Chet took a stand, insisting Darlene allow him to go alone to the clinic. She refused. *To spend the afternoon driving through the mountains or getting drunk at a bar, only to claim you went? No.* He found it eerie how well she knew him and sulked back to the garage.

Pacing the small, beige room, he took in the wide berth of pornographic materials sprawled out on the table (and tucked on the shelf like great works of banned literature). Waves of disgust, resentment, and shame overtook him. He already knew what story his ejaculate told – that he would never father a child. That the history of his family ended with him, that he was a cul-de-sac where his ancestors were collected and snuffed out. He didn't need its inadequacy magnified beneath a microscope, entered into some cold database and stored, bouncing back and forth between routers and servers when called up at a moment's notice – that was a step too far. It was ironic that the only immortality he would achieve would be the testimony of his inability to procreate.

Pulling a chair out from the jerk-off table to the middle of the room, balancing himself upon it, he yanked at the smoke detector until it came off in his hands like the disregarded shell of some oceanic crustacean. Inspecting its inner guts, he was unable to identify a camera but remained unconvinced. Tossing it on the recliner against the wall, he shook his head. Just as he had surrendered to Darlene and this horrific request, he surrendered to the bidding of the room. He settled on a Hustler and got on with it.

Once finished, he slid the little door open, set his non-life-giving material on the lazy Susan (how meager it seemed in its current foggy form), spun it around, and slammed it shut again. It was distressing how quickly he heard the door on the opposite side slide open. *Right,* he muttered. What a job that was. Just waiting while he yanked on his shit? Then collecting, labeling, and transporting it to some apathetic doctor or RN to interpret its results under a microscope? He didn't speak to Darlene the entire ride home.

When the clinic called at the end of the following week, he knew the results of the tests before the voice on the other end had even finished speaking two words. Hell, he knew by the silence before she had uttered a single syllable. It was leaden with anticipatory dread. She had clearly hoped to give the grievous news to his voicemail.

There was no need for the call. The nurse practitioner (it is never the doctor) would inform him that he was cursed with a pre-existing medical condition. Her conveyance would imply that this was supposed to ease his mind, that this a priori state relieved him of some measure of responsibility, at least when delivering the news to Darlene. He had already Googled the word as the nurse went on in her measured, rhythmic tones and stared at the glowing screen. Oligospermia. It was as ugly and impersonal as the doctors intended it to be, camouflaging the pain behind bureaucratic jargon. *Low sperm count.* His chance of impregnating a woman – of her conceiving his child naturally – was essentially zero. His stomach tightened. The nurse's voice droned on. When it was bad news, they always went on. They couldn't help themselves. He only caught some of what she was saying. There was no need. She would rattle off alternative methods of how he and Darlene could possibly conceive a child. That all hope was not lost. Of course, she would keep it vague. Making no promises. She would be more than happy to email him a list of contacts and phone numbers, if he so desired, to set up appointments, and so on. Here, her voice brightened for the first, and only, time. This was not mercy or hope. Nor was it cruelty, exactly. It was partly the due diligence of bureaucracy. Really, it was just fear of silence, of allowing for that space where his humanity, his flesh and blood, might creep its way through the cold fiber optic cables, and he would blossom into a person. Mercy would have been giving him time to process the fact that his dream of becoming a father had been summarily snuffed out by the Googling of that one word: oligospermia. He was about to cut her off (mercifully, if you will) and decline any further help when something completely unexpected happened. "Wait, what?" Exiting his office, he walked the length of the parking lot over to the dumpster. He dialed Darlene's number.

"The clinic just called," he said. Before she could ask, he offered the verdict, "My boys are fine."

"Oh," she uttered, with a grief that, despite her best efforts, was palpable to Chet.

"Well, you're the one who wanted to know so badly. It's not me. Not what you expected?" he barked cruelly.

"I never said that."

"Sure, you did. Repeatedly."

They stood in their respective positions on opposite sides of the city, silent, as their world was irrevocably altered forever.

"I thought you never used protection. Were you lying to protect me?"

"No."

"Then what?"

"Dumb luck."

There was a long silence during which Darlene seemed to regroup.

"What about in-vitro? Or a surrogate?"

"With what money?"

"We can at least—"

"Dar, stop."

There was another long silence.

"When will you be here?" she asked. It certainly didn't go unnoticed by Chet that Darlene asked when he would be 'here' not 'home.'

"The usual time."

"I made pork chops," she said, adding, "It's me? How can it be me?" she asked and started to cry.

That night, they picked at their dinner in silence. Chet watched the last half of a baseball game and got drunk while Darlene pretended to read in the bedroom. By the time Chet came to bed, Darlene was asleep. They never spoke about that phone call again. It was too raw. They entered an unacknowledged agreement, an understanding that their life would not include children. The years passed, but the yearning for a family never ceased, and though they would never admit it, they silently blamed one another. Now Willow was on her way to their very doorstep. It was supposed to be the concluding movement of the piece that was started when she asked him for a ride so many years ago, but not twenty-four hours before that conclusion could occur, everything would be soured by a simple phone call.

Pulling himself out of bed, Chet showered, shaved, and got dressed. In the kitchen, he forsook the freshly brewed pot of coffee Darlene had left for him every day since they started living together and went straight for the freezer. He grabbed a bottle of Jack Daniels they had received as a Christmas present three years ago, broke the seal around the cap, unscrewed it until it fell gently into his shaking hands, and took a hit, then another, then a third. It was mellow and biting simultaneously. He felt its effects directly. Winding the cap back on meticulously, he lowered it into a brown paper bag and exhaled deeply.

"What's that?" a voice came from behind him, still clouded by sleep.

"A little lunch. I told you I have to go into the office for a bit," Chet said, stubbornly refusing to face Darlene. She knew he was lying on both counts but didn't call him on either. Taking a step forward, she placed a hand on his back, which immediately tensed up. Chet stood for a moment, angry at her, not only for catching him in his deceit and for the sympathy she was offering, but resentful at having her in his life. It so often seemed the case that those things which were designed to comfort only repelled us, got in the way of what perhaps were supposed to be solitary moments. He pulled his arched back away from her caress and left.

    Backing out of the driveway, Chet circled the block and parked around the corner from their house. Sitting in his car, windows up, radio off, and intermittently sipping from the Jack Daniels – every synapse in his head humming like a failing air conditioner – he watched the cars that crawled past, wondering which one carried the delivery from his past. There was nothing about her impending arrival that boded well for him (or his relationship with Darlene, which suddenly felt like an afterthought), but he didn't care. She was driving across the country to him. Whatever message needed to be conveyed could only be done in person. In that, he sensed urgency, and in that urgency, hope. It was two and a half hours before Darlene finally called, confirming that Willow had arrived (as he had insisted she do). Rubbing his smooth face with his hand, it occurred to him, for the first time, that free will was a myth or, at best, had strict limitations. That we were just the yo-yos of fate – only allowed so much leeway to doodle about indiscriminately before yanking us back and shooting us off in an entirely different direction with utterly no purpose. Exiting his car, Jack Daniels in hand, Chet walked up the sidewalk and took a seat on the curb across from his front door next to a large green recycling bin.

    The last time Chet had seen Willow had been under eerily similar circumstances. While still in college, he had made the decision to relocate to Utah. Before this final exodus, he made his way to the red brick building where Willow lived and sat in a patch of woods across the street, his eyes fastened to the second-story window. He observed her as she floated from the kitchen to the cavernous high-ceilinged living room (a framed poster of the Indigo Girls monitoring him) and back to the kitchen. She meticulously poured herself a cup of coffee and briefly fell out of sight. This was his soundless goodbye, not only to her but to his current life, the only life he had ever known.

He was a mess. A horrible sweaty red-faced mess. He was certain he needed medical attention. Pants around his ankles, ass thrust out, he squatted, shitting his brains out. *This was the only position that allowed you to shit outside and avoid a nest full of runny turds dropped in your pants and smeared into your butt cheeks when you pulled them back up.* It refused to end, and there was sure to be blood. He continued, grunting and squeezing as noiselessly as nature would allow. Finishing up his business, he yanked a handful of leaves off a hovering branch, wiped, took a quick look (indeed, the leaves had a suggestion of scarlet), and fastened his pants, rubbing the sweat from his brow, exhausted.

Taking a few tentative steps forward, he lowered himself onto a stump. Willow had reappeared outside, already seated on the front steps, legs together smartly, holding an oversized coffee mug with both hands, a cigarette inserted deftly in her mouth. He could smell her perfume, abundant and sickly sweet. Raising her porcelain face to the sun, she closed her eyes, her bottom lip protruding slightly. He felt a sting. He recalled sucking that bottom lip, thick and pink and mildly chapped, into his mouth like a section of an overripe orange. It was hard to believe they had ever been together. Had laughed. Shared meals, spoken about dreams, planned a life – *a couple of architects* she would jokingly call them (she was always a superior wordsmith than he was). Even more astounding that he had seen her perfectly-formed body naked. A mere fifteen feet away, she was no longer a flesh and blood person but, rather, a star in the heavens, hidden from him by vast distances.

He observed her for a few minutes more. He could have sat there forever just to be witness to her otherworldly presence. If by chance she would see him, huddled in the shadows, cowed and unsure, framed by the trees and branches and beckon him, he would call the entire endeavor off. Repugnance overcame him. Even after all the forethought and mental duress and final finals, he still wasn't sure if this was what he really desired. His internal struggle had not abated moments before he was to depart. By some miracle, it nearly came to fruition when he broke a twig with his heavy, forlorn footfalls, and her head snapped in his direction. He stood frozen, like an escaped prisoner under an omnipotent and cruel spotlight. But she did not call out his name. Her body relaxed. She went back to observing the sparse traffic and occasional jogger, nonchalantly sipping her coffee. He tiptoed to his rusted-out Ford Bronco he had abandoned several blocks back and fired up the engine.

The truth was, had she caught him lurking outside her apartment (yet again), she would not have been so forgiving. After the last incident, she had promised, in no uncertain terms, to get her father involved, swiftly and without mercy. This was something he wished to avoid at all costs, and she knew it. Every man fears a woman's father more than the police. The consequences were far graver. Police have policies and procedures, rules and regulations. Fathers have none of these limitations imposed upon them. Little did Willow know that her father had discovered that Chet had been stalking her and wasn't about to sit idly by as his daughter was terrorized.

It was the fifteenth day of his stakeout. He sat, parked outside the Caribou Coffee where she worked as a night manager, waiting for an opportunity. What that opportunity entailed, Chet couldn't articulate. To unwind the past. To be seen as he wished to be seen, not as he was. To make love one last time. To blot out the world sans the two of them. To covet. To devour. It was all so unclear in his mind, which was a tuning fork that wouldn't stop vibrating. In practical terms, he was waiting for her to appear outside, to smoke and get her alone (these things must be done alone) under the flimsy guise of returning the (admittedly few) items she had left behind in his dorm room and would never, ever want back if it meant she had to see him again. But that was of no consequence.

He had been slouched in the driver's seat for five hours when he drifted off to sleep as the sun was setting, covering his body in a cool, uncomfortable dew. He was awakened by a knock on the window. Waking with a start, he came face-to-face with Willow and a stern-looking security guard standing close behind her. She motioned at him to roll his window down. Sitting up, he fumbled at the door handle. The security guard shook his head and mouthed the words, *just the window*. Chet cranked the ignition, and it slid down.

"What are you doing here?" she asked before the window was completely hidden inside the door.

Grasping at the grocery bag that had been on his passenger seat for the better part of a month, was crumpled and torn, he thrust it clumsily at her.

"I don't want that garbage," she said, refusing it. "Anything else?"

He had waited so long for this moment, and now that

it was here, he realized he hadn't mapped out one word to say. He had no strategy. All his energy had been expended in the waiting and the watching: of faceless buildings, of her static car outside of buildings, at maps charting her various routes. Staring at her exasperated, impatient face, it was slipping away. She was already in the rearview mirror of his beleaguered life. And pregnant with another man's child, no less. Leaning back, he moaned, much to the consternation of the security guard.

"No," he said, cold and heartsick.

With that, she was gone, swallowed up by the coffee house. The security guard remained behind. Leaning forward and whispering in a low, threatening tone, he said, "Never make an appearance here again. Understand?"

"Yes."

Then he was gone too.

When Chet pulled into the parking lot of his dorm, Willow's father was waiting. Chet didn't see him at first. But as he exited his car, he appeared from behind his Yellow Datsun. How he had discovered his stalking, Chet didn't know (and never found out), but the sense of dread at seeing him was overwhelming. He was unsure if he was there to merely threaten him or to actually physically harm him. It was a real possibility. Unlike fathers of sons who foster a sense of self-reliance to the point of cruelty in their boys, fathers of daughters are irrationally protective. Chet had made many mistakes, had done many disgusting, regrettable things. To be forced to reckon with those things in the bald nakedness of this man's judgment was too much to bear. On top of this, ever since Chet was a young boy, grown men had instinctually loathed him. They seemed to revel in intimidating and humiliating him, making him feel small and insignificant. At times, he believed their aversion hid a real desire to hurt him.

In junior high school, after years of playing slow-pitch softball, Chet and his best friend, John Kelly Kirby, decided to try out for baseball. Before tryouts had even been completed, they went to the coach (and Social Studies teacher, a young man and favorite of the young eighth-grade girls) Mr. Jorgenson and told him they were out. The switch from slow pitch to fast pitch was terrifying. Flying into a fury, Mr. Jorgenson berated them in front of the other boys, labeling them cowards, demanding they get off his field. Months of teasing ensued. Similarly, in high school, Chet was dating a very pretty, chaste young girl, Daphne, from a blended protestant family. Her stepfather, Stan, was suspicious of him from day one. Chet was rarely allowed to visit and, even then, under the strictest of conditions. On one of these occasions, they were watching a movie (one preapproved in advance) in the family room, where all blankets had been extricated and with every light laser-focused upon them like the eyes of God, when a light snow began to fall. Chet was asked to leave ostensibly for his safety. He was barely at the edge of the gated community when his car died. After trudging back the half mile to the house, Stan begrudgingly agreed to assist him. When he ascertained that Chet was ignorant about the inner workings of car engines, he pointed to the nearest service station, got into his SUV, and fled the scene. Chet, too embarrassed to notify his father, called every friend he knew who owned a car. It was two and a half hours before he was able to reach Tim, a freshman, and convince him to make the journey and give him a ride home. Daphne was subsequently forced to end the relationship.

And now Willow's father. Directing him to a bench adjacent to the tennis courts, they both took a seat.

"Well, go ahead," Willow's father began.

Slowly, Chet unfolded the events that led up to the current situation. How Willow had dumped him for another man without notice, without explanation, and how his life had spiraled out of control since. Chet did his best to minimize these incidents (of which there were many more than her father knew), attempting to present most of them as misunderstandings, unpremeditated acts that never put her in any real danger. He finished by adding that, as a consequence of his reckless behavior, he had to withdraw from his *Existentialism and 19th Century Literature* class (pushing his graduation past the traditional four years) and was fired from his job at Arby's.

At this, Willow's father stood up abruptly.

"So, *you're* the victim?"

"No, sir."

"What part are you culpable for?"

Chet had no answer. A junior couple Chet recognized entered the tennis courts and began volleying the ball.

"I don't give two shits about who dumped who or if it was done in a respectful way. That's life, pal. You put my daughter in danger," her father said in the most deliberate, frightening tone Chet had ever heard. "She was terrified, boy."

"I know that now."

Pinning him down to the bench with the same menacing tone as the security guard, he said, "Never, ever talk to my daughter again. Don't call. Don't show up at her apartment, at her place of business. Don't even think about her. Understand?"

Both students stopped what they were doing and looked Chet's way, the tennis ball dropping and rolling off to the corner of the court.

"I said, do you understand?"

"Yes, sir."

Then he walked with purpose to his car and was gone. The sound of the tennis ball bouncing off the clay court once again resumed. Chet made his way to his dorm room, drank four beers in quick succession, and considered slitting his wrists.

In the following six weeks, Chet did not have any communication with Willow or her father. With her completely cut out of his life, it became, in every sense, a living hell. His stomach was constantly in knots. After shitting his pants in a grocery store and sprinting to his car, feces racing down his legs and into his socks, he stopped eating after ten in the morning, then for a time stopped eating altogether. The iron judge he kept beneath his bed, and that made appearances at dawn, dusk, and noontime, told him he had lost twelve pounds. He was drinking constantly. He ceased attending his classes. He moved all his belongings out of his dorm and into the back of his truck in the middle of the night (without so much as a word of explanation to his roommate who had bugged out and was either staying with his boyfriend or had temporarily moved home) and stopped showering. His paranoia raged unchecked. When he creeped out of his dorm room after eight days inside and caught sight of a crow overhead, he became convinced his death was imminent.

Those months with Willow were the most rapturous he had ever experienced. Pure ecstasy. How did she repay him? She took everything from him twice. First, when he had given his love, his time, his body, his self-respect. Anything she asked, he had willfully sacrificed (and which he would enthusiastically do again). The second, when she had severed their relationship, without warning, and taken with her his heart, his self-respect, his future family, and had given it to another.

    A year earlier, he hadn't even known Willow. By outside appearances, he was just another faceless student with a fifteen-dollar haircut at an average University, working on a generic business degree. But he was a young man who arrived at college with a specific plan. Growing up, Chet was in awe of his Uncle Donald and Aunt Marie. Unlike his parents, who seemed to communicate only at high volumes (or not at all) and were continually on the edge of financial ruin, his Uncle Donald was a decorated salesman, and his Aunt Marie was a stay-at-home mother who was active in their community and ran their household with the efficiency of a military operation. He longed to duplicate that template in his own life. In order to fulfill this desire, he needed to succeed (so he surmised) academically, socially, and romantically.

    He dutifully attended to his studies, was a regular at the dances and weekend parties, football and hockey games (during their respective seasons), joined a fraternity, and augmented these experiences by making an impromptu jaunt to the Badlands while on mushrooms, qualified for State in golf, saw the Beat poet Gary Snyder read, and helped build a shanty town in the University center. All while pursuing women with as much vigor as any red-blooded American man. All that was left was to find a partner who could run their house and raise their children. At one point, he thought he had found her.

Her name was Maddie, a tall, red-haired girl from a blink-and-you-miss-it township in North Dakota. Told by her high school English teacher she had promise in creative writing, she came to college with aspirations to write the great American Novel. Quickly overwhelmed by the more talented and disciplined writers, and having discovered she loved weed, mushrooms, sex, and the Violent Femmes more than the daily grind of editing page and paragraph of a boring Bildungsroman, another dream was mercifully put to rest.

Chet and Maddie shared a couple of English Literature Survey classes and had friends in common. After rescuing Maddie from a drunk and dangerously aggressive hockey player at a fraternity party who had her cornered in a bathroom, they enjoyed a friendly flirtation and eventually began dating. So certain was he that she fit into his plan that he requested they be exclusive on their second date, which she agreed to. From that point on, they were inseparable. They studied and ate together. She spent most nights and every weekend in his dorm room. When spring break approached, they decided to take a bus westward to Santa Barbara. At the time, it was the best trip either of them had taken. They shared quiet, intimate dinners, walked along the beach where they shared their views on life, art, and music, relished the hotel hot tub (even skinny dipping one night after too much wine), and indulged in plenty of sex. On the way back, on a stop in Salt Lake City, they were both robbed of their backpacks. The thieves acquired nothing of value, mainly dirty clothes and some cheap souvenirs they were going to bestow on their friends and family with much aplomb. They took it as a sign and were set to move in together the following fall and had even started touring apartment complexes when Chet met Willow. Now, his life was in shambles.

Eventually, his father was alerted by a still heartbroken Maddie that Chet was spinning out of control. The following Saturday, he showed up unannounced. His imperative was to get his son's life back on track. That a woman was the cause of his pathetic state came as no surprise. Ever since Chet was a young boy, he was easily washed out by the fairer sex. Taking him out to Perkins, he listened as he walked him through the entire saga. The details (of which there were many) were irrelevant. In his opinion, the pedestrian fact was that Chet loved a woman who no longer loved him. It happened every day. Time was the only remedy. After finishing up their lunch, he purchased his son an abundance of groceries, a 12-pack, and deposited him back to his dorm, convinced that once another woman turned up, everything would fall back into place.

Sunday afternoon, after a lovely morning together, father and son were saying their goodbyes when Willow appeared on the opposite side of campus. *That her? Yeah. Pretty. Yeah. You can do better, son. Give me a second.* With that, Chet's father watched in horror as his son wandered away, making his way through the crowd to Willow's side. Once there, he pelted her with questions, gesturing wildly, throwing himself on the grass, begging her to take him back. Even at a distance, it was obvious she was unmoved and eventually disappeared behind the library. Walking over to him, Chet's father lifted him up from the grass and escorted him back to his room. Groceries and clean clothes were not the panacea for this bewitching – not this time. Drastic measures were needed. Grasping him by the shoulders, he told him plainly: *You're no longer able to function at this school* and made a case for his son to come home, enroll in a trade school, and get his head straight. If he didn't get him away from this woman, he was finished. Chet reluctantly agreed. They silently packed up Chet's remaining belongings into their vehicles. Yet when the time came to leave, Chet adamantly refused. No amount of cajoling or threats was effective. They ended up in a screaming match outside his dorm. His dad wasn't surprised. He had no choice but to leave him to his fate, inadvertently taking half of his belongings in the process.

By the time Chet got back to his dorm room, he had already decided. He would transfer to a new school. Not just a different college in Minnesota (anything within a day's drive would be a disaster). No, he needed to go far away, somewhere he could finish his degree and start his life anew, free of all burdens. An unknown city where he had no ties: no family, no friends, no foundation; a foreign skyline where he had no affinity for any sports team, could name none of its elected representatives, where he was easily lost among the streets. Where, in every sense of the word, he was a stranger. With that distance, both physical and existential, Willow would alchemize into just another memory, and he could meet a new woman and start a family. He looked west. Chet knew if you were an American explorer looking to seek your fortune, to start over and reinvent yourself, you ventured westward. There was something quintessentially American about that instinct. It is ingrained in our DNA, so he figured. The Gold Rush of 1849. Route 66. Jack Kerouac. Haight-Asbury. The Beach Boys. Manifest Destiny. Bruce Springsteen's Thunder Road, "*It's a town full of losers/And I'm pulling out of here to win*" resonated deeply. It filled Chet with a sense of possibility and wonder. It seemed almost patriotic. Not to mention, even at his young age, he had grown tired of the punishing Minnesota winters. Rising from the bare mattress and looking over the map spread across his dorm room desk, he concluded that he would make his new home Salt Lake City. The very place he was robbed, he would reclaim his life. He withdrew from all of his classes. His truck was already packed. He just needed to look upon Willow one last time.

Watching her from his burrow inside the small patch of woods across from her apartment, for the first time in six weeks, vibrating like a tuning fork, his ass moist and raw, he found it hard to resist the urge to scream out her name, to run into her arms. This time was different (he had convinced himself). He was not here in the same capacity as all the other times. There was no bag of junk to return. No words in desperate need of utterance. There were always words you *could* speak, but he had exhausted every syllable that could be offered to the air and have an effect. In fact, everything regarding Willow had been exhausted. She was pregnant with another man's child. It was growing right now. It felt like a death to him, his plan. *Was he bereaved? Perhaps he had been for some time.* Picking back up his reverie – he just needed to have one final look at her. *Yes, he had said that every single time he had lurked outside her apartment, place of business, bar, house party, or random parking lot.* She was just so damn easy to fall in love with. It was nearly impossible not to blame her for his condition and uncontrollable behavior. He did his best not to this time. To be a man. To have integrity. To be a morally centered person. To remind himself that this time was fundamentally different. The stakes were higher. All with little success. Turning away from her statuesque beauty, he was certain of one thing – that dropping out of school, moving to Salt Lake City away from his family and friends, everything familiar or safe, and starting fresh was the right move. He had never been more certain of anything in his life. Pulling onto the interstate, his leave-taking took on the grandest of metaphysical proportions in his mind. In simple terms, he was proud of himself (something that never came easy). Rolling the passenger window down and feeling the air rush through the car like the breath of God, he sighed. He was finally at peace.

He wasn't eighty miles into his journey when he screeched into a gas station parking lot. The needle on the fuel gauge turned away, ashamed. Chet didn't need gas. Not for a long while. He stared at the grim grey cement blocks that made up one wall of the gas station, the two unmarked bathroom doors, the public telephone booth, and two thick telephone books encased in metal frames hanging motionless. Not far to the right was a rotting wood corral housing a rusty dumpster with its small rust-frozen feet like an old crabby bull. Through the large glass windows of the gas station, he could see a single woman behind the counter, flipping through a magazine.

Sweating profusely, he fantasized about what it would be like to take her to a nearby motel and have unbridled, passionate (even rough) sex with her. It was possible, he postulated. Movies and television made it appear simple. Two strangers meet and have undeniable chemistry. That was the entirety of the necessary ingredients. At that point, it would smash cut to them in bed in the throes of passion. Often, they were unable to make it to the bed (or get their pants completely off) and screwed right up against the wall, the ills of existence wiped away through the communion of their bodies by one transcendent act of lovemaking.

He knew better. Nothing like that had ever happened to Chet. Not under the best set of circumstances. Even when there was obvious bestial attraction, it took weeks to make it into the bedroom, and it was never, ever transcendent. Well, maybe once, but it was his second cousin, and after they had consummated, she ratted him out to her father, and it almost destroyed their family. Even with Willow, the apparent love of his life, sex had never come naturally. The second time they attempted to make love had been a disaster. *The first was completely orchestrated by her and seemed to have very little to do with him.* Willow had been distant the entire evening. Eventually, they began to mess around. After an elongated period of time, both shirtless, he dared whisper, 'Take your pants off.'

'Why?'

Rolling onto his back, he was stunned into silence. Eventually came the sound of her indifferent snoring. It was weeks until he made another attempt.

He entered the gas station, the electronic bell dinging loudly. The clerk could not even be bothered to look up from her brightly colored pagan hymnal. Chet ambled up and down the aisles, amazed at the variety of certain items such an isolated place stocked: cat food, fake nails, dreamcatchers, and not of others: potato chips, pornographic magazines, and condoms (the sight of which momentarily gave him hope). His body felt a chill as he passed the wall of refrigerators. Approaching the counter, he set down two Hawaiian punches, a Snickers, and a pack of Big Red gum.

"Will that be all?"

He glanced around nervously.

"Anything else you'd recommend?" he asked and raised

his left eyebrow provocatively which she failed to notice.

She looked at him sluggishly, freezing in midturn, the page being held hanging in midair, "What?"

"No, that's it."

Plopping the bag down next to him in disgust, he inserted the key in the ignition but refused to start the truck. This was not an insubstantial proposition he was undertaking, relocating his entire life to a foreign place. Yes, it would be a pivotal moment in the story of his life when told to his children – the hero arriving at his new home after his arduous journey, a stranger in a strange land ready to plant his flag, meet his wife, mother of his children and begin constructing a life. But at this moment, Willow needed to know, to fully appreciate the endeavor he was undertaking and the part she had played in it.

Getting out of the truck, Chet slammed the door and raised his head to the heavens. This time, the woman behind the counter looked up in horror, no doubt petrified he was reentering the store with an unwanted proposition. He could see the reasons she couldn't accept his invitation forming on her brow like fault lines that threatened her peace of mind if he dared not accept them: *I have plans. I just got out of a bad relationship.* And the tried-and-true, *I'm a lesbian.* Why they rarely opened with "I have a boyfriend" always confounded Chet. It was checkmate. It was occasionally the closer. Perhaps it was a desire to let you know it's *you* they don't want? For a moment, he considered reentering the gas station, partly out of curiosity, partly obstinance, just to see what grenade she would lob at him. Or maybe, just maybe, she was interested? Realizing how pathetic he was, he made his way to the phone booth.

He pulled out his wallet and focused on the picture

of Willow, which appeared grey and dirty, ensconced in the plastic sleeve in his wallet. *You're the easiest person in the world to fall in love with,* he said tenderly, before pulling every coin from the depths of his pocket and laying them neatly on the tiny ledge of the phone booth, dropping them in the slot until a dial tone registered and entered her number. There was a delay before it connected, a lonely echo reminding him he was already far away, physically and psychologically, that his future was drawing him even farther afield, that he didn't want to go, that it didn't matter and most heartbreakingly, that his past would never be finished with him no matter where he landed. He also knew that she would hear the hollowness of the line in the instant before he could even blurt out a ridiculous "hey" and realize the call was long distance, that it was him. He considered hanging up. Then, like a needle being dragged unceremoniously from the inside groove of a record to its outside and off, it ceased, and the warmth of a physical presence on the other side filled the void.

"Hello?"

He again contemplated replacing the receiver.

"Hello?" the voice said with marked annoyance. Then, like a hypnotist breaking a spell, she said, "I know it's you."

An involuntary guffaw belched its way through his teeth, followed by a hot sob of tears. Then the line went dead.

"Hello?" he gasped through a slosh of excessive salt water, barely clinging to the phone. "Willow? Willow?"

Letting the receiver drop onto his shoulder like a baby needing to be burped and shooting a quick glance to the window (he could no longer see the clerk), he lunged at the ledge for more coins. The first time he called back, she picked up and hung up. The second he heard giggling before the line went dead. The third, fourth, and fifth registered busy. Finally, she answered with a curt, "What?"

He managed to corral his tears (which had made an unholy mess of the front of his shirt and left sleeve) and blurted out in a set of sloppy sentences the opposite of what he had planned. He was scared. That he had made mistakes; with her, with their relationship, with the break-up. He adored her. Maybe was in love with her. He would beat himself up for years for that single word: maybe. That she should leave Brayden (this was the first time he had said the interloper's name aloud) and run away with him and start fresh to raise her baby together as a family. In Canada. Or Europe. Or he could race back. Either way, they should move in together. Of that, he was one hundred percent certain. Or live in separate locations and date if she thought that was a better idea. He would prove himself worthy of her. Of her child. And so on. This time, when the line dropped, he hung up the receiver, slumped back to his car, and sheepishly pulled out of the parking lot. What was intended to be a reprieve had metamorphosized into its pathetic opposite.

By the next day, he had arrived in Salt Lake City. It was larger than he had envisioned, more industrial. Less like the utopian paradise he had been imagining. He spent a week in a hotel, devouring unholy amounts of fast food, watching a strange mixture of the Golf Channel, Animal Planet, and the Food Network. After that, he got off his ass and found the strength to rent a studio apartment and land a part-time job at Subway before his money ran out. A few weeks after that, he was registered for school for the following semester. With the exception of a few drunken calls, his life in Minnesota and Willow was firmly set in stone. On those occasions when he called his decision into doubt, he would call his dad, who was more than happy to remind him of what a selfish twat Willow was and to get on with things. Even if he didn't understand why the fuck he had to move all the way to Utah, he was glad he no longer seemed in agony and, most importantly, he was away from that woman. So, he did get on with things. Slowly, the semblance of life became recognizable through the fog. He received his degree a year later, got a job shortly after graduation at an accounting firm, a few years later, a better job at a bigger, more reputable company, and eventually met Darlene.

Now this phantom from history had been resurrected and sat like an angel of death inside his house, anticipating his arrival. Taking three more generous sips from the bottle of Jack Daniels, he stood up and brushed the dirt from his ass. He was about to drop it in the recycling bin and greet his destiny when the door unexpectedly opened. It was Willow. In a panic, he took cover behind the recycling bin. He sat, knees buried in his chest, poking one of his eyes with the bottle. Had she seen him? He listened intently. Nothing. Then that voice. Closing his eyes, he attempted to decipher the words. It was in vain. Listening harder, it was different. These were not the lyric notes one speaks to a lover. The tone was loving, tender, and sweet. She was talking to a child, her child. Chet's shoulders dropped. His fists tightened around the neck of the bottle. Eventually, the voice ceased, and she reentered the home, his home. He took a long, steady sip from the Jack Daniels, stood up, and approached the door.

* * *

Willow was not the only apparition to rise from the grave. Not twenty-four hours earlier, as she was lost in the great, lonely expanse of these United States, Chet received devastating news. Before he arrived at work, his cell phone had started ringing. He did not recognize the number, and having a backlog of work to do, he ignored it, immediately forgetting about it. Throughout the day and with greater frequency, the calls kept coming. Eventually they became impossible to ignore, like a great sin coming to light or sickness forcing itself from your belly. He was not alarmed. It was more than likely the usual culprits: marketers attempting to pick his pocket, political campaigns with urgent messages about the state of the country (which, no matter the year or party in power, was in dire straits), the three or four independent contractors he had contacted about painting the house. In a quiet moment, he answered the phone.

"Chet?"

"Yes."

"This is Adele Hennings," she began. "I don't know if you remember me, but I am Willow Hennings' sister. You two dated in college."

The introduction was wholly unnecessary. Chet had only known one Adele his entire life. And even after nine years, Adele's voice, coarse, impatient, preemptively pissed off at what you hadn't even said, was immediately recognizable. To say he was astonished would be an understatement. He never thought he would hear from Willow again, much less see her, but a call from her loathsome sister (and only a few days later) was something he had never, ever considered. Truly, the fates were swirling about him.

"Are you still there?"

"Yes."

"Jesus Christ," she muttered. "Do you not know how to carry on a conversation?"

"I do."

"Anyway, Willow got pregnant when you were dating. She had it taken care of."

For a moment, Chet was relieved. At the sound of Adele's unpleasant voice, he was certain that Willow, the love of his life (and those were the words that had immediately come to him as the opening of her eulogy), the woman who had pushed him out of his chosen school and halfway across the country, away from his family and everything he loved, had died on the way. He was ashamed of how relief flooded his senses. Then the import of Adele's words sunk in.

"What did you say?"

"I said, Willow aborted your child," she repeated. "I thought you deserved to know."

"What the hell are you talking about?"

"Planned Parenthood in Minneapolis."

"When?"

"I just told you, you dumb motherfucker. When you were in college. She wanted Brayden. But she couldn't very well agree to be his girl if she was knocked up with another man's child. So, she had it taken care of. I think you know the rest, how she had his baby and married him. Attempted a normal life."

"You're lying," he blurted out, although something told him she wasn't. The timing was suspect, especially considering the nature of Willow and Adele's relationship and the fact that Willow was nearing his doorstep like a heat-seeking missile for unexplained reasons to once again blow up his life. *God, why did it feel so good?* "You're lying."

"Am I?"

"I don't understand this."

"She'll be darkening your door shortly for you to ask yourself."

Then the line went dead. Almost immediately, it began ringing again.

He picked it up and shouted, "Fuck you, you hateful bitch!"

"Chet?"

It was Darlene. He felt the blood rush out of his entire body.

"Eh?" he muttered before hanging up. Or so he thought. He could still hear her voice, staccato, panicked. He pushed at the screen until it disconnected. It began ringing immediately. He fumbled to turn the phone off, dropping it on its belly. It continued buzzing at him. Picking it up, the screen was shattered. He finally managed to turn it off. Standing at his desk, phone still in hand, he cursed himself. It felt like his insides were on fire. He knew the logical thing to do, the emotionally mature thing to do, would be to turn his phone back on and call Darlene. She was an astute judge of character and always knew what to do. He did neither. In that moment, he hated both Adele and Darlene with a fury unbeknownst to him before, and wanted nothing more than Willow standing before him, no matter what she did or planned to do or what the outcome was. *That, he knew, was true love.* The better angels were always capsized by his demons inside.

In a flash, he recalled an affair he had with Zoe, a twenty-nine-year-old co-worker, not long after he and Darlene moved in together. It was a disaster. The memories were spotty but forceful. The two red velvet chairs in the lobby of the hotel. Straightening his tie in the mirror as he proceeded to the room. The way she brushed the hair out of her face like a teenager before kissing him. The sound of coins inserted into the vending machine outside of their room, followed by the hard rumble of the can. Each of them turning off their cellphones.

The sex was tremendously mediocre. He took a long time to get and maintain an erection. Neither one of them came. The moment they were finished, he blurted out, "Was it the best you ever had?" like an asshole. She responded by gathering her clothing and disappearing into the bathroom. Eventually, the toilet flushed, and she emerged fully dressed, picked up her purse, denied him a goodbye, and left. He never heard from her again. He never told Darlene.

Calmly and swiftly, he made his way to his car and onto the highway. It would appear he was headed towards home. It's a universal truth that the pull of home is stronger than the gravitational pull of the sun on its children to a man. However, that wasn't Chet's destination. At that moment, he had only one purpose: to throttle his vehicle to its utmost limit and send it careening into a foundational block of the nearest bridge, ending his life. For if what Adele was telling him was true – and he was convinced it was – he believed that killing himself would be his life's crowning achievement and would give him a list of accomplishments that had thus far evaded him in his thirty-odd-years of living: it would punish Adele for her mindless cruelty, allow Darlene to find a man to give her a family, and deny Willow the forgiveness she was so obviously seeking and allow him peace by reconciling him to his unborn child. It was decided. Immediately, there was a lightness to his touch, a playfulness as he bobbed and weaved out of traffic. He pushed his car harder. 65, 70, 75. He drew the car into the left lane, then onto the shoulder, and finally the ditch. The car began to shake. A little at first and then more aggressively. 80, 85, 90. The bridge grew in size. Chet began to howl. Then was heard the long swishing and popping of dirt sliding beneath rubber as he slammed on his brakes. *What a loser, what a fucking loser.* He banged on the steering wheel. He wanted to extinguish his life and never set eyes on Darlene again or hear about starting a family or painting the house or continuing earning money just to pay the bills ever again. He just wanted to see Willow a little bit more than he wanted to die.

Inching the car back onto the highway, Chet took the first off-ramp that presented itself and came to a brief stop. Whipping a left before the light turned green, he was nearly t-boned by an oncoming semi, which laid on the horn hoarse and wide-throated. His surroundings were unfamiliar to him. It didn't matter. It was an American suburb overflowing with restaurants, department stores, bars, gas stations, bookshops and grocers, strip malls, and farmers' markets. All bustling with cars, buses, and bikes, and with pedestrians rushing up and down the pavement, in and out of buildings, zig zagging in every direction. Families with children and dogs, working women in skirts and jackets, businessmen with briefcases, teenagers bunched together like atomic particles, hordes of young men on the prowl. Eventually, almost without warning, strings of houses appeared with small, well-maintained lawns and single garages. Children squealing. Lawnmowers purring. The beep of construction vehicles reversing. A train barreling off in the distance. Not a newly planted tree in sight. Although he was in the midst of paradise, he was denied access to its fruits. He began to weep.

In time, he found himself at the road's end. He sat at a stop sign dumbfounded. The events of the last few days were impossible to believe. After nearly a decade and thousands of miles, he was back exactly where he started. His attempt at a new life had been wiped away like a mosquito off a windshield. Looking to the left, a condominium development was under construction, bordered by wild, untamed fields. To the right were grain elevators, the headhouse, and its many bins stretching to the sky. Further on in both directions were farms and small towns waiting for the cruel hand of industry to seize them. His phone began buzzing anew. His demons, patient as cancer, refused to cease giving chase. Looking up to the sun, he sensed them swirling overhead, attempting to ascertain his location. Adele had called Darlene. Of this, he was certain. How she had gotten her phone number (or discovered her identity) was a mystery, but Adele was as shrewd as she was vicious. Even if it was difficult to ascertain her motives, it wasn't difficult to imagine the havoc she was willing to unleash. How was he supposed to proceed? Drying his eyes, Chet caught a glance of himself in the rearview mirror. He did not recognize the image staring back at him. For a brief moment, he thought there was a stranger in his backseat. He quickly turned around, only to find the vacant backseat. Making a U-turn, he began to drive towards the airport.

He did stop home first. Discovering he had beaten Darlene there, he made his way to their bedroom and searched every drawer of their desk until he found his passport and pocketed it. Rummaging through their closet, he pulled down a suitcase, tossed it on their bed, and began to fill it. Not knowing where he was going, he chose clothes appropriate for any climate. Once he was finished, he exited through the front door, not bothering to close it behind him, walked down the street to his car, and screeched away.

Barely off the plane, he couldn't comprehend what he was seeing. But there it was. Out of the throngs of people going about their business, in a tuxedo no less, was Chet's older brother, Gary. He carried with him no luggage. He was just strolling languidly down the left side corridor of Ronald Reagan National Airport.

Chet ducked into a Taco Bell to his left and sunk into a booth. Somehow Gary had gotten word that his little brother had once again had a meltdown and abruptly excused himself from whatever celebratory event he was attending to clean up whatever mess his little brother had made. He entered the Taco Bell, approached the counter, placed an order, and waited patiently for it to be fulfilled without so much as looking in Chet's direction. Taking his tray to the booth, he took a long hard sip of what Chet knew was a Diet Pepsi.

"I gotta thank you."

"Why?" Chet asked, his face wrinkled in anguish.

"For whatever all this is. I've been dying for a diet soda all day," he said and chuckled in that easy way that immediately put Chet at ease. He unrolled the wrapper of his soft taco. "I would have preferred White Castle, but I don't think they have those out here. Pity."

Chet watched his older brother consume the taco in two massive bites. Dabbing the corner of his mouth with the small brown napkin and setting it on the tray, he made a face. Chet knew this meant he was prepared to get down to business.

"What am I doing here?"

"I didn't ask you to come."

"Cut the shit, Chet. What the fuck is going on? What am I doing in Washington D.C.?"

Chet leaned back and closed his eyes; tears began rolling down his cheeks. Wiping them away, he muttered, "Willow—"

"No. I do not want to hear that name," he said, gritting his teeth. It couldn't be the same woman who had caused his little brother to drop out of school and abandon his family, miss his father's funeral. "You know, I had a feeling. I thought it couldn't be, even after all these years. But somehow, I knew. That bitch never goes away. Well, spit it out."

"Her sister, Adele, called today."

"The nasty one, right?"

Chet nodded.

Gary stood up, walked over to the soda machine, removed the lid from the cup, topped off his drink, placed the lid back on, and sat back down.

"Why?"

"To tell me Willow got pregnant with my child and never told me."

"Right. I got it."

"Stop it. Stop it right now."

Chet cried for some time.

"Why now? How do you even know she's telling the truth?"

"She just is."

"Assuming that's the case, how did you end up here?"

Raising his head and sniffling loudly, wiping his nose on his sleeve, he said, "After she told me, I got in my car. I was going to kill myself. I thought of you and Darlene, and I just couldn't."

"I hardly believe that."

"I didn't know what to do. I couldn't find the strength. I just ran. I ran out of my house, to the airport, and onto the first departing flight."

"To what end?" he asked, passing him a napkin. "Wouldn't it make more sense to go to her?"

He didn't have the heart to tell him she was already on her way to Utah.

"Jesus Christ, Chet," Gary said, pounding on the table. "When is this nonsense going to end? How long are you going to let this woman control your life?"

"I moved halfway across the country."

"That means nothing."

Chet flinched.

"Don't you see? Until you face all this crap, you could run all the way to China, and it's the same as going nowhere? Get up."

"What?"

"Get up," he said, standing up, taking his little brother by the elbow, and marching him out of the Taco Bell. Looking left and right, he dragged him through the throngs of bustling people to the screens announcing arrivals and departures.

"There is a flight for Minneapolis in two hours. You're going to be on it."

"No, I'm not," he said, yanking his arm away.

"When you get there, you're going to get this out of your system once and for all. Then I don't care what you do. Just lose her."

"I appreciate you being here—"

"Do you? I left a fundraiser because my little brother, who I haven't seen in ten years, is having a meltdown yet again. Over a nobody."

"I'm sorry."

"Then lance this boil," he said and started to walk away. He was no more than twenty feet away when he turned around and added, "Pick up a phone once in a while."

Chet did board a plane several hours later, but it was back to Salt Lake City. Afraid Darlene would be waiting for him, Chet parked down the street from his house. He stood at the sidewalk's end and took in the entirety of his house. The front door stood askew, beckoning him. He couldn't go in. Adele's call had exposed the truth of his life: *it was one he never wanted.* He thought about the years he had spent there. The expense poured into it. The effort put into its upkeep. The blood. The sweat. They were walls built with the compromised portions of himself. The third-string parts. The rejected bits that made him feel diminished. It was strange, disorienting. He had felt nothing but sincerity, even joy, during its design and execution. Even now, it stood real and accomplished, with its own goals and desires. He could have lived the rest of his days here without reckoning. What, then, were his options? To run back to the airport and purchase a ticket for the next departing flight? Only to what? Land in Seattle? Brazil? To what end? If he ran, he was only running from himself. Worse yet, if he razed it to the ground, he would still be destroying part of himself. In front of him stood a monument to that which was denied him, the only structure he was capable of building: a life without children. Oddly, he felt the urge to laugh, but not really. Not knowing what else to do, he walked the half mile to Dakota Park, where

Darlene found him on a swing.

Kneeling next to him and placing her hand on his back, she asked, "Everything all right?"

Staring at the woodchips beneath him, he took a long time to answer.

"The day after Willow and I first made love, she told me to meet her after class at her dorm. We were going to trek out to Little Blue Lake to have a picnic, get stoned, and make love again. At least, I hoped so." Here he lifted his head and smirked in the most heartbreaking manner Darlene had ever seen, and, for the first time, she truly understood how profoundly Willow had hurt him. "After class, I rushed back to my room, took a shower, and ran over to the girl's dormitory, only to find her exiting the building with friends, laughing in that slightly mean-spirited and conspiratorial way that is terrifying and—"

"And? What?"

"She was surprised and embarrassed to see me. She pulled me aside and asked what I was doing there. When I reminded her of our plans, she blanched and shushed me. *Oh that,* she responded with a wave of her hand. *We'll have to reschedule,* she said and got into the car filled with the most beautiful women I had ever seen. Leaning out the window, she yelled, 'Later Gator' as it sped off. Later Gator," he repeated, shaking his head.

"And there you stood."

There was a long pause before he spoke again.

"Adele called me today," he said.

"Willow's sister?"

Chet nodded, still looking at his feet. Darlene didn't rush him.

"She told me that Willow got pregnant when we were

in college."

"With your child?" she asked too quickly.

He nodded.

"She got an abortion. She aborted my child. Without telling me. How could she do that without even telling me?" he said, wincing, his eyes welling up.

"I don't know, baby." Darlene waited a long time before saying, "Is that possible?"

He shrugged. "Do you think she's lying?" he asked again like a little boy.

"No, I don't. Let's go home. I have thoughts."

Chet knew what Darlene was going to do but was too devastated to resist. She could attempt whatever she wanted when Willow arrived. She took Chet by the hand and walked him to their home.

* * *

Chet, more focused on his malfunctioning brain and the bottle of Jack Daniels, didn't see the non-descript car stop in front of his house. Neither did he see Willow gracefully exit the said vehicle and stand for several moments at the end of the sidewalk, staring at the brown house, trying to work up the courage to knock on the door. By the time he looked up, she was out of sight.

"The famous Willow," Darlene declared, propping the screen door open with her left hand, staring down from the entryway. There was a barely contained fierceness coiled up in her fading jaded eyes that forced Willow to take a half-step backward. "I suppose you are looking for Mr. Chet Huber." Her stout solid frame and short economic haircut gave Willow the impression that she was an old-school dyke.

"Is he here?"

"You were supposed to arrive last night, weren't you?"

"I ran into some difficulties. Are you expecting him back soon?" she asked, peering past this woman into the house enveloped in shadow.

"Hard to say. He's tied up with work."

"I came from far away. It took me a long time to get here."

"Close to a decade, it seems," she said, her eyes narrowing.

For a moment, Willow considered listing for this brute, harsh woman the litany of Herculean-like struggles and petty indignities she muddled through, from gracelessly exiting her sister's wedding and being harassed by her ex-husband over parenting choices, to having her car stolen and taking a bus manned by a racist, before finally arriving at this stop. On the other hand, it was difficult to resist the old urge to run. She did neither. The handicap Willow had lived with her entire life was the inability to distinguish between who she was and the actions she performed. Whenever anybody was critical of her in any way, large or small, vocally or silently (and it need not be a person of authority), she was devastated. It made her unable to confront any problem directly. On top of that, this woman looked as sympathetic as a cornered wild dog. And there was nowhere to run. No man's arms to fall into and commiserate with who would agree the world was a vindictive, heartless place. This was of her making. Nine years ago, it was Paul's cruelty she had used as a patsy to set into motion a series of events that were still in play, and forty-eight hours ago, it was Adele's wedding. She had feigned an urgency for this very trip that did not exist. Standing there, face to face with this person she did not know or expect, there was no reason pressing enough that could extricate her from the situation. Not the miles traveled, or the indignities suffered. Not even Chet's inexplicable absence. She was stunned into paralysis.

It was no different now than when she was eight, maybe nine, suspended on the high dive at the community pool coerced upwards by Adele. Staring at the rippling water from the thin, prickly perch, the children's laughter harsh like the cackling crows, unable to move forward or backward, she remained frozen. Eventually, she was escorted by the lifeguard down the ladder, Adele having disappeared into the girl's bathroom.

"But this is where he lives? He mailed me a letter with this as the return address," Willow said, pulling the paper from her purse, thrusting it towards this woman who took it after a prolonged delay and, even then, hesitantly, before inspecting it thoroughly.

"I was surprised to receive it. Not unhappy by any stretch of the imagination, just surprised," Willow said to fill up the widening silence between them. "As I read it, I kept waiting for the bomb to drop."

"Bomb?" she asked, her eyes rising then falling back to the paper.

She let the sun radiate upon her face. "Like he was sick or coming to Elmwood."

"That would be a bomb?" she said, snorting. "Coming back to his home? Chet hasn't been home since you two… well, you know. Not even for his father's funeral."

Willow had not been aware of this miserable fact. Had someone, this very woman perhaps, told Willow this even twenty-four hours ago, she would have found it impeccably delicious and used it like a nail to hold up the failing slats of her battered self. Now, it just seemed like pathetic histrionics. She was also certain that this bulldog of a woman knew every sordid detail about Chet and Willow's relationship, including Chet's dark fascination with her when their relationship ended, which she confessed to herself for the first time, wasn't all that interesting.

"That just seems stupid," Willow said, rolling her eyes.

Darlene's entire body drew taught, although Willow failed to notice.

"Chet's an accountant?"

"A very successful one."

"And takes Karate," Willow said, lifting her head to the sun as if taking communion.

"Tae-Kwon-Do, actually," she said, her large nostrils flaring (they seemed to do this whenever she inhaled). At the same time, her top lip didn't appear to move when she spoke, which made Willow distrustful of her.

When Brayden and Willow sat down with his parents and announced they were pregnant with McKenna, all hell broke loose. They didn't approve of Willow. In their eyes, she was just a girl he was fucking. Once he got tired of the sex, he would move on to someone they deemed more appropriate. They were incensed this hadn't happened. Brayden's father, in particular, lost his shit, pacing, bellowing, going off in a million directions like a malfunctioning firecracker, repeating over and over: *this wasn't the plan*, grilling Brayden about birth control, condoms, his disintegrating future, all the while refusing to acknowledge Willow's presence. When he finally gave Brayden a chance to justify himself, his son's faltering responses: *she was on the pill, we used condoms,* and the pièce de résistance, *we are in love,* only made matters worse. *Love* is the kryptonite that every child uses to break their parents since the implicit message, lurking like a ruinous undertow beneath that simple syllable, was the threat of marriage. When Brayden's father was unable to sway them to terminate the pregnancy, he stormed off to his car and squealed away. All the while, his mother sat at their kitchen table drinking wine, smirking incoherently as if she always knew her boy would make such a stupid mistake with such a stupid girl. This butch woman in the doorway had that same ruddiness in her eye, all before Willow had stepped foot in the door or confronted Chet.

"There's nothing in here about coming to Salt Lake," she said, scrutinizing this figure from Chet's past. Willow, in turn, scrutinized her and the eyeliner applied with all the subtlety of a Van Gogh brushstroke. If she were to hazard a guess, it would be that it was the first time in years, if ever, she had employed it.

"I guess there isn't," she said with a wry smile. Willow felt an ease with herself she hadn't felt since puberty. Was it that easy? Like the flipping of a switch? Where did it come from and was it grace? And who bestowed it upon her? She had turned a hard, wild shoulder to God so long ago. Even if he had returned to offer reconciliation, her shame ran so deep – it gave her pause. She had taken enough drugs, prescribed and otherwise, to know it was usually temporary. A moment's bitterness arose out of its center. She dismissed it. Whatever transformation had occurred, she merely hoped it stuck around.

"This is your idea," she said, poking at the letter about before handing it back to her, which Willow folded up and placed in her purse like a delicate and precious talisman. "To drive halfway across the county without provocation?"

"Can I get some water? It's been a long couple of days."

"Days, humph. Yes, of course," she said, waving her inside languidly with her right hand, pulling the screen shut loudly behind her.

The living room was stuffed full of furniture and was casually messy. Besides the couch, there was an oversized easy chair, two large end tables, and a chest being used as a coffee table, on which were two ashtrays, cigarette butts racing to the ceiling. Similarly, the dining room table was too large for the space, with elephant-sized legs sprouting out from a tree-trunk base and lazy brontosaurus feet oozing out the bottom. The top was scratched all to hell. A half-eaten meat and cheese platter (with no crackers) set out as welcome. On the kitchen counter was a stack of dirty dishes and the kitty litter box, a stick of incense shoved into its corner, burning silently. A large grey pot sat on the stovetop, a saucepan next to it, a large wooden spoon protruding out of both.

"Don't be shy," she said, turning her back to Willow before making her way into the kitchen.

Willow stood in the entryway much as she had the first time she was deposited at her father's house when she was a child, trying to decide if it was worth the effort to wait for Chet or simply to spin around and leave. Hesitantly, she stepped forward and into the dining room, taking a seat. "I said don't be shy. I don't bite."

"Is Chet coming back?" Willow asked. "I'm a long way from home, you know?"

"Have some cheese. I'm sure you're hungry from your trip."

"I'm lactose intolerant," Willow demurred.

"That's made up."

Willow's face screwed itself up by way of disagreeing. She placed a square of the cheese cautiously into her mouth. She took a single bite before swallowing the piece nearly whole. This seemed to please this strange woman.

"If you were starving, you wouldn't say shit about being lactose intolerant," she said, handing Willow a half-filled glass of lukewarm water.

"Do you live here?"

"I do."

"And you are Chet's—"

"Cousin, yes. Darlene. Although a lot of people say we look more like brother and sister. What do you think?" She leaned back from the stovetop. The heavy, ugly bags beneath her eyes confessed to prolonged sleep deprivation or stress.

"People say that?"

"All the time," she said, slowly stirring the pot.

Willow found this hard to believe as there was no resemblance but felt it unwise to contradict her.

"It's very flattering. Chet's a very attractive man, don't you think? Well, you already know."

Before she could respond, Darlene was moving on.

"You have a daughter, don't you?" she asked, stirring more vigorously.

"Yes."

"It's not Chet's daughter, though."

"No," she said with emphasis.

Speaking about McKenna in this place felt somehow heretical, like giving a handjob in a church gallery. She glanced around the house casually for a cat she suspected had gone missing or was dead. Enmeshed in the shadows was an unmistakable gloom, as if from a recent death or divorce, but certainly a loss of some sort. Even the cheese, which was hard and slightly discolored on the corners, seemed affected.

"You got pregnant immediately after the two of you called it quits with another man's child – do I have the timeline correct?"

"Not immediately. But something like that," Willow said reluctantly.

"And a sister?"

"Of sorts."

"And what is she like?"

Darlene turned from the stove and looked Willow up and down, during which she seemed to be assessing her very character and her intentions for her appearance in her home. Regardless of who lived here or who was on the lease, whether she was Chet's cousin or not, there was no doubt in Willow's mind that this was Darlene's home. The politics, athletics… warfare, really, of competing women was petty, vicious, and demeaning. It also explained Chet's absence. Darlene needed to ascertain Willow's true purpose before allowing him back into his own house. Or perhaps Chet had no plans of meeting her at all. Conceivably, they had ascertained the purpose of her visit and were determined to deny her forgiveness – posting Darlene as a gatekeeper was an act of revenge on their part. In any case, if he didn't show soon, she would grab an Uber to the airport, find an overpriced souvenir for McKenna, and fly home with a clean conscience.

When it became apparent Willow wasn't going to answer, Darlene's eyes narrowed, and a flash of anger flickered intensely across her face. She seemed poised to launch another in a series of questions when something started buzzing. Willow believed Chet had arrived and was relieved as Darlene headed towards the entrance. She was quickly proven wrong (*why would Chet ring his own doorbell?*) when Darlene stopped before a front hall closet, its doors replaced by a wall of beads behind which stood a washer and dryer. Extricating a wet lump of clothes from its belly, she tossed them into the dryer, saying over her shoulder, "He was surprised to get your call." Returning to the oven, she continued, "Even more surprised when you announced without warning that you were to arrive in a couple of days. Clever, messaging him on Facebook for his phone number." Adding, "See, the cheese sits fine."

Willow thought of the night she seduced Marco. Not the clumsy first kiss on the patio at the bar in a remote part of town or the awkward sex in the backseat of his hatchback. It was several weeks prior when she refused his hand and said to him: *You don't want to get messed up with me*, knowing damn well that he did, that her objection was the moment their affair truly commenced, the instant she truly broke her wedding vows. In the same manner, here was this woman, showing such faux astonishment at her arrival in Salt Lake City when they both knew (all three of them knew) that the moment of initiation to this benign ménage à trois had been when Chet had penned that stupid fucking letter.

"I suppose I could have given a little more warning."

"You're like a dog in heat."

"Excuse me?"

"Probably the first time you've been called a dog in your life," she said and chuckled meanly. "There ain't no reasoning with an animal in that condition. And so here you sit in my home. For a reason which has yet to be revealed."

Willow turned away in disgust. She had only been here a few minutes, and she already loathed this woman.

"The last one, Alyssa, was an awful little creature. Chet tied himself in a million knots trying to please her. She could convince him he was stepping off a curb when he was being shoved off a cliff," she said, her eyes shining like Vaseline. "She was pretty. They're always pretty. What am I saying – look at you. Lovely little creatures like you chew up as many boys as there are stars in the sky. The damage doesn't even track."

"No," Willow said in defense of herself (and all beautiful creatures, apparently). Watching this woman try to give her a dressing down, it occurred to her that Chet's weakness was not exclusive to her – it was an essential component of his character. The seeds of his angst over their demise were planted the day he offered her a ride home that cool, crisp autumn day. Perhaps before they had ever spoken.

"She came over one afternoon. To open a joint bank account with Chet. Can you imagine the carnage? I told her over coffee that, under no circumstance, was that going to happen. Before she could raise any objections, she blacked out. When she woke up, we were on the edge of town in a deserted cul-de-sac. *Don't ever darken our door again.* Then I kicked her out of the car and sped off. We never heard from her again. We've been together ever since. Are you shocked?" she asked too quickly.

"Puh," Willow burped out involuntarily, pushing aside the glass of water.

This brazen display of territory marking was not only embarrassing but unnecessary. She wasn't even sure if she was telling the truth. Nevertheless, it set her back on her heels. All she wanted to do was right one wrong. She had no interest in getting into a bigger-dick contest with this woman. Whether it was the universe, God, or her shitty karma – some agent in the world seemed determined to make her every effort exceedingly difficult and bound to fail.

"I'm going to go have a smoke if you don't mind."

"Do as you please. It seems that's what you're best at."

Exiting, Willow stepped to the right of the door and leaned against the house. Closing her eyes, she exhaled seemingly for the first time since she arrived. She pulled a cigarette out of her purse and lit it. She wondered if Adele was awake yet. Or if she was still spent from a night of celebrating and finicky lovemaking. She sincerely wished her happiness. She wasn't sure if she deserved it exactly (*who did?*), but she wished it for her, anyway.

"You all right out there?" Darlene barked.

"I'm fine," Willow clapped back. She took several steps forward and sat on the front steps.

Looking around the sleepy, middle-income neighborhood, she found it uncanny that Chet had landed in Salt Lake City. Not that she had imagined him anywhere else: in Houston, Texas, or San Sebastian, Spain, or the moon, for that matter. Or somewhere more affluent or impoverished. The world was so large and complex that she was dumbfounded as to how anything at all happened: how people ended up where they did, with the jobs they performed, partnered with the people they loved, and so on. What conclusion could one reach? Adele and Braydon would have cynically concluded that it was proof of a random, indifferent Universe; Mark and her mother just the opposite, that it signaled the workings of fate (and romantic fate at that), maybe even of a supreme being. Her dad would have been more pragmatic, no doubt believing one's life was partly the sum of your choices but also a combination of dumb luck and circumstance. Thinking about it left her with a sense of overwhelming melancholy. Raising her eyes up over the city, the morning clouds had dissipated, revealing the silent, steadfast mountains. For the first time, it occurred to her that there was a real possibility Mark might never forgive her. That gave her more pain than she would have ever imagined.

"Fuck me."

At Scott's funeral, Adele was the last to speak. Making her way to the front of the room, she looked so slight, so unlike herself. Without lifting her head, she said, "*The Divine Comedy* is the best book ever written. If Dante had stopped with the *Inferno*, it would be the most honest book ever written. In my experience, there isn't redemption," and took her seat. There was an uncomfortable silence after she spoke, a mixture of awkwardness and embarrassment that filled the quiet, as if to give Adele the opportunity of a redo. Willow knew better. Her sister had said exactly what she wanted and had meant it. She never believed Adele loved Scott. Her eulogy did nothing to dissuade her of this opinion. Sitting in the front row, high as shit and a touch hungover, Willow was disgusted by her sister's behavior. It seemed selfish and lacking in mercy. She wasn't even convinced she had ever read Dante. Now, so many years later, her sister appeared to her, despite the bluster and rancor, a tragic figure. She longed to call her. Adele would answer (she always answered). She would be a cunt, but she would know exactly what Willow should do.

"Hey, baby."

"Mom. Where are you?"

"Salt Lake City. I made it."

She cooed a little. "Have you gone to the Space Needle yet?"

"That's Seattle, honey."

"What's in Salt Lake City?"

"So far? Not much. The mountains. Are you behaving for Grandpa?"

"Yes."

"Good girl."

"Mom?"

She sighed and looked back up at the stubbornly recalcitrant mountains. She hadn't the heart to ask about the wedding. Not out of embarrassment for missing it. Even had she been there, she would have had little interest in the ceremony, the food, or if Mia had stolen a bottle of wine for her room. She only wanted to know if anyone had inquired about her: why she had missed her own sister's wedding or if her presence was in any way missed. This filled her with deep shame. Especially since at the other end of the line was the daughter she had left behind and hadn't given a passing thought if she had enjoyed herself.

"I'll be back soon."

"Can you bring me a present?"

"I'll bring you a little something. I'll talk to you soon and see you even sooner."

Placing the phone in her back pocket, she flicked the exhausted cigarette butt into the front yard, pulled open the screen door, and reentered the house, determined to leave, that her business, although incomplete, was finished.

"Everything okay with your daughter? McKenna, is

it?" Darlene asked.

Willow turned her head, but she already knew what she was going to find. The window adjacent to the living room was raised, the curtain waving slightly in collusion with Darlene. Not only was the house, but the whole goddamn state was conspiring against her. She noticed that the cheese tray had been removed from the table and was balancing on top of the kitty litter box.

"I would have loved to meet her. Although, that may have been difficult for Chet. But you already know that don't you?" When Willow did not immediately respond, Darlene added, "My mama was very protective of me, too."

"I've made a mistake coming here," she announced. "I'll be on my way." It wasn't just that she didn't believe Chet was coming, or that she wasn't being played in some manner she hadn't quite figured out yet. This woman certainly was a bully screwing with her. It was more than that. Somewhere along the stretches of the grey firmament, something happened. She no longer gave a damn. She was done. If Chet showed up or remained incognito, if he found out about the abortion or was forever kept in the dark – it no longer mattered. She didn't owe anyone anything. "I'm going to call an Uber. I can just wait outside. It's been interesting," she said with a flick of her hair and turned towards the door.

"I noticed you didn't arrive in a car. You couldn't have taken an Uber all the way from Minnesota?" she asked incredulously, unphased by Willow's declaration, ready to call bullshit on everything she had ever heard about this beautiful creature.

"My car was stolen early this morning. It's not your problem," Willow said with effort.

"What?"

"I befriended a woman in Colorado. She had just left her husband and offered to drive with me to Salt Lake to make a fresh beginning. Turns out she got cold feet and needed my car to hustle her way back to her piece of shit husband," she said, turning back to the door.

"Nothing worse than a bitch in love," Darlene said bullishly, although a hint of sadness crept through. "You took an Uber all the way from Colorado?"

"I took a bus from Colorado and an Uber from the bus station. Like I said, if Chet's not coming—"

"Is that right?" Darlene asked, lowering herself almost involuntarily to the couch. "Yeah, that's right," she said, softening despite herself.

Darlene had the most bewildered expression on her face, as if, with those few words, she was experiencing Willow for the first time, free of prejudice, through her own eyes, not Chet's. "Chet is taking an awfully long time. He's wanted to see you for such a long time. Maybe we should see where he is. Get his ass moving a little."

"That would be appreciated."

Darlene pulled her cell phone from her back pocket and, within seconds, had Chet on the line. Willow stood in utter disbelief and wanted to scream *This is fucking bullshit*, but she knew better. She couldn't.

"She's here. Not long. Right in front of me."

Darlene smiled awkwardly at Willow.

"That is unacceptable, Chet. For this to get resolved, you need to be here. She's threatening to leave, and I know you, we don't want that."

Darlene was listening very intently, pushing the phone hard against her ear to prevent Willow from hearing whatever Chet was saying.

"*Yes. Please. As soon as you can.*"

A long silence followed. Darlene's eyes darted from Willow to the floor. Her face grew ashen. She seemed reluctant to answer. She lowered her voice when she finally responded. It almost sounded as if she were whispering out the words, the way one does in a confessional, afraid to utter them aloud, even to God. "*Are you shitting me? That's what you're concerned about. She looks fine. Pretty. Very pretty.*" She closed the phone and set it on the coffee table. "Chet will be here shortly."

Almost immediately, the door was thrown open, startling the both of them. Chet stood, damp with sweat, breathing with effort, visibly overcome by mania but otherwise looking nearly identical to nine years earlier. No one moved. Before anyone could respond, he took three steps in, swinging the bottle of Jack Daniels wildly. Placing his free hand over his head, he shrieked, "Don't look at my hair," and dashed into the bathroom, slamming the door shut.

"Bring back memories?" Darlene asked sardonically before cautiously following him to the bathroom, stationing herself in front of the closed door.

"Chet?" she asked. "You alright?" She delicately turned the knob, but it was locked.

"Can you get me a glass? I've been drinking from this bottle all day."

"Maybe you've had enough, don't you think?"

"No."

Hesitantly, Darlene did as he requested. While still in the kitchen, Chet reappeared. He pushed the hair out of his eyes. He scanned the room and took a swig from the bottle.

"Do you remember that time we stayed at the Super-8 in St. Louis Park, for... I don't remember why. Some fancy event. Do you remember that?"

"Yeah." Willow slowly answered.

"I was taking a bath, and you were so mad. She hated that I was taking a bath. Can you imagine?" He took another drink, slurping loudly. "I'm trying to remember. But I'm – I don't know – blocked. Why were you mad?"

Willow looked from Chet to Darlene, who was holding the glass he had requested. "The heat from the water made it hard to get my make-up on correctly. The mirrors were fogged."

"That's right, that's right," he said and then fell silent as if in a private reverie. "Oh, we laughed." He stopped once again. He brought the bottle up to his mouth, held it there, and lowered it. "We laughed. Remember how we used to laugh? On this occasion, we were laughing uproariously because you turned around, and the tip of my penis (and here he pointed at his crotch with the bottle of Jack Daniels) was poking above the waterline, through the bubbles – yes, I like a good bubble bath (*he said to no one in particular*) – and you said it looked like a bobber. As if you've ever been fishing, beautiful princess. Do you remember? Do you remember that?"

"I do." Willow noticed that his hair had been gone over meticulously with a brush, the damp strands pulled dangerously back into place.

"I'm sorry, I'm sorry," he said. "That's a strange story to remember right now, isn't it. How is it that something so long ago can feel like it just happened? How is that possible, I'm asking."

"I think sometimes—" Darlene started.

"I'm asking Willow," he said harshly, pointing at her with the bottle, his eyes suddenly ablaze.

"I don't know, Chet. What are you doing right now?"

The authority with which she spoke to Chet made Darlene instantly furious.

"Everything seems blurry, like a dream. But real. Like I've been here before, but I haven't. Or I'm imagining it or have imagined it, and it's coming true. My dad and brother would hate this, that you're here. Thought you had bewitched me. *He's a fool, and don't I know it.* Called you a twat. Repeatedly. *I'm in love and don't I show it.* If he was here right now, he would look at you and say—"

Before he could finish his thought, the bottle of Jack Daniels slipped out of his hand and onto the floor where it shattered, dousing his and Willow's shoes in alcohol, shards like ice making a perimeter about the spill. An expression of sheer terror overcame Chet's face. He dropped onto his knees. "Fuck, shit, fuck." He pulled the bottom of his shirt outward, dabbed at the liquid, and picked cautiously at the pieces of glass, dropping them almost immediately. "This is not how I wanted you to see me."

Darlene got up and calmly made her way to the kitchen. She came back with a handful of dishtowels. Before she could apply them to the spill, Chet drew a Swiss Army knife from his back pocket and stuck it hard into the floor, as if claiming a piece of land for the sovereign. Darlene gasped. Willow leaned back on the couch.

Placing the knife against the carpet, he pulled at it in fits and starts, dragging the blade in a straight line for ten or twelve inches.

"Chet, what the hell are you doing?"

It tore with difficulty. Yanking the knife out, he took a deep breath, reinserted it at the original point of entry, and tore at the carpet at a forty-five-degree angle for another ten or twelve inches. Once finished, he tossed the knife aside and yanked on the loose piece, exposing floorboards and glue. Heaving at it until blue lines riddled his forehead and sweat poured down his cheeks, he was able to yank up a swath of material. Exhausted, he collapsed sideways onto the floor and vomited. The torn piece of carpet fell back into place like a loose flap of skin.

"That's really nice," Darlene said before retreating to the kitchen. "Way to make our guest feel at home."

Willow counted the eyelets on her shoes, and a calico cat crawled out from underneath the couch, sauntered about the shards of glass, sniffed at the whiskey, and mewed vehemently in protest.

DAVID HAIGHT

Chapter Four
Bill Evans

THOMAS BATTEN normally relished the long commute north on Highway 170 from his office in the heart of Salt Lake City (the greatest city in the world as far as he was concerned) to the remote gates of Ambrose Commons high up in the mountains. In his black BMW, window cracked, tie loosened, the Dave Matthews Band thundering in the background (who he had seen in concert 24 times – 7 times at Red Rocks), he would drift above the not-insubstantial pressures of his career as a Senior Property Accountant at Spartan Investment Group. The twenty-to-thirty-minute drive allowed him to decompress and not be a vicious troll when he burst through the front door of his home (which had been a problem when he lived a brisk seven-minute walk from the office, nearly ending his marriage). While it was true he lived in one of the most gorgeous states in the union, he was generally oblivious to its exquisiteness and, at times, was even hostile to it, feeling pressure to enjoy an aesthetic he was just not drawn to. He didn't much care for the long stretch of sycamore trees that lined the two-lane road leading out of the city. Or the large smoldering sunset. Or the unending fields. What thrilled him was how those trees eventually led, like an outstretched arm, to an inauspicious sideroad blocked by a heavy iron gate with the ironic words *Ambrose Commons* draped across its thick, dull bars. Holding his keycard out the window, the gates would suspiciously part, and he would drive unhurriedly up the winding road, past the mansion-packed hills that were situated like massive uncut jewels along the shore of some great untamed river, leading directly to his estate. While it was true that his four-bedroom home wasn't at the peak of the mountain and, in fact, stood at the lower end of the Common's gated populace, with dozens of larger, more palatial estates staring condescendingly down upon his not-insubstantial home, it was grander than most of the homes in Colorado. Nevertheless, it was a point of contention for Thomas. Only on a handful of occasions had he journeyed up past his own drive (such was the image Thomas Batten maintained of himself that he believed he stood at the peak of every summit). Even when he sat at night on his deck, cocktail in hand, he faced due east, down the mountainside, to maintain this illusion. This was all done reflexively with an animal quickness, as Thomas was not one to indulge in introspection, something he considered a symptom of a moribund mind. On the rare occasion he did turn the magnifying glass upon himself, he would conclude that if he was not happy (a word that suggested a finality he was uncomfortable with – there were too many things to do, too much to maintain, not enough yet acquired – he was proudly a man of action), he was at any rate not tortured. He often recalled Father Marquard pontificating on Hell and those occupying it; they were not tortured (God did not torture his creations, he assured his congregation), they were *tormented,* being separated from God by the very acts they themselves committed. In reality, Thomas was neither tortured nor tormented but self-satisfied and a bit exhausted, like an overstuffed pig that's eaten too much and was unwilling to pull itself from the trough. But not today.

Oh, sure, there were the persistent bugaboos rapping upon his conscience, like steps accelerating behind you. The house that was never finished. The endless array of social activities, both professional and personal. The more extravagant vacations that the wife seemed to demand. And speaking of the wife – for the last number of years, he just had no desire for physical intimacy. This was not based on any defect on her part. She was beautiful, gorgeous even, and not just for her age. She could legitimately stop you in your tracks. He was just as attracted to her as the day they met at their church social so many years ago. It wasn't as if he was pining for the touch of another woman, of any age, not that his office wasn't filled with the most nubile of young women vying for his attention. There was just nothing south of the border. It was as if the electrical grid in his brain had shorted out. Was it his age? A manifestation of stresses elsewhere? Had he morphed into some awful asexual monster? In any case, her patience was wearing thin (a person can only be rebuffed and bedroom romps rescheduled so many times without consequence). One morning, after a stupidly expensive brunch and far too many mimosas, she slammed her champagne flute onto the table, shattering it, and stormed out of the restaurant, taking the car with her and refusing to return home until evening. All these beasts he attempted to keep at bay partly with alcohol and exercise but primarily by working harder, longer, taking on whatever projects came up. This was an easy fix because it never stopped. It was just an insatiable machine. Nevertheless, these weren't the goblins that were chasing him down today.

Finishing his Red Bull and plopping it into the cupholder, he attempted to focus on the drive. Nothing seemed to assuage his melancholy. Not his upcoming yearly bonus. Not the Dave Matthews Band, which, for the first time, he was forced to shut off (enough with the acoustic guitars, already). Turning his locus of attention outward, he surveyed the landscape, trying to garner some zeal for it. It was such a winsome stretch of road: fields littered with wildflowers, drained-out rows of corn, the unremitting sky, its natural beauty only marred by the occasional faded billboard of cherub-faced infants decrying the horrors of abortion. Over the years, he had flown in guests for various anniversaries and celebrations who had commented on what a slice of Colorado beauty he was lucky to inhabit. He had one of two responses depending on his mood: I am a blessed person, or the State of Colorado has plenty to lure tourists here, neither of which he put much stock in. He concentrated, attempting to find something more. You need to live in the moment of your immediate surroundings, he had been repeatedly told. By his wife, children, and Pastor. He did not sense what Father Marquard had called the mystery and awe of existence, the transcendence of the living God behind its majesty. It only reflected back his internal condition. Banal and dulling subjectivity. It was confounding to him that these depressive moods (like a deep azure) occurred the more successful he became. Normally, these fits of melancholia dissipated watching the gates of Ambrose Commons shutter behind him. Not (as one might suspect) from a condescending sense of haughtiness, a barring of some vaguely defined 'have-nots' or a lurking shadowy criminal element. It had more to do with watching the rope ladder of a tree house being pulled up on the fat little boy he once was and had worked so hard to leave behind.

It was normally the most joyous time of year for the Batten family and Thomas in particular. Beginning the day before Thanksgiving and continuing until the day after Christmas, the residents of Salt Lake City flocked to the Commons for the Festival of Lights, a decades-old tradition where the Ambrose Commons community lined the streets of their neighborhood with thousands of white candles covered with brown paper bags and opened their gates to the general public. Initially, cars lined up to catch a peek behind the curtain of the wealthy, of the gargantuan houses and their extensive Christmas decorations, but as time went on, the main attraction became said candles – something so simple and inexpensive. Making your way up through the hills, it felt as if you were viewing the thoroughfare to heaven.

Thomas Batten had been fully invested in the Festival of Lights since he moved into Ambrose Commons sixteen years ago. Sure, there was satisfaction in being one of the houses being ogled over – a sense that he had won. But it was more than flaunting his material wealth before a train of anonymous cars that endeared the festival to his heart. Its preparation always brought a special closeness to his family. The weekend before its kickoff, he hopped into his beloved BMW with the kids and raced down the mountain to run the necessary errands for its preparation. At the grocery store, they gathered up the ingredients for a grand family breakfast, more than any sane family could eat: eggs, steaks, cinnamon buns, bacon, waffles, Texas Toast, and champagne (apple juice for the kids) – the extravagance, part of the point – along with the requisite paper bags, before stopping at Seedling Gifts and Books (a Christian Specialty Store) where would procure the hundreds of candles he had pre-ordered (at a pretty penny), loading them into the trunk of the car. Next, they would stop at the t-shirt-making shop at the mall. Every year, they would design and have custom shirts made up, inevitably involving their name: Battling Battens, Bruising Battens, and so on, which, since his daughters had entered the latter part of high school, he had been doing alone. The day before the event began, they all rose early, prepared and then devoured the large buffet breakfast together. Once finished, his wife, Amber, warmed up Thermoses of apple cider before they bundled up in sweaters and gloves and trekked down to their allotted section of the neighborhood from the entrance (up a half mile and, of course, in front of their house) and began. It was his youngest daughter, Morgan's, job to measure and place the candles and his oldest, Andrea's, to place the bag over them while he secured them. Sipping the warm apple cider, chatting with the other neighbors along their assigned routes, reveling in the abundant laughter, working up a sweat in the winter cool, Thomas would get lost in his thoughts, feeling blessed. It was always Amber, the managing director, who made sure they kept on schedule. That night, in front of the fire, they would roast marshmallows. Even if his children's interest had waned since the onset of puberty and prowling boys, they managed to keep the core of the tradition alive, even as the girls entered college.

However, for the first time since moving to the Commons, Thomas's heart wasn't into it. He had ordered the candles (he had convinced himself that Seedling Gifts depended on his order to hit their yearly budget) and the truncated ingredients for breakfast. Over the last few years, the sprawling breakfast he so enjoyed had gone through many transformations. As the girls had entered the ladder part of their high school years, he was forced to cut down on the ingredients, and once they had both entered college, he canceled it entirely. Not only did they refuse to wake up to help fix it, but their dietary habits had also drastically changed. Morgan had become a pescetarian, Andrea, a vegetarian. Initially, Thomas attempted to grow, buying food to fulfill everyone's very specific wants and needs, but found he couldn't figure out how to prepare the recipes that had been requested of him (although Morgan was sweet about the entire thing). On top of all that hassle, for the first time in their family's history, they had told him in no uncertain terms they were not interested in keeping up the tradition and that he would be flying solo. He was disappointed but not surprised. He knew this was a natural evolution in the lifecycle of a family. Even these developments were not the reason for his melancholy.

Making his way to his three-season porch, he surveyed the booze and what food he had purchased, trying to calculate if he had enough. Not only was it strange to have children who drank, he forgot how much young people could and would consume if given the opportunity. In his entire life, he never felt comfortable drinking in front of his parents. The first time he got intoxicated with either of his parents was with his mother after his father's funeral. In her tiny, dusty living room, she asked to share a scotch with him and subsequently shared six. Once inebriated, they stared at one another in silence and never spoke of it again. Even as a young man, he kept any drinking far away from his parents. Only on one occasion was the subject broached. Home from college, he staggered into the kitchen, attempting to hide a hangover. Preparing to call in sick to work, his father took the receiver from his hand and set it sternly back down. *You're not sick. You did this*. He insisted Thomas go to work. It was subsequently the most grueling day of work Thomas ever bungled through. He never called in sick with a hangover again. A signature of the changing times and relationship between parents and children, Amber let the girls do whatever they wanted (Morgan was not of age but regularly drank with the family). Cataloging the tofu burgers, hummus, vegetables, beans (and other items he didn't recognize or find remotely appealing), along with the many cases of domestic and imported beer, he blanched to think he would have to do this all again for Thanksgiving and Christmas with a plastic smile. Glancing at his watch, it would only be a few hours, and his entire family would be congregated at his house, not to celebrate any national or religious holiday or his beloved Festival of Lights (which, again, he would be doing alone for the first time), but to celebrate Andrea's twenty-first birthday.

    On each of the girl's birthdays, Amber would give Thomas an assignment. She would force him to reflect on their relationship, the importance of the particular age to both her and him, and so forth. She started doing this not long after Andrea was three or four when she felt he was not bestowing the appropriate level of weight upon significant milestones. It was preposterous. He could vividly recall both of his daughter's births. He was honored that he witnessed them drawing their first breaths. He recalled their first steps, each losing their first tooth. The list was endless. He refused her request this time around. He wouldn't indulge in any aspect of Andrea's twenty-first. He was keenly aware of how momentous an age it was, how she was closing out a major chapter of her life and beginning a new one. None of that mattered. It was not, in actuality, Andrea's twenty-first birthday. That was not until May of the following year, and he was not going to pretend otherwise, no matter how much Amber bullied him. In fact, he wished he could scrap this entire ridiculous celebration.

He had planned to surprise her with a trip to Martha's Vineyard for a long weekend and her first legal drink. Their last daddy-daughter trip together before launching her off into the world (he had no illusions about either of his daughter's activities in college, he just had one strict policy: *no details*). Then she appeared, at home, unannounced, several weeks ago, 'with news.' There was something about her demeanor that told him it was not a visit he was going to revel in. There were not going to be celebratory dinners similar to when she ascended to captain of the swim team or went abroad for a semester or was awarded a scholarship to university. Before she had spoken a syllable, he knew Martha's Vineyard was out. She asked she be given the opportunity to completely finish speaking before he (and not her mother) objected. That was when he knew that Amber was not only privy to the entire proceedings but had already signed off. She had decided to take some time off of school to drive across the United States with her girlfriend (were there any more dreaded words to a parent than "take some time off school," except maybe "I'm pregnant").

With those few words, Thomas Batten saw his eldest daughter's entire future which he had worked so hard to facilitate, end in a flash. It was like watching a state-of-the-art unfinished skyscraper collapse in a controlled explosion, making way for some new, lesser structure. He could do nothing but acquiesce. There was the issue of her mother's powerful alliance, yes. But also, children in adult bodies with half-formed minds and bull-stubborn will do what they will, regardless of Mom or Dad. This was just a courtesy. This was compounded by the fact that he didn't handle her coming out as a lesbian the previous fall (another bombshell his wife knew about well in advance) with any sort of grace. While he always thought of himself as an accepting person, it turned out that was only applicable to other people's children or in the abstract. She hadn't spoken to him in months. Not until his wife's intervention. As far as everyone was concerned, he had "come around." In reality, he just faded silently into the background when the subject came up or whenever Tammy was around. This was difficult as Tammy sought him out like a missile as if sensing his disapproval. She talked exclusively about the trip she was taking with his daughter. What a great opportunity it was for them to get to know their native land. That he needn't worry, she would protect his firstborn. All the counterarguments that he could have made, about Andrea only needing one semester to complete her degree, her desire to go on to graduate school and start her career, that this trip could be taken at any time since the chances of anyone re-enrolling in school after dropping out, were basically nil, were made moot by the argument to trump all arguments; they were in love. All he could do was let her go. "Sounds like you have it all thought out," was his one and only response.

He made a drink, recalling the brief period when Andrea was three or four before Morgan was born when she called him both Mommy and Daddy (much to Amber's chagrin). When he was her everything. Days long since passed. He downed the drink quickly and made another. It would be one of many. The doorbell rang.

"She's here," Amber said, floating in from the kitchen, a dishtowel thrown over her shoulder, rubbing his back. "Twenty-one," she added as if everything were proceeding normally and was not, in fact, a complete disaster.

"She's not twenty-one," he said to her receding form, raising the glass to his lips.

"Dad," Andrea said, appearing in the doorway with the hugest least self-conscious smile on her exquisite face. Why did it have to be for this person and this decision? If only she knew what he was prepared to offer for her graduation. "You remember Tammy."

"Where are your manners?" Amber asked. "Shake her hand."

"Tammy," he said, wiping the condensation from his drink before offering his hand. She was in brown cargo shorts, sandals, and a man's dress shirt that was much too large, her crop top of blond hair purposely styled to appear messy. She had a pleasant smile, though. She shook his hand so tightly that he nearly winced.

"Tom-Tom. Good to see you, friend. Looks great in here. You're sure sending us off in style."

"Come on in," he said. "You want a beer?"

"Absolutely."

About an hour into the gathering, the doorbell rang.

"I wonder who that could be," Amber asked.

* * *

Darlene's glance was firmly fixed out of the passenger window, not at the static, oversized houses bending suspiciously over her but at the invisible fate that she felt was rushing to greet her and the plan she had set in motion the morning she overheard Andrea explaining her need for financial independence from her family to Tammy at the supermarket last fall.

"You're sure about the timing on this thing?" Chet asked as he directed the car up the hill. What, exactly, the gameplan was had not been articulated, and it wasn't in Darlene's nature to improvise. He was hoping at any minute she would come to her senses and instruct him to turn the car around.

"It's perfect," she said flatly.

These were the only words she had spoken the entire day. When it was time to depart, she rose, put on her windbreaker, and exited the house, assuming he would follow, which he did. Starting the car, he headed towards the destination. It felt like one of those heist movies where it was nakedly obvious that the mission was bound to fail. That is to everyone except the mastermind of its design. The drive took twenty-five minutes. Chet sat outside the gate of *Ambrose Commons* until someone exited, and he gunned it before it could deny them access.

His follow-up question, "Were you even invited?" was acknowledged with a curt, "Who cares?"

It wasn't long before they were in the driveway.

Looking up at the magnificent and unwelcoming house, Chet knew that Darlene's monomaniacal desire was blinding her to its certain failure. Yet here he sat. Reflecting upon the many questionable choices he had made over the past ten years, Chet wondered what his life would have been like had he given his decisions the weight they deserved rather than reacting like a frightened rabbit or subsuming his will to the desires of others. As it stood, he had been pulled so far off course that getting back on track now seemed impossible. His life was foreign to him. The worst part was it was all irrelevant – he had no other choice but to press on.

"Darlene?"

"It doesn't matter."

"They don't know we're coming?"

"Surprise," she said sarcastically. She was halfway to the house before he had shut the engine down. He reluctantly followed, whispering 'no' at her back. He even stopped walking, taking a stand she neither saw nor would have acknowledged if she had, before catching up to her with a start. He pleaded with her to abort the mission, insisted they were a family just as they were. She smiled saccharinely. Then, still looking into his eyes (which, despite the situation, nearly made him swoon), she rang the doorbell. He knew at that moment that, even under the best of circumstances, we were all strangers. The only authentic connection was the pain. He also knew he would pursue her through hell. Eventually, Andrea appeared.

"Darlene. I wish I could say I'm surprised. I thought you were in San Diego this weekend?"

"I would be remiss if I missed your big day."

"You and I both know it's not my actual birthday."

She stared nervously at Darlene before immediately disappearing, pushing the door closed.

"Why did she think you were out of town? This is bad. Let's get out of here," Chet said. "This shit is dead. This was dead the last time we drove out to their apartment."

"Shut up. Shut the fuck up," she whisper-yelled back at him.

"Why would anything have changed?" he pleaded.

When the door reopened, Andrea had been replaced by Tammy.

"I'm glad you're here," she began, propping the screen door open.

Before Chet had met Darlene, he had dated Derby, a dental hygienist. She had been involved in a serious skiing accident, making it impossible for her to work or take care of herself. Chet not only nursed her back to health but supported her during her convalescence. He took on a second job, drove her to doctor's appointments, never once complaining, even as she accused him of being selfish, unloving, and neglectful (the more helpless she felt, the more she resented him). This carried over to her first days back at the dental clinic, where she began flirting with a new hygienist named Blake. She knew she was risking her relationship with Chet. She did it anyway. When her best friend, Alyssa, chastised her for her behavior, Derby ended the friendship. When she first was injured, she told Chet she wanted them to move in together. He was convinced, until the day she broke things off, despite all the evidence, it would happen. That's how he knew Tammy was about to tell Darlene they had changed their minds. Darlene must have suspected as much, too. Why else would she insist they show up unannounced at Andrea's birthday party?

"This isn't really the time. But I guess, it's as good as any. We've made our decision. We're going to pass."

"What?" Darlene gasped. Chet reached for Darlene's hand. She yanked it away.

"Here's your check. I'm sorry," she said, handing it to Chet.

"I don't understand. We had a deal. Things are in motion. We've made appointments. Set schedules. You can't say no now."

"We've made our decision," she said, stepping back into the house, the screen door banging shut.

"Just wait, wait, wait. You haven't thought this through. Think of what that money can do. The two of you would be able to go wherever you wanted. Alaska, Cambodia, Europe. What about Andrea? Do you really think it's wise for her to drop out of school with one semester left? I know her family would prefer her to finish. Think of the goodwill you'll engender."

"I appreciate you looking out for us, I really do, but our minds are made up."

"I don't understand."

"Let's go, honey," Chet said, taking her by the crook of the arm.

"Get off me," she said, pulling away. "Take the check back, please. We can figure this out."

"Let me be clear – we are not having your baby."

"This is utter bullshit. What happened in the last 48 hours? We both know Andrea wants that money. She craves independence." Darlene squeezed the bridge of her nose, furiously attempting to process what was occurring. Then it hit her like a meteor. "Maybe it's too much independence. If she gets that money, maybe she doesn't need you. You're the one who came up with this trip. You want to get her away from her family and this opportunity."

"Don't contact us again."

Darlene prompted Chet, who held out a large yellow envelope.

"More money isn't going to change things," she said, refusing to accept it before shutting the door.

Darlene lurched one more time half-heartedly towards the doorbell. Chet grabbed her arm. This time, she didn't pull it away. Posting the envelope through the front door at Darlene's urging, he then led her back to the car. They weren't half a block down the street when Tammy burst out the door, the envelope in hand, screaming, "What the fuck? What the goddamn fuck?"

"What was in there?" Chet asked, rapidly accelerating, the motor letting out an unexpected roar, Tammy quickly receding into the distance.

"A copy of her background check. She has quite the criminal history. Imagine if Andrea's parents found out before they go on this stupid trip," she said, her eyes narrowing.

Chet sat back in the driver's seat, intermittently checking the rearview and side mirrors. "Jesus Christ."

Darlene didn't utter another word the rest of the way home. Over the next few weeks, they went about their normal business, neither mentioning Andrea or Tammy. One evening, Chet came home from work and found Darlene collapsed on the floor sobbing, the kind of tears you release, hot and loud and unashamed, when someone irreplaceable dies. Picking up an envelope from the kitchen table, the same envelope they had left at the house that day, Chet pulled out an 8x10 photo of Tammy and Andrea at the Grand Canyon, gleefully giving them the middle finger. He walked it directly out to the trash to the piercing sound of Darlene's wailing.

* * *

I wasn't two steps out the front door when my left foot slid out from beneath me, and I was sent flying down the two concrete steps on my ass. Investigating the underside of my shoe, I shook my head. "You can't be serious." In my rush to get out and away from the crazy clown circus that was Chet and Darlene, I had trampled through Chet's vomit.

Hearing a deafening crash coming from behind the front door, followed by the sound of shrieking voices, I jerked myself from the ground and huffed it to the end of the decaying sidewalk and down the street. Nothing had unfolded as planned. Not that I was expecting to walk Chet through my announcement in as clean and precise a manner as a mathematical equation. But, if I was going to enter an overheating nuclear plant, it would have been nice to have an instruction manual to avoid a full-on meltdown (or at least told him about the abortion). After speed-walking several blocks, I cut over a block, running a parallel course in the same direction. Regardless of how I was to proceed, I needed to ensure I was at least out of eyeshot. Once they regrouped, they would come for me. Of this, I was certain.

It wasn't long until I came upon a business center tucked away in the midst of the unending suburban sprawl, two strip malls cradling a man-made lake. Joggers went by at regular intervals. Men in suits had deliberate conversations. Stay-at-home mothers pushed strollers, bathing their faces in the sun. A large contingent of fat, crabby geese kept their heads to the ground, pecking and squawking, hissing in that ugly way if anyone got too close.

At the end of one of the strip malls was *Heartbreaker's*. It was just the place I needed to unwind and stay out of sight while I considered my next move. I hustled over and entered, frazzled and sweaty, taking a seat at the bar that ran the length of the place and where a bearded man sat in an army jacket, nursing a drink, reading a paper that was spread judiciously across its surface. There were two tables, three booths. At the far end were the restrooms, the doors designed to look like vending machines.

I was greeted by the bartender, a tall, brunette woman in her early thirties, hair pulled back in a tight ponytail, a large tattoo of an ouroboros emblazoned across her neck.

"You look like you've had a rough one," she said, dropping a coaster in front of me. "What's your poison?"

"Corona."

As she was pulling the beer from the cooler, I caught a glance of myself in the large ornate Budweiser mirror hanging on the wall. The image looking back at me, sallow eyes, sunken cheeks, and hair so moist that it appeared painted on, was so foreign as to appear a completely different person.

"When you travel to China, you're fingerprinted when you get off the plane," she said to the man with the newspaper.

"Oh yeah?" he said without looking up.

"You have to register where you're staying with the police, too. Fucking surveillance state," she said, pushing the bottle towards me. "Remind me not to go there. Not that there was any threat of that."

She waited for a response. When none came, she began wiping down the bar.

"You're divorced, right?"

"A few years ago. After twenty-six years. Told me I was a bad husband and a selfish lover. That I could have lived without. She should have just said it was over. Why do you ask?" he said, finally raising his head from the paper.

"My partner wants out," she said, growing gloomy. "She's demanding we sell the house so she can have her share of the equity. I'll lose everything and have to move in with my mother."

He shook his head and went back to his paper.

I could imagine squandering the rest of my life in this place, silently drinking every day into oblivion and skulking home after dark when my demons were too tired to give chase. Because, as of right now, they were swirling overhead, preparing to strike.

My phone began to ring. It was my father.

"Hey, Dad," I said, only half-listening. The bartender and the man at the bar had moved on to conversing about the Monkees (and if they qualified as a legitimate rock-and-roll band) in their odd, staccato rhythm. Like all subjects that arise within the confines of a bar, regardless of the day or hour, that you would never consider worthy of discussion, I was immediately captivated. My father went on about Coco and the squirrel, the upcoming meat raffle at the legion, and an exercise bicycle. It was only when the subject of Adele's wedding arose that I returned my attention to him.

"A hot mess," he said with a chuckle. "And that was even before the ceremony began."

"A hot mess? How so?"

"She got in a fight with the maid of honor, the caterer,

and the groom, even me. Poor thing – even on her big day, she just can't give herself a break. She means well."

"Since when?" It was amazing how we so rarely (or accurately) see the objects positioned directly in front of us. "What was she so upset about?"

"Nothing was up to her exacting standards. It was the darndest thing; each time she spotted one mistake, it led her to discover another one. By the time the ceremony was about to begin, she was so worked up she nearly passed out from rage. She doesn't know how to navigate her way through relationships the way you do." There was no reason to listen. My father liked to parade out his Adele-as-ugly-duckling metaphor whenever she floundered at love, which admittedly was most of the time. Scott's suicide only solidified this view. His lack of compassion for my suffering (as if my relationships were a string of gold medals) made it difficult for me to feel sympathy for her and hardened me to him. "Everything looked fine to me."

"You should have told her to bail."

"Funny you should say that? Before walking her up the aisle, I whispered in her ear, 'You can always get a divorce pigeon,'" he said with a chuckle. "I was trying to lighten the mood. Weddings come with so many expectations. I just wanted her to be in the moment. Before you realize it, shit has passed. I wasn't serious."

I laughed heartily, downing the rest of my nearly full beer, signaling for another. "You're the only one who could have gotten away with that. Did she actually go through with it and get married?"

"Of course she did."

"It's not beyond the realm of possibility for her to tank the entire event. You know, get everyone there and undermine it on feminist grounds or some shit."

"I don't know why you talk about your sister that way. Just once, I'd like for you to take her side and empathize instead of criticize. Would that be so hard?"

"No."

It crossed my mind to confess everything that had transpired thus far – to catalog for my father the ways this expedition had already misfired. How my car was stolen, and I hadn't reported it to the police, only to be greeted by a drunken Chet who cut up his living room carpet and vomited before I could reveal the abortion. All of this, compounded by my decades of lost potential, along with the stubborn fact of my birth, would give him license to admit he never wanted me (or my mother), that he didn't love me (and never had) and give him ample reason to finally end our relationship.

"Bye, Dad."

I finished my beer, reluctantly paid for my tab, and came back out into the afternoon heat. Not knowing how to proceed, I began circling the man-made lake, gleefully disturbing the geese. I wasn't halfway around when, like a lioness upon its prey, Darlene inched her way up to the curb parallel to me, passenger window down, and gave her horn a stern toot. I headed laconically towards her. Barely within earshot of the car, she was already talking, "Chet can't handle spirits. Not as long as I've known him. I don't know what he was like in his college days. You'd know better than me. I'll need to call someone to repair the carpet after you leave," she said, popping open the passenger door. We remained stalled in our respective positions. This is what being the pawn of fate is like. It's not abstract. I've discerned it in retrospect before, but I could feel it happening now in real-time. There's an actual physicality to it. "I know you aren't leaving until you say whatever it is you have to say." I got into the car. Not because of Darlene. There was no reason to resist, and who knows what would rain down upon my head if I did. Anyway, the bitch was correct.

Within one hundred and twenty seconds we were back at their front door and back inside. A grubby bathmat had been placed over the torn carpeting, and Chet sat very still at the kitchen table, an untouched glass of water in front of him. Darlene made her way into the kitchen, still messing with the same pots on the stove as when I arrived.

Pivoting on her heel, Darlene pulled one of the chestnut cabinet doors open. It creaked its dissatisfaction as if it were awakened too early, as a skyline of jars and random items – vegetable oil, herbal teas, salt and pepper, a large yellow flashlight, a pack of cigarettes, and several sagging cookbooks with broken backs – greeted her. She lifted the pack of cigarettes and pulled a joint from deep within its belly. "Chet doesn't like when I smoke weed when the sun is still our companion. He believes it's indicative of a problem – don't you, babe?" she asked, lighting it, taking a hit. She thrust it towards me. Unable to resist, I took it from her and took a drag.

"Yeah," he mumbled unconvincingly.

We passed the joint until it was finished. Darlene ran it under the faucet and dropped it down the drain.

After a moment, Chet rose and stepped towards Darlene, the thick shuffling of his shoes filling the air, his drunken frame consuming the tiny kitchen. He attempted to kiss Darlene on the mouth. She offered her forehead. Pushing past the flashlight in the cabinet, Darlene snatched the oversized box of Morton salt, held it over the sink, and sprinkled a small crystalline mountain in her palm. Turning back to the stove, she dumped it in the pot and began stirring.

"Chet always insists on using this old steel monstrosity. It looks like something from an old cowboy movie that should be over a fire on a prairie somewhere."

"Have you ever been camping or even made a home-cooked meal?" he asked after a long silence, perhaps attempting to snap himself back to soberness.

"It's slow to heat and takes forever to cook anything. I… we," she said carefully, leaning against the opposite cabinet, "have newer pots that cook more evenly and are easier to clean. But here we are. We grow attached to the strangest things, don't we?" she asked, turning to me. When I didn't answer, she continued, "Like this knife, I got it free at a Home and Garden Show by flirting with the attendant," she said, displaying the blade flashing it this way and that.

I wasn't exactly sure what Darlene was attempting to accomplish with these little personal anecdotes. Were these pieces of misdirection or an attempt to build trust? In either case, neither was effective.

"Oh yeah?"

"A couple of years ago, Chet had it in his head we needed some home improvements – as if he would ever spend the money."

"You've had designs on our money for a long time."

She shot him a quick disdainful look.

"Off we went to the Home and Garden Show – which if you never have, do, it's more interesting than it sounds. Chet was going around to all the window company booths collecting quotes when this guy offered to have a show-mance with me. It was his coinage – show-romance. He even winked. Isn't that stupid?"

"Kinda clever, I guess," I said.

"The knife is high quality, though. Expensive. And slices like a wonder. I named it Michael Meyers," she said, pleased with her own cleverness, cutting an unwrapped stick of butter into four unequal sections, tossing each into the pot. "We've had it for years, and I've grown attached to it. Would you mind stirring the sauce?"

I did as requested.

"Maybe you just regret not accepting the man's proposition," Chet mumbled.

"It was his grandmother's. The pot, not the butter," she said, ignoring him. She extracted a piece of the still-stiff pasta and inspected it. "I don't think we're in a hurry, are we?"

Chet shrugged his shoulders.

"We'll eat your meal," I said with warmth. "Right?" I asked, making eye contact with Chet.

"Of course."

She smiled indulgently and continued stirring the pasta with the big wooden spoon. The pieces dodged and darted around the wide bowl, round and round, quick then slow, like minnows narrowly escaping the mouth of its natural predator. I watched the dancing yellow bits and the rotation of water the spoon created, an underwater tornado rising and then trailing off into nothingness the moment the spoon broke off. She saw me watching her.

"It has often struck me that cooking pasta is like bringing something back to life. It starts from a rigor mortis-like state, slowly growing more life-like. Don't you think?"

"I've never thought about it."

"The water here's being sneaky. It's showing no hints of boiling."

Snatching a towel off the counter and wiping the dots of red acne it was burping onto the surface of the oven, dipping her chunky pinky into its warm gooiness, shoving it into her mouth greedily. "It's not quite ready. Not too good either. Nothing like the beautiful Italian farm sprawled out on the jar," she said, presenting it to us, chuckling wryly. "I bet you're anxious to get back to your daughter."

I confessed that I was.

"Do you have shared custody of her with your ex-husband?"

"I do."

"That must be hard. If I had a daughter, I'd never want her to leave my sight," she said, adding, "Chet and I are unable to have children of our own."

"I think Willow and I are going to take a walk," Chet abruptly announced.

"I thought we would eat first, and then you two could have some time to catch up," Darlene said as casually as she could, although there was a palpable tension behind her words.

"We're going to take a walk first," Chet said, refusing to look at either of us.

Darlene stopped everything she was doing. "Can you wait for Chet outside? It'll only take a minute."

I waited at the end of the sidewalk fifteen or twenty minutes before Chet again appeared.

Chet seemed less drunk and more relaxed when he emerged from the house. His hair had been over-combed, the sweat had been toweled away from his face and neck, and he had spruced up his outfit by adding a brown sweater. For the first time since I had arrived, I was able to get a good look at him without the interfering eye of Darlene. He was taller than I remembered but still much too loose-limbed to be thought of as athletic. The newly sprouted goatee gave him a more bohemian appearance, but he wore it much too wide at the neck, spreading out from his mouth like an avalanche. In the light, his eyes appeared darker and a bit hollowed out, although that could have been from the alcohol. He motioned for us to walk down the sidewalk in the opposite direction I had fled a few short hours previously. We didn't speak. It was an odd sensation finally being alone with this person with whom I had shared such a tumultuous history, but that time had made a stranger. It was like revisiting your old neighborhood where the streets remained but most of the buildings had been replaced. After walking a few more blocks, he silently steered us to the right down a tree-strewn lane covered in shade.

"You obviously made a deal with the devil," he finally said without glee.

Now that we were alone, really alone, it would start. I could only imagine the phantasmagoric release of the repressed and half-realized, half-decayed emotions about to come forth. All one could do was allow them to run their course and pray they do minimal damage or hope they perish once hit by the light of day.

"I guess I shouldn't be surprised by that characterization. What with the whole vanishing routine you pulled ten years ago."

"Excuse my staring. You haven't aged a bit. You look exactly the same as you did when we were together," he said, although he hadn't once looked upon me since we had left his house. I sighed with great sadness.

"Compliment accepted."

The sound of our footfalls, which initially were a jumbled mess of clattering teeth, had fallen into sync. He was much taller than me, and it would have taken sustained effort on his part to slow his gait to match mine.

"I still can't believe you're here with me in the flesh. It's like a dream or something you imagined coming to life. You know I think of those as the best days of my life?" he said. The unoccupied air swallowed up his words as we ventured forward.

"You did send me a letter."

"About that," he said, grimacing embarrassingly. "I had ordered some absinthe from Prague. Have you been to Prague?"

I shook my head.

"I understand it's one of the most beautiful places on Earth. Anyway, when I cracked the bottle, I hit it really hard, and it hit back with equal strength. I barely remember writing it. Next thing I know, I got your message." He chuckled falsely. He might just as easily have said, 'I hijacked a plane to Brazil,' 'I am a woman trapped in a man's body,' or whatever ludicrousness one could imagine. The contents were irrelevant, all equally absurd, and empty of meaning. Everything flowing from his lips was completely false, rehearsed, or both. Perhaps he could no longer differentiate them, like watercolors running together. "I'm sorry you came all this way. I feel terrible. I didn't think you'd answer me, much less take a cross-country trip to my doorstep."

"Why wouldn't I answer?"

"Here we are," he said. Before us stood an old-fashioned park, the type I played on in my youth, complete with a rusted-out merry-go-round, wooden seesaw, and iron slide dimpled with tiny dents. He made his way to the far side of the park, taking a seat on one of the swings. I took a seat next to him, the brown serrated mountains silently looming over us.

"You're an accountant?" I said, pushing myself gently into the air.

"After I left Minnesota, I decided to pick something there would always be a demand for, something recession-proof. It was either accounting or funeral director. I landed on accounting. A strictly pragmatic decision. Not the most exciting of fields, but it pays the bills," he said, kicking at the woodchips beneath his feet. "I thought that might surprise you."

"Not at all."

"Really?" he asked mildly, disappointed. "Not even ten years and 1200 miles can dull that incisive brain of yours."

"You used to read mystery novels all the time—"

"Still do, I'm happy to report," he said, thrusting himself into the air.

"You always had a deep fear of ambiguity, so it makes total sense you'd choose that as a career. The ledger has to balance, and the killer has to be discovered. Your love of sitcoms hinges on the same premise – everything is resolved and is status quo by the next episode. There's comfort in that shit," I said, perversely proud of myself for retaining and remembering all of that information.

"Damn," he said, his breath taken away. He was astonished not only at the sight of time collapsing in front of him but at being vindicated. It had finally been confirmed that if you were patient enough that which you loved would eventually return. What he misunderstood is that the past cannot return in the same form by which it left. As memories age, they are transformed into something almost unrecognizable. In a sense, as I stood before him, I no longer existed. Everything he was currently undergoing emanated not from me (or what once transpired) but from the aftershocks of those experiences. When the ghosts of long-gone days are not relinquished, they can only deign to destroy you.

"I'm surprised you remember," he said. "I didn't realize you paid such close attention to me."

Easing himself off the swing and drifting over to the merry-go-round, he pointed to it as a form of invitation.

"We dated for two years. I was bound to notice something."

Examining his overeager face, a groundswell of repugnance overcame me. The very attributes that made Chet an easy mark were the exact qualities that made him repulsive – an utter lack of belief in himself coupled with a constant need for affirmation. Even now, pointing down at the merry-go-round as if he were the gatekeeper to Xanadu when we both knew it was I who held the keys, made it difficult not to crush him all over again.

"Is it weird if I even miss that?"

"Yes," I said, rolling my eyes, taking a seat.

"There we are," he said, setting it in motion. I watched him watch me as it spun around several times before he hopped on. We laid back, staring at the mid-afternoon sky. It was a while before either of us spoke.

"Do you remember that house party we went to in St. Paul for Squirrel's 20th birthday?"

"Vaguely."

"We had only been dating a few weeks." I spoke unhurriedly like a lizard warmed by the sun.

"Tom was going on and on about Lester Young. Do you remember?"

"I didn't know who he was or care," I said. "I still don't."

"Not only wouldn't he shut up, but he was so wasted I couldn't understand most of what he was saying."

"Wasn't he dressed like William S. Burroughs?"

"I forgot about that," he said, laughing loudly. "You didn't know who Lester Young is, but you knew who William S. Burroughs is. Is it any wonder I was entranced by you?"

"I'm an enigma."

For whatever reason, perhaps pity, perhaps knowing that the recently dismissed Mark was still resentfully feeding my cat (along with the multitude of various other transgressions from my past), I indulged him. Those aftershocks are mighty indeed.

"You just took my hand and led me straight to the door. Once outside, we spontaneously started running down the street to my car, our jackets flapping in the wind and ended up at that all-night café. At some point, a drunk wandered in, commandeered that enormous organ in the back, and played John Lennon's 'Mother' over and over again."

"Dubins," I said without enthusiasm.

"Dubins," he said with a great life-affirming exhale. He reached back and took my hand. "We talked for hours."

"I don't even remember seeing Squirrel."

"He was passed out, shirtless, his great mass of a body shining under the lamps at his own party."

He had it half correct. We did make an early exit from

Squirrel's birthday party that night, but we went straight back to the dorm and played foosball. It was on another evening after I convinced Chet to do my pre-calculus homework (on the night we had first made love, the reason the memory left such an indelible mark on him) that we ended up at Dubin's, drinking coffee and smoking cigarettes. It was a massive Drag Queen who overtook the organ. She was playing the Velvet Underground's "I'm Waiting for My Man" (not John Lennon's "Mother"), pounding out its repetitive chords like an out-of-control train.

"How about that time we went to the bed and breakfast? The one with the all-Teddy Bear décor?"

"I missed one of my finals because of that little surprise."

We stayed hand-in-hand, the merry-go-round spinning slowly, dialing us further back in time, the sun and clouds keeping a suspicious eye on me.

"Are you seeing anyone?" he asked cautiously.

It was obvious he had been wanting to ask me for some time, no doubt since the moment he had laid eyes on me again.

"There's someone in my life."

"I figured," he said.

"Well, there was until a day or so ago."

"Do tell," he said, attempting to sound more casual than he was. He gave the merry-go-round another shove with his foot. He was driving us back in time to a location where he believed we were at our happiest, our most content, in the thrall of first sex, but before the suffocating blanket of contentment begins to smother all pleasure in one another. It was a place that never existed, not for me anyway. Where I needed us to be was still too raw for him, even after all these years, and would be confounded by the information I had yet to release.

"On the way out here, I met a woman in Nebraska, and we hung out for a bit. She was a real firecracker. The kind of woman I would have wished for as a sister. Easy to talk to. No bullshit. While we were in the bar, we got a little lit up – well, a lot lit up – with these local guys, and I ended up making out with one of them."

"You never could resist," he said without bitterness.

"I don't even know why I did it. I didn't even like him. That was bad enough. I could bury it with all the other bodies. Then, as we were driving to a hotel, my boyfriend called, and she told him about it."

"People love to spread misery around," he said in a gloomy kind of way.

"She acted as if she was doing this for my benefit."

"How so?"

"I told her that I didn't love him, and she thought I needed a little shove to end it. She was right. I'm slow to act, obviously," I said, giving his hand a squeeze. "I just would have preferred to do things at my speed."

"And how did he take it?" he asked, the merry-go-round slowing, then stopping.

"I've been trying not to think about it. He didn't scream or cry. He's not that kind of person. He is such a big dumb sweetheart, loving and considerate with a gentle soul," I said, touching my heart with my free hand.

"But?" he asked.

"I really wanted to love him. I tried. I stayed longer than I should have because he loved me. But when it's not there, what can you do? It's just me. I'm broken. Well, that's over now, and none of your concern. Believe it or not, that wasn't even the worst thing she did. She and her husband were having trouble. That's how we bonded. Over you men. My coming out here gave her the courage to leave him. She decided to tag along and make a new start. It was a lot to take in, actually. It scared me, but it was exhilarating, too."

"She couldn't just blow up her life."

"What do you mean?" I asked.

"Changing your life is scary. Too final."

"You did it."

"Nevertheless," he said with obvious pain. "So, she blew up yours too. By doing that, you were in it together. Mutual destruction is the only form of courage some people know."

"Shit, I never thought of that," I said. "In any case, she chickened out. We had stopped to eat. She excused herself to use the bathroom. Next thing I know, the bitch stole my car. She lifted the keys from my purse."

"Leaving you alone with the blown-up life."

"Even worse than before, if you can imagine. I still have to find a way home. I'm not sure I have enough for a plane ticket back."

"Let's see what I can do about that."

I really hated this man. For a moment, I was looking forward to smashing his heart upon Dead Girl Grey until I recalled the clinic, the pain, and the aftermath, the years of drunken nights alone on death day.

"Any word from the police?"

"I never called them," I said shamefully. "Don't even. I feel bad enough already. My dad would lose his shit if he knew."

"Is that why you were late?"

"Late?" I asked, letting go of his hand.

"You arrived a day later than you told me."

There was a slight but perceptible shift in his mood.

"My car was stolen, Chet. It wasn't like I was late on purpose," I said, sitting up. He got off the merry-go-round and faced me.

"If it hadn't been that, it would have been something else. In fact, it was something else. You found time to make a new girlfriend and hook up with a guy. It sure doesn't sound like getting here was top of mind. I do have a life that you didn't give any consideration to at all."

"I dropped out of my sister's wedding to be here."

"Don't turn this around," he said.

"Sorry to disappoint you. I always did, though, didn't I?"

"Things went on for me after I left Minnesota. I had my adventures. My time in the sun. My share of lovers."

"I'm sure."

"Don't do that – don't condescend to me," he said, pointing a finger at me. "I had to start completely over when I came out here. Do you have any idea how difficult that was? I was alone and brokenhearted. I had nothing and no one."

"You did that. You made that decision."

"Yep. I did."

"I won't bear the responsibility for all this. I just won't. We broke up. Relationships end all the time."

"It happened to your boyfriend not a day ago."

"Don't throw that in my face. Mark would never do that. You have no idea what you're talking about."

"Don't I?"

"You're no martyr. Moving here didn't absolve you of all the terrible things you did to me. It doesn't erase the fact that you demanded all of my time, pushed my friends away, and stalked me. Mark would never do anything like that. You know what else Mark would never do? Quit his job and run halfway across the country over a woman."

"Fuck you."

"Who does that?"

"I guess I do."

He paced back and forth in front of me. "I thought I knew what I would say to you if I ever saw you again."

"I'm right here. Be a man for once in your life."

"What are you doing here, anyway? My letter wasn't an invitation. What shit have you been carrying around?"

"I thought if I came out and saw you, it would all make sense. That if I could right this one grievous wrong, I could, I don't know, right my entire life."

Chet burst out laughing, a mean, heartless cackle. "How many miles did you rehearse that in the rearview mirror? It takes a lot of gall to say that." He shook his head and paced more rigorously. "You didn't like that? Your feelings are hurt? Good. You should feel some pain. Do you know what it was like watching you and Brayden parade around campus, giggling and kissing? Flaunting your newfound love?"

"No one cared."

"I cared. You were telling the entire world that I wasn't good enough. That's what your ex-boyfriend is thinking, by the way. That he isn't good enough. I saw my future in you, and you didn't trust me with it." He stopped in place. "I couldn't figure out why you picked Brayden. What made him special? Then, when I saw you today, that all changed. You may not have loved me, but you never loved him either."

"I didn't love my husband, the father of my child?"

"You're not married now," he said, kicking at the woodchips.

"People split up, Chet. Divorce is not a case against love."

"My bet is you got tired of him like you get tired of everyone else. Did you cheat on him?"

"No."

"I don't believe that either. You used to always say that no one ever broke your heart. It was like a badge of honor. Either way, you didn't do too much thinking about the consequences. In fact, you seemed to take a perverse pride in the pain you caused. And still cause, apparently."

"You're not making this easy."

"Good, good," he said forcefully, walking back to the swings. "Didn't you ever feel bad? Once, in all those years?"

"No," I said. "Not then. Not a year ago. Not a week ago. I do now. That's why I'm standing here right now."

After nine years, nine death-day blackout drunk anniversaries spent alone (Brayden knew what I had done but refused to acknowledge it, jealous that McKenna wasn't my first child), I was finally prepared to confess. Regardless of the consequences, I was ready.

"Chet—"

"Jesus, Willow," he said, grasping the chain of one of the swings, "You really do believe you're the only person in the world. You're not here because you feel guilty about how you treated me. You're here to tell me you had an abortion, right? You didn't trust me with that either."

I was speechless.

"You knew?"

"I would like to say that I figured it out. That the only

reason you would have shown up here would be to tell me about our child. To show some remorse for what you took from me. But I was blinded by my feelings for you like I always have been. And to my great shame and embarrassment, I never even considered it."

"You thought—"

"That you were here for me, yes. The minute your sister called—"

"Adele?"

"She's the one who told me. She called yesterday after you were already on your way."

"After I dropped out of the wedding?"

"Yes. And the minute you said you were coming, I was ready to throw my entire life away again – this time to run away with you. That's how big a jackass I am. The same jackass I was ten years ago nipping at your heels like a begging dog. Which you're not. You're not here for me. You're here for you."

"But I'm not. I needed you to know."

"Not five minutes ago, you said you were trying to… what did you say? That you were trying to right your entire life? This has nothing to do with me. You drove thousands of miles for you. Like it once was and always will be. You should have stayed home," he said, dropping, sitting cross-legged in the woodchips.

"I wanted to talk to you. I did," I said, holding back tears. "But I was young. We both were. I was scared and high all the time. I tried telling you. In my dorm room. On those walks, we took late at night. At Dubin's. I couldn't. I didn't know how. I knew you would want to keep it, and I couldn't."

"You don't know that."

"I do. You would have forced me to keep it. It would have ruined both our lives. I couldn't withstand the onslaught you would have come at me with. I got rid of it. I did. I did. I didn't know what else to do. I'm sorry. It was horrible. It took me years not to think of it every day. I was so alone with it for all these years."

"You didn't even give me a chance. I was the child's father."

"I didn't love you."

Pulling his car keys out of his pocket, he wriggled one off the silver loop. "My car is parked one block up and over from my house. It's the first car on the left. Take it to the airport. Buy yourself a ticket. Go home. Leave the car on the ramp."

"What?"

"Darlene and I have tried for years to have children. All she wants is a family of her own. When it was obvious it wasn't going to happen, we looked for alternative routes. We've gone to a phonebook's worth of doctors, taken all the tests. Every waking thought of our lives, every penny we earn, revolves around this fantasy. But she can't let go. We have no retirement. We don't travel. We've been consumed to the point that there's no joy in our household."

"I'm sorry. I didn't know."

"Why don't you leave?"

"I would expect you to say that," he said. "Once Darlene found out what you did, she decided you owed me, owed us. If we go back to my house, she's going to ask you to donate your eggs to us for a procedure called reciprocal in vitro fertilization. Doesn't that sound warm? It's a process where we collect your eggs and my sperm, have them fertilized, placed in her uterus… it doesn't matter, here take the key."

I stepped forward and did as he asked.

"You know I can't do that."

"She's willing to offer you a large sum of money—of our money," he said with a sad smile. "She's persuasive and very persistent."

"This would be our baby, Chet. She's trying to make a family by resurrecting our baby from the dead." He shrugged indifferently. "She's manipulating you. Leveraging your feelings for me, leveraging my guilt."

"How is that any different from you?"

He stood up.

"When I left Minnesota to come out here, I had convinced myself it represented something larger than me. That it gave purpose to what I was doing. You said you felt that coming here. It's doesn't," he said without rancor. "I was just running. I wasn't even running towards anything, just away from you. I imagined the void I left in your life. Of course, you weren't thinking about me at all. We assume there's reciprocity in the conjured-up memories between people in relationships or who share experiences. When, in truth, it's like that see-saw – we all assign significance to wildly different things to make memories rise to the surface. But there was no turning back. One night, I just sat in my car, a vodka bottle in my hand, watching as the sky lowered itself over the earth like a coffin lid.

"Eventually, I walked up to a local bar. I was ready to unload the pathetic state of my life on this bartender, the only person in the place. Before I could say anything, she told me about her dog, Bill Evans. She had put it down a couple of days earlier. It had inoperable cancer. She had no family, no career. Just the dog. She had got its ashes back the day before. Picture a grown woman lying on the floor around a cardboard box of ashes sobbing, she told me. Her eyes were shining with pain. I was furious."

"Furious? Why?"

"That dog was put out of its suffering. You had actively inflicted and were still inflicting suffering upon me. There was no comparison, and I told her so. I expounded on the many sins of Willow Hennings. You know what she did? She took my hand. *Suffering is not an Olympic sport. Pain is pain.* I felt so ashamed. You better go; she'll only wait so long before showing up here. She really wants this baby, and it's not as simple as saying no," he said, wiping woodchips off his pants.

"I don't think I have enough money for a plane ticket."

"The bus station then. It's the best I can do," he said, chuckling ruefully. He looked at me in the eyes, long and hard. "After Adele called, I decided to kill myself. I was on the road, speeding towards a bridge pillar. I was determined to meet my child."

I turned and started walking away. I could feel his eyes on me. I made my way out of the park and up the street. Once out of sight, I dropped to the ground and started bawling. I don't know how long I cried, but eventually, my phone began to ring. It was Brayden.

"This isn't a good time," I said, wiping my eyes.

"Some surprising news." I nearly hung up. "Your boyfriend came by my house this morning. Not sure how he knew where I lived, but that's a discussion for another time." I rolled my eyes. They burned intensely. "Setting that aside, he had in his possession your house key which he placed in my possession and wanted me to return to you upon your imminent return."

I rubbed my eyes. That fat fuck couldn't have just slid it into my mail slot like a normal human being. He had to light a stick of dynamite and toss it where he knew it could inflict damage upon my already fucked life. My sister was right – men couldn't keep their pain private.

"He said not to call him back this time."

"Thanks for taking the message," I said abruptly, hoping that would halt any further inquiries, knowing that it absolutely would not.

"Something happened?"

"Nothing that doesn't happen every day, and nothing that concerns you."

"He mentioned a call with some rather nasty, abrupt woman claiming infidelity on your part. Sounds like you got more than you bargained for on your little road trip."

"Brayden, it's nothing."

"Sounded familiar," he said. "It's over, I assume?"

"What do you think?" I said, closing my eyes tightly.

"If I may say—"

"You may not, but when has that ever stopped you?"

"Every time you called me post-separation to hang out, I always thought I had a chance. That you wanted me again. Yes, you were clear about the ground rules. You told me we were friends. That door was forever closed. But ninety percent of communication is non-verbal. Not to mention, why would you be calling to hang out if there wasn't some other motive?"

"You're right," I said, my eyes still closed.

"You're doing it again. You always accused me of never being able to let go of you. Now I'm realizing, finally, it's you. It's always been you. You can't let go."

"Right on all counts."

"If you're not going to take me seriously, that's fine. Agree with me to dismiss me, clever as always. Don't forget to pick up McKenna a little something."

"I won't."

I opened my eyes and lifted my face to the sun.

"It's just that you said you would, so she's expecting something. It doesn't have to be anything big—"

"I won't forget."

"Okay, good. I won't cover your ass this time."

"I'm sorry about Marco, Brayden."

Since our divorce, this subject was rarely discussed, and not without rancor. It brought our conversation to a standstill. I understood his trepidation to speak. How distasteful it was to have people in the world who knew all your vulnerabilities and fault lines able to crack you in two. He was an animal caught on an open plain, assessing a perceived threat, afraid to run lest it should be mauled. In practical terms, that meant he was waiting for the addendum I added to every apology I had ever offered him, which usually ran something like this: *I am sorry but…* or *I wouldn't have done this had you not done that first.* It was a terrible pattern I had engaged in as long as I could remember, instantly walking back any culpability I was responsible for and trivializing someone else's pain. See, we are not merely stuck with specific people forever but also with their unchanging, exasperating behaviors. It was just further proof to him that we should never have met. Nevertheless, I was determined to break new ground in this dusty, well-worn relationship.

"By the end of our marriage, I was so angry with you that I was convinced I was justified in my actions. I wasn't. You didn't deserve that. I'm sorry," I paused before adding,

"That's it. That's all I have to say."

There was another long period of stillness, his mind racing like quicksilver to discover an ulterior motive and a reason to reject my act of goodwill. If none was found he would be left with a decision to make: accept my apology at face value or withdraw the poison he had stored since discovering my infidelity and strike back. Knowing what a weak, petty man Brayden was, it would not be an easy choice.

"Brayden?"

"I'm here."

There were a few seconds of silence before the line went dead. I guess there was a third option.

I stood up, took a deep breath, and started walking. There was a modest breeze and homes with tiny patches of brown and green before them. Rounding the corner, Darlene sat on the top step outside her house. If I did not know her, would I be able to recognize from appearance alone that here sat a woman whose singular dream was passing? Was already gone? Wasn't it true of all of us? I don't know if I had made the correct decision to come to Salt Lake City. Nevertheless, for the first time in years, I felt something akin to grace. Cutting over a block, there sat an old blue truck devoured by rust. The driver's side door was locked. The passenger side, as well. Perhaps, in haste, Chet had only given me the ignition key. The window was down a quarter of the way. I squeezed my arm through and lifted the knob. Opening the door, I shimmied to the driver's side and ran my hands over the steering wheel. With any luck, I could get to Rawlins or even Cheyenne before stopping for the night. I would call my dad and McKenna. Perhaps even Adele. The key didn't fit in the ignition. Forcing it, it snapped. As the pieces lay in my hand, it was clear – this wasn't a car key. Nor was this Chet's truck. Ache filled my body. I needn't go back to the park to know that Chet was no longer there. At the house, the driveway was empty, the shades were lowered, and it was completely dark. Taking a seat on the step where I had seen Darlene not fifteen minutes earlier, I took my head in my hands and sobbed for the second time that day.

Drying my eyes, I grabbed a taxi to a cheap motel and collapsed on the bed, too exhausted to take my clothes off, and fell into a deep, hard sleep. The following morning, I went early to the bus station. I didn't have enough money to make it all the way back to Minnesota but boarded the first bus east. Anything to get out of Utah. Four hours later, I arrived at the small, dismal bus terminal in Cascia, Wyoming. A square, flat brick building, only the greyhound sign affixed to the front of the edifice indicated that civilization had briefly swept through before completely forgetting the place. There were few other buildings, no cars, and a low murmur of the wind from the mountains passing over the grassland, which was shorn like a buzzcut and burnt to the ground from the relentless sun. I took a seat on the low cement curb, gazed down the two-lane blacktop, and prayed that Adele kept her promise.

It was a long wait. The heat lulled me to sleep. I awoke once to the hiss of a bus releasing its compressor like a whale surfacing from the deep and again when I felt a rough hand upon my shoulder and found my sister looking down upon me.

"Let's go."

Dragging myself to the compact rented car, I strapped myself in and laid my head back, grateful this dreadful affair was nearly over.

"I'm not going to last very long. I'm exhausted," she said.

"Alright."

Much to her consternation, we didn't come across a hotel (much less a gas station, fast food restaurant, or a town) for several hundred miles. It was just the highway unspooling cruelly before us, the sun and our resentful silence pressing up against the car windows. Eventually, a wooden sign appeared with the non-descript word 'Motel' painted in blue, the simple qualifier 'one mile' etched beneath it. With no foreseeable options, Adele took the exit ramp and followed several more of these signs until we were deposited in front of a long dirt road at the end of which stood a simple two-story structure, a staircase running up either side, with four faded white doors on each level, and a picnic table off to the side, a rusty aluminum sign propped up against it which read '*Sunset Inn.*'

"What do you think?" Adele asked.

"Not very promising."

"I just drove half a day. I need a few hours rest."

"I'm capable of driving," I said, noticing what appeared to be the tail end of a brown El Camino peeking out from behind the building.

"I didn't add you to the insurance."

"That makes sense," I said, rolling my eyes. "Just look at the place."

She had already grabbed her bag and was headed for the door furthest to the right, where a small sign reading 'office' was haphazardly taped in the corner window, a dim yellowish light glowing from behind the blinds.

We entered reticently. The waiting room was small,

decorated with two red chairs, a stout round table, and several old magazines stacked sloppily upon it. There was no one behind the counter.

"Hello," she called out, dropping her bag. There was no response. "Why don't you check out back?"

Doing as she asked, I found an open field stretching several hundred yards, bordered by a row of darkened pines. There was a firepit loaded with blackened soot and cigarette butts. Three bicycles stood propped up next to the back entrance, above which an exposed lightbulb fought the daylight. The brown El Camino had three flat tires. The only sound was that of the heat in conversation with the crickets. I reported this all to Adele.

"Looks like there's a small kitchen that way and a basement where some lights appear to be on."

As she headed to the lower level, I made my way down the hallway. The walls were covered with old black and white photographs without an obvious relation to the motel: a couple of old men ice fishing, an obese woman in a lawn chair knitting, unsmiling children on a rusted swing set, a semi-truck stretched out lazily in a parking lot. The kitchen was more modern than the rest of the motel, a sea of shiny aluminum countertops and surfaces. Although, it appeared as if none of it had ever been used. I opened one of the cabinets. It was completely vacant. I opened a second only to find the same. One after another, there wasn't an item of food in the entire kitchen. The refrigerator was dark and humid.

"You're not going to believe this," I began to say, only to find that Adele was now gone, the lobby once more abandoned. I peered out the front door. The car was unoccupied. Stepping over to the stairwell, I found her at the bottom, staring intently at something or someone.

"Anyone down there?" I asked.

Turning her head towards me, she signaled with a nod that I should join her.

"Huh?"

She focused her gaze on me without uttering a word.

"There's no one here, and the kitchen is completely barren. There's no food. It's a freak show."

She widened her eyes but remained completely motionless. It confused and then alarmed me. I made my way to her. Before I could inquire what the issue was, I was shocked to find she was surrounded by three Mexican men. Surprised at my appearance, they took a seat at a small table at the other end of the room.

"What's going on?"

No one moved or responded.

"Do you speak," I was about to say 'English' but one of them, the middle one with a thin wispy mustache, cut me off with a curt, "No."

My breathing became labored, my ribcage tight.

"They speak English," I whispered to Adele.

I glanced back up the stairs. The doorway seemed miles away, nothing but a blinding whiteness. Whether by design or accident, we had wandered into a wolf's den. We were smaller, outnumbered, isolated, and could not communicate freely (the thought that I was about to become a statistic shot through my mind like lightning). Unless we made a move quickly, the outcome would be grim. I grasped Adele's hand and gave it a squeeze.

The next thing I knew, we were in a full sprint up the stairs. The sound of a thousand footfalls came crashing up behind us, mixed with the guttural grunts of animal pursuit.

Somehow, we made it out the front door, the sun screeching like a siren. I was petrified that I would get snatched in the short distance from the hotel entrance to the car. "Go, go, go," I screamed, pounding on the dashboard, unable to process the fact that the men had congregated in the doorway. Jamming the car into reverse, Adele maneuvered the car down the long drive, dust consuming the vehicle. Hitting the asphalt of the two-lane road, she spun the wheel madly, and we spiraled all the way around, facing the hotel. The three men remained motionless, almost inhuman in their stillness. Straightening us out, she floored it. I was still shrieking as the wolves and the 'Sunset Inn' faded into the distance.

Finding the highway, we continued forward to the sound of our breathing like exploding waves.

"That was nuts," I said, pulling a cigarette from my purse, cracking the window, and lighting up. These were the first words either of us had spoken in ninety minutes.

"Fucking men," Adele said. The adrenaline now having drained from her body, she had been restored to the same prickly, difficult person I had known my entire life. "Can you believe that shit?" She motioned for the cigarette. "Worthless. They're completely worthless."

I watched as she maneuvered the thin cylinder up to her mouth, stuck it bluntly between her lips, and inhaled. Her fingers held it gracelessly, fidgeting and rolling it, attempting to find a comfortable way in which to maintain it, her lips puckering bitterly. She extracted it from her mouth and considered it briefly, disapprovingly, before handing it back to me.

"It kind of reminded me of that one winter in college when we went up to Canada to drink."

She scowled, attempting to make a connection between the two seemingly disparate events.

"We went a few times," she said, attempting to stifle a cough. "I remember driving forever in the unending snow."

"It was you and me and Jon. It was late, and everyone was tired and high."

"You two were high," she said derisively. "So far, this describes every trip we ever took to Canada. Can you blow that smoke more directly out the window?"

I lowered the window completely and held my arm out. The heat was stifling despite the fact that the sun was blunted by a blanket of clouds. "It was pitch black, and we came around this hill... well, a small mountain, really—"

"It was a hill," Adele countered.

"—And there was this huge factory, all lit up, its smokestacks pumping relentlessly. When Jon, who was obsessed with World War II – I think his Jewish grandparents sold out other Jews to save themselves – screamed, 'It's Auschwitz!'"

"I remember," she responded suspiciously.

"As if on cue, the car started spinning out of control, and we were tossed in the ditch," I said, dropping the cigarette out the window and closing it. "There was nothing, I mean, nothing around. We were stranded."

"Where, instead of helping dig us out, you two started getting cozy. It almost cost us a ride. When that old man in the pick-up finally stopped, he thought we were a bunch of perverts and nearly left." She looked at me, then back at the road. "How did our almost getting accosted, possibly killed, remind you of that? There is absolutely nothing about these two events that are similar."

"It was something memorable on a road trip."

I reached for another cigarette, but before I could extract it from the pack, the car decelerated and was eased over to the shoulder, hazards flashing.

"This is not a road trip. What is wrong with you? You're lucky you weren't killed."

The depth of rage in her voice was restrained but palpable. I could see the gears of her mind in motion. She had me alone with no one to come to my defense. It was the perfect opportunity to use the comparison I had just made between the 'Sunset Inn' incident and our Canadian road trip not only to blast me for my impulsively organized trip to Utah but as a springboard to level a major indictment against the very person I was (something I sensed she always had longed to do), the men I loved, the career I chose, how I raised my daughter – every choice I had ever made. But she couldn't, and she knew she couldn't. She was the one largely responsible for my trip's undoing. She was its catalyst.

She squeezed her eyes shut, took a deep breath, and redirected.

"We need to make a decision. Are we going to actively look for a place to stay or push all the way through to Minnesota?"

"I can drive. There's nothing and no one out here. I'm sure I can get us home without incident."

Flipping off the hazards, she put the car back in drive, checked the mirrors, and eased us back on the road. "That's fine. If I get tired, I'll let you know." That was the odd thing about resentment; it circumvented all logic (and virtue). In other words, I wouldn't be driving.

"How was the wedding?"

"What do you mean?"

When my dad first told me about Adele's behavior, I immediately dismissed it. It wasn't out of character for her to act out. Reflecting on it further, I was convinced there was a guilty conscience lurking behind her conduct.

"It wasn't anything out of the ordinary. In the end, I gained a husband, if that's what you're asking."

"It was merely transactional then?" I asked with a smirk.

"Hilarious."

"It's just that Dad seemed to think it was a little rough for you."

"Nice of him to fill you in. There were a few minor hiccups," she said, stressing the word minor. "Nothing that any bride-to-be wouldn't lose patience with. There's already an immense amount of pressure to begin with as all eyes are on you, and that's before shit starts to go wrong. Why?"

"He couldn't figure out why you were, well, so you, since from his perspective everything seemed to be running smoothly. I was wondering if maybe there was anything else on your mind."

"Like you?" she asked, her voice rife with sarcasm. "Not out of your wheelhouse to somehow make my day about you, even without your presence. No, I wasn't thinking about you. But I'll let it pass. Dad filled me in on your little misadventures as well. Your car didn't break down. Chet's not having it fixed and driving it back. It was stolen before you even got to Salt Lake City, and in your infinite incompetence and laziness, you didn't even report it. I mean, Jesus, Willow. When are you going to act like an adult?"

"Is he pissed?" I asked.

Picking at some foreign object in her teeth for some

time before answering, she grimaced contemptuously. "I wouldn't say pissed. He wasn't surprised, either. Disappointed, but he took it in stride. You know him. He figures everything will work itself out."

"He refused to come and get me," I said, leaning my head against the window, watching the telephone poles whiz by. "How is that supposed to make me feel?"

"To be fair, he does have McKenna."

"He could have brought her. She loves to travel. Not that she's gotten to do a ton of it. It would have been a great opportunity, just the three of us. So, I guess you know about Mark, too?"

I could see from her reaction that she did not.

"The same lunatic who stole my car broke up with him for me," I said with a weary chuckle.

"Sorry?" she asked cautiously. "What you were doing with him was a complete mystery."

"It's for the better. I knew he wasn't the one pretty early on."

"Then why waste your time?"

"You know those last unfinished Michelangelo sculptures?"

"The Hall of Prisoners? I've been to Florence."

"I used to think of being in a relationship like those statues — as people trying to liberate themselves from the stone, reaching out to the world, trying to find an authentic connection. Now I see them as figures attempting to recede back into the stone," I said, completely full of shit. Much as I was loathe to admit it, I respected her intellect and was always trying to impress her. "No matter how hard I try, love leaves me with less than what I started with. It's no wonder I finally earned my Kerouac eyes."

"What in the hell could that be?"

"When I was in college, there was this guy I was seeing—"

"Naturally."

I stopped irately.

"Please go on," she said, urging me forward with her hand.

"—Who was obsessed with him. We walked the fifteen blocks to a Midway bookshop every day to scour the place for his books. Personally, he left me cold. The one thing that did catch my attention was his eyes. They were so full of sadness. I had this idea that I wanted my eyes to look like that one day."

"Romantic nonsense. Didn't he die an alcoholic, living with his mother?" she asked, tilting her head, attempting to recall and verify the biographical information. "It just glorifies defeat, right?"

"You think, as a feminist, you'd let another woman have her voice," I said and waited before continuing. "I wanted to be able to say that I had lived. That I had seen things. Then, in that putrid bus station bathroom, I saw those eyes looking back at me and realized what a fuck up I was. I didn't have any special insight. I wasn't wiser. I was older. Certainly not richer. My life was passing me by without the benefit of anything."

"Be careful what you wish for, I suppose."

"On the plus side, I think I squared things with Brayden."

"Brayden? What happened to him? And when did you find the time for that?"

A semi-truck passed us on the left side, its weight and momentum pushing our entire car to the shoulder. I watched as it sped off into the distance, several compact cars trailing behind it like tiny fish after a shark.

"I apologized for what happened with Marco for the first time."

"The first time ever?"

I was about to lie out of reflex, shame, and embarrassment, but for whatever reason, decided against it. "Yes."

"How'd that go over?"

"He hung up."

"Progress? Right?"

I agreed that it was.

"And how did things end up with Chet?" Adele asked cautiously, her eyes still set firmly on the firmament in front of us.

I lifted my head and scanned the movements of her eyes, the contractions of her forehead, and the corners of her lips for any admission of what she had done. I wasn't sure if I should detest her all the more or admire her ruthless cunning.

"Are you really asking me that?"

"Yes, I'm really asking," she said. "I just left my new husband to pick you up in the middle of nowhere. I think an update is appropriate." She was like a criminal who had that strange compulsion to return to the scene of the crime, unsure herself what she wanted, or more accurately, who demanded credit for their crimes (no matter how heinous), reveling in their destruction but ultimately forced to their kneels to repent. Such creatures of hubris and woe.

"John's mad that you're here?"

"Of course he's mad. He barely knows you. You dropped out of the wedding, and right after I agreed to become his wife, I am off to a Wyoming bus station to collect you because you ran out of money and couldn't get home. Don't pout. We don't leave for Cancun for a few days. He'll get what he wants then, and all will be forgiven."

"That's a little cynical, isn't it?"

"You're one to talk."

"Fair enough. You'll find out anyway. When I arrived, Chet was drunk. He muttered a bunch of incoherent nonsense, cut up his living room carpet, and vomited. And that was before I had even said a word."

"He's still in love with you," she said, checking the rearview mirror and abruptly changing lanes.

"You knew that before I left. Other than that, I didn't accomplish much. But you knew that too."

"Yeah. I did," she whispered, a shadow of shame falling across her face.

"What was that?"

Adele seemed to be wrestling with an inner demon, a range of emotions fluttering across her face like different shades of light.

"Towards the end – before the event – Scott's walk changed."

This was not what I had expected her to say. Adele rarely spoke of Scott's suicide. In fact, she normally spoke of it only in response to an inquiry by someone else and never to me. It made me nervous (and slightly suspicious) to hear her refer to it so directly now. I slowly sat straight back up in the seat.

"His walk?"

"I was unaware of all the financial trouble we were having. Although it was obvious to even the most casual observer things were moving in the wrong direction for this man. He had started to drink. He was quiet and moody, quick to anger. He seemed to be carrying the weight of tragedy in his labored gait."

"I didn't know."

"How would you? He never talked to me, and I never talked to anyone."

"Not even Dad?"

She chuckled bitterly. "No. I remember one morning waking up simply because he wasn't in the bed next to me. You know how you sense the emptiness?" I nodded. When Brayden was raging at the world, which was most of the time at the end of our marriage, he decamped to the garage and played music until the house shook. When it stopped, he crept back inside to the couch in the basement, moving up to our bed at dawn. It was only when I felt his weight on the mattress that a sense of security befell me. It took me years after our divorce to be able to sleep soundly alone. "I searched the house. He was in the bathroom with his laptop, very drunk. I asked him what he was doing as if he were a naughty dog. He just smiled a drunk smile as if he didn't know who I was and turned back to the computer. Then it started happening regularly. He began missing work. We began getting calls from collectors."

"What did you do?"

"Willow, nothing." She registered my shock and chuckled. "Yes, in the beginning, I yelled, pleaded, coerced him into promises he couldn't help but break. It didn't matter. Somewhere deep inside, he had made his decision. I couldn't understand. I still don't. Maybe he didn't either. So, I did nothing. Well, that's not one hundred percent true. I did my best to make sure no one found out."

"Dad didn't know?"

Adele laughed ruefully.

"We missed Thanksgiving one year. He almost... you all almost found out then."

"You said you had your own family and that you wanted to start your own traditions, right?" I asked more to myself as a form of recollection than to her.

"And here, I never thought you paid attention," she said. "We had been separated a few months by then. He ended up in the hospital for attempting suicide the first time. He was convinced I was leaving him, so he would only communicate with me by phone – no emails, no texts. He was certain I would use these as evidence against him. As if he had anything. But I was so mad at him that I wouldn't take his calls. Can you believe that?"

I could.

"I had forgotten I was even in love with him." Here, she stopped and fought an emotional uprising so strong I could see she had difficulty maintaining her composure, her hands tightening around the steering wheel. Once it was quelled, she asked, "Isn't that strange?"

"No."

"It wasn't a rhetorical question. You think with all the time it took you to finish college you'd recognize one. God dammit," she snapped.

"One semester. I was in school four years and one semester."

"You're really unpleasant."

"Me?"

Despite her sudden rage, she couldn't stop. The dyke had been broken. Whether she wanted to confess this piece of her history to her little sister, I truly don't know, but it no longer mattered – the rocket had been launched, and there was no shutting it down.

"How do you forget something like that? That you loved someone? Now, I'm asking. I'm asking you. There's no one else here. Not that I think you know or anything."

"I think it's really easy."

"Mm," she muttered and seemed to fall into a reverie for many moments. She continued, "On the way to the hospital, a song I hadn't heard in years came on the radio, and don't bother asking, I'm not going to tell you. Despite everything, that first flush of love overcame me. It stopped me in my tracks. I had to pull the car over. Can you believe that? Talk about being a dramatic bitch."

I had never heard Adele talk like this about Scott or anyone.

"What happened?"

"So nosey," she said playfully. "We agreed to work it out. Those are my last memories, the two of us silently playing gin rummy in the hospital. When he got out a couple of days later, he killed himself."

"Why?"

"The note said: *I saw the papers*. When I had gone to the hospital, I had a stack of ordinary work papers in my purse that he assumed were divorce papers. He thought that my agreeing to work things out was a tactic. When he was discharged, he killed himself in that stupid carwash parking lot."

"There wasn't any note."

"Yeah, well, who wants anyone to know that? That particular piece of shame I kept from everyone until this very moment. Yes, even Dad. You feel like sisters now?" she said coldly.

I turned back to the window.

As the sun began its descent, we pushed through Wyoming and into Nebraska, and I thought about the day I snuck out to my father's truck and fell asleep. I awoke in the dark before Adele rose to shower and endlessly primp for school and the boys who never showed any interest. Sitting up in the blackness, my fingers danced beneath the bed like spider's legs, searching for the clothes I had covertly hidden there the night before. It was my favorite turquoise blue dress with pastel parasols and brown leggings. Putting them on, they were cold on my body. Through my curtained window, I could see the sky getting brighter, although the sun was still bashfully hiding. Adele, her hair still in braids, began to toss. I remained absolutely still. My instinct was to rush over to her bedside and cover her bare shoulder with the knitted blanket my grandmother had crocheted me (yet mysteriously ended up at the foot of Adele's bed). I stared through the shadows long after she had stopped moving, slipped on my dark red leather shoes, and wetted my fingers, giving a quick shine to the gold buckles. I lowered myself to the ground. The hardwood floor registered my weight, every step tempting my father, a notoriously light sleeper. I tiptoed to the stairhead. At the bottom, the door stood closed. It was like a faceless prison guard, merciless and unkind. If either of us had to use the bathroom, we had to find our way past this sentry, down the narrow hall, and to the bathroom, kitty-corner from our father's room. Without fail, our former cat, Buttons, would leap out, eyes on fire, scaring us to death before immediately retreating into the kitchen, its pace slow and untroubled. Our father would be yelling, sending us back up the stairs, bounding into our beds and under the covers. Unable to coax myself back to sleep, I wished only to go back to my home. I was ready to make my move, but at the last second, I shuffled back to Adele, covering her glowing white shoulder. She roused and made the sounds of sleep and deep contentment (which she never made while awake).

Back at the stairhead, I made my way down until I stood face to face with the door. I turned the knob and cracked the door. All I heard was the buzz of the refrigerator and hum of the kitchen sink light, and nothing more. I slipped past, through the house, and to the front door. Pulling the brown wool coat off the hook, I opened the front door and pulled it shut behind me.

Outside! The morning air and waning darkness was a rush to my senses. Creeping down the sidewalk and the abandoned street, I stood before the large brown delivery truck. I crawled inside, where I promptly fell asleep.

It was not the jostling of the truck or the roar of the engine that woke me. It was the unmistakable sound of my father whistling. He did this continuously. In a completely unselfconscious, joyful way. In our small kitchen while making dinner, reading the paper, or watching the news. From behind the refrigerator, I would watch him mesmerized. Opening my heavy lids, I sat up and saw myself in the rearview mirror. The whistling trailed off and then stopped completely.

"Holy shit," he exclaimed. "Willow, where did you come from?"

I stared back at him, terrified. I expected repercussions so severe that my childish imagination could not at that moment conjure them into existence. Then the strangest thing happened. He smiled. It was the first time I realized he didn't have his canine teeth. Shoving packages off the front seat, he said, "Come up here." In a flash, I was beside him.

We made a handful of deliveries, then stopped at Ember's and enjoyed a leisurely breakfast. I had always glossed over this fact to focus on Adele's response when I was dropped back home. Ignoring why I was put in that cab in the first place. He was late for work. He had given me exactly what I wanted and needed, the reason I had woken early and snuck out to his truck in the first place. I had wanted to share time with him alone.

"Did you know Dad wanted to be a baseball player?" Adele asked. "It was his big dream. It went unfulfilled, obviously. Like so many. Sometimes, I think that's all life is – the shedding of your dreams to face reality. He was pretty good at hockey, though—"

"Why wasn't he at the hospital when I was born?"

"What?" She was shocked at the unencumbered directness of the question and the abrupt halting of her nostalgic reverie, the type that is articulated for no one other than the one speaking but must be uttered aloud. "You're asking me? How would I know?"

"You seem to know everything else. You talk every God damn day."

"Why does that burn you so much?"

"I'm lucky if he and I talk a couple of times a month."

"We aren't lovers, Willow."

"You're best friends."

"You think that just happened? Well, it didn't. It was work. I invite him to do things. I always go to his house; he never comes to mine. I cultivated the relationship like an adult. I call him. He doesn't call me," she said, reaching out and clicking on the radio.

"Ever?" I asked, reaching out, shutting it back off. "He raised you, and he never calls you? Bullshit."

"That's the God's honest truth. If you want to talk to him, then call. Who's stopping you?"

"I'm his daughter. He should take it upon himself to foster our relationship."

"I know you think that's how it works. Maybe it should. It just doesn't. Not for our family, at least. He's a lazy, selfish man. I love him, but he's got his flaws, like we all do. I lived with him for a long time, and if there's anything I know about that man—"

"We all know the incredible story of your liberation. I've been hearing it literally my entire life. Spare me from hearing it again. I can recite it from rote." She raised her hands in surrender. "Do you know how I first became aware of our father? It wasn't some storybook rescue. He had just visited my mother, like anyone else would. After he left, I was told, 'That was your father.' Who meets their father like that? I was four years old. All it leaves me with is questions. Why didn't they tell me together? Obviously, I had seen him before. Who did I think he was? Up until that point, did I believe I was fatherless? What was the plan moving forward?"

"You lived with him too."

"After my divorce. I was a grown woman, for Christ's sake. It almost killed you, me having him to myself if I remember correctly."

"My point," she said, exasperatedly, "is that you had the opportunity to ask him these questions yourself. Why didn't you? Your problem is that you're incapable of confronting shit directly."

"Of course, insult me. Can you go ten minutes without tearing me down in some way? We're supposed to be sisters. Take the next exit. You heard me. Take the next exit. I want to drive."

"I'm not letting you drive."

"We need gas."

Examining the fuel gauge and finding (much to her consternation) that I was correct, she scowled and said, "I'll stop, but you're still not driving."

"Whatever."

I was out of the car before it had completely stopped moving. Moving briskly across the parking lot, I entered the gas station. Wandering through the narrow aisles and densely packed shelves, I paid attention to nothing, consumed as I was with resentment and self-pity. Wishing I hadn't had my car stolen like a pathetic loser. Sensing I wanted to be alone, Adele soon caught up to me. Rushing to the end of an aisle, I turned and began down the next. On the opposite side of me, Adele picked up an aluminum wall sign with a large fish in the middle that read *Don't worry, Be Crappie*, and presented it to me. Failing to respond, she turned up another sign – a large jumping fish mouth open with the words *Bite My Bass* – to which I rolled my eyes and wandered away.

"You ladies need anything?" called out the man behind the counter with a patch over one eye.

"We ladies are just fine," barked back Adele.

She tried on an oversized red construction helmet, then large sunglasses, lenses shaped like hearts. Having enough, I marched out of the place, spotted a frontage road, lit a cigarette, and began walking.

"Where are you going?" Adele called, leaning out of the gas station and propping the glass door open. I ignored her and continued on. "I'm not coming after you. I'll leave. I swear to God, if you don't come back, I will. Fine, you can drive for a little while."

I followed the serpentine road past a small school and several dilapidated houses. I tossed my cigarette and lit another. About a quarter mile up, I came across a county road that passed beneath a railroad bridge and down a slight incline to what appeared to be the edge of a cemetery. It was protected by an iron fence and bordered by a three-foot-high stone retaining wall. Hopping on the retaining wall, I followed it all the way to the entrance, where large iron gates were propped open by heavy cement bricks. Taking a seat on the coarse bricks, I watched as the sun began its further decline until it was hovering just above the horizon, the sky a deep azure blue. Eventually, Adele found her way to me.

"Are you serious with this?" she asked, positioned directly in front of me.

I ignored her and entered the cemetery.

Adele followed reluctantly, "All right. We'll do this your way. For the moment."

We tread along the dirt path. Twenty feet in, it split left and right, leaving an island of larger, more ornate headstones and bushes and trees separated from the rest of the dead isolated in the middle of the cemetery. Veering left, we passed a long row of flat markers. The grass had crept over their borders, many of the names and dates no longer visible, the earth making its final assault upon the deceased. How lonely and forgotten they seemed. I wondered how long it had been since they were graced by a living set of eyes and a beating heart. Behind these were tall, thin headstones, none of which stood upright but bowed at frightening angles. It would take nothing but a tap to send them careening over. I stopped before June Wildhaber, a woman the same age as my mother when she passed, now but a name and date, her life measured not only by the short dash between when she lived and died but by the unending stretch of eternity surrounding it on all sides which she interrupted for but a blip.

"Do you ever dream of your mother?" I asked, kneeling down, unsuccessfully fighting back the thick green turf over her marker.

"Mm-hmm," she mumbled, standing behind me. "I wish I didn't."

"No? I'm always pleased to see her."

"Even when you wake up and she's gone again?"

"It's like a new memory."

"The real ones are difficult enough, and most of those are fading away," she said, bending down, tugging the grass from the marker. "I don't even remember her voice. I tell myself I do, but I don't."

"For a long time, I thought her appearances were symbolic since she usually showed up at specific times of the year or if I was particularly stressed. But I could never figure out what she was trying to tell me," I said, brushing away the dirt encroaching on her grey nametag.

"You always bought into that new age crap."

"I'm really lonely without her. She was the only person who always thought I was great. No matter what I did, no matter how bad I fucked up. She was always my biggest fan."

I waited for the rejoinder, but none was forthcoming.

"I was always jealous of your mother."

"You were?"

"That willowy hair and those endless legs, she was impossible not to notice. She had an impeccable sense of style, too. My mother used to say she had three men in her life: Dad, Jim Beam, and Jack Daniels."

"Sorry."

"You don't get to choose the cards you're dealt."

"Suppose not."

I plucked a flower from a well-maintained grave covered in fresh flowers and set it on the marker of a child several markers back.

"This is for you—" I paused. It was no longer appropriate to call her Dead Girl Grey. I looked up to Adele, "I don't have a name for her."

"Don't look at me. I think this entire thing is maudlin," she said and wandered down the dirt pathway to a patch of green and black tombstones surrounding an immense angel, arms and wings spread wide as if she were blessing the entire cemetery and its brethren. I rose and made my way in the opposite direction. Finding a large, white obelisk, I ducked behind it.

"My god, can we go now? We have a lot of road left," I could hear Adele complaining. "Willow? Willow?"

My back up against the column, I yelled out, "Why did you tell Chet about the abortion? You fucked up my whole trip."

There was no response.

"You had no right to do that."

Again, the cemetery was permeated by silence. Eventually, the sound of Adele's footfalls upon the unforgiving ground could be heard as she immediately began to search for me. I listened intently, swearing I could sense the entirety of her prickly, unforgiving personality in those deliberate steps.

"Adele?"

"I don't know," she answered. She was still moving, swiftly, methodically, determined to find me.

"Bullshit. That's not good enough," I hollered, my head tilted skyward. The moon was out, the day nearing its close. She refused to answer. Peeking around the marble monument, her back was to me, head scanning left and right. I tiptoed deeper into the cemetery, taking solace behind a large mausoleum, that of an Agnes Littlefield (1856-1932), and again cried out, "I drove halfway across the county to tell this man something that he already knew, something that was our business and ours alone. Why would you do that to me?"

"I was getting married."

"So that's how it is? I ruined something of yours, so you ruined something of mine, is that it?"

"No."

Behind the massive stone crypt, the hard, unforgiving stone pressed into my back, I said, "Then what? Just say it – why is it so hard for you to say you wanted me in your wedding?"

"Why do you need to hear it so bad?"

Her voice was very near. She was on the opposite side of Agnes Littlefield's mausoleum. The effect was disarming. What would she do when she discovered me? Such is the nature of all discovery, a sense of exhilaration and foreboding. I braced myself for the moment when she would appear. Instead, I heard her slide down into a seated position and the sound of her feet displacing pebbles.

"At the beginning of my marriage to Scott, I got pregnant. We were still in the honeymoon period. Although to be perfectly honest, I'm not sure any man is blessed with one with me," she said without humor. "He was so excited to become a father."

"And?"

"I miscarried."

I didn't know if this was true. It probably was. Just another major event in the life of my sister that I wasn't privy to. It didn't matter. This was her trump card. A tragedy being weaponized to marginalize what she had done to me. How long had she kept this in her back pocket for an occasion such as this?

"Willow?"

"You can't hide behind Scott anymore."

Before she could respond, I sprinted straight ahead as hard and fast as I could, taking solace behind an austere Virgin Mary, her head bowed towards the ground, my entire body supported by her draped legs. I pinched my eyes tight and refused the tears that were insisting on being released. It wasn't long before I heard Adele patiently making her way once more through the graveyard.

"I'm not going to play cat and mouse with you all day. The sun is almost gone, and I have a long drive. It's ridiculous."

"Of course, I'm ridiculous."

"I didn't say you were ridiculous. Do you ever listen to the actual words I say to you?"

"You really must hate me to go to such lengths to humiliate me."

"I don't—" she began loudly, "hate you," she said, her voice dropping as she rounded the Virgin Mary, coming to a full stop face-to-face with me.

I immediately stood up and marched to a waist-high headstone and sat upon it.

"Christ. Stop running," Adele barked, reluctantly following me, taking a seat across from me on an identical stone. "I'm sorry, okay. I'm sorry. My feelings were just so hurt when you dropped out of my wedding—"

"Stop lying," I said, stepping to the opposite side of the stone, placing my hands on it. "This isn't about your wedding, and you know it. It's about you and me. How you've always resented me, never wanted a sister, how I ruined the life you had with Dad—"

"I'm not getting into this again. Anytime things go wrong for you, out comes this lamentation. It's bullshit. You can't lay everything at my doorstep. Take some responsibility for your own failings," she said, rising. "I'm going back to the car. If you're not back in fifteen minutes, I'm leaving."

She began for the entrance.

"My failings? What a laugh," I said to her backside. "After what you did, you still let me get all the way to fucking Utah, knowing it would blow up in my face. You engineered it. This was so important to me, and you shit all over it. How ironic that this is the first time you're here for me, and it's not to help or comfort me but to witness me at my lowest, to witness the depths of my humiliation. How can one person be so continually cruel?"

She turned around, rubbed her forehead with her right hand. "I shouldn't have told him. I should have stopped you."

"You're just one of a pair. Look around. Where is Dad? He didn't come running, did he? We both know if it had been you in this exact situation, he would have dropped everything just like he did before, like he always does. You're right, even when I lived with him, I couldn't get close to him."

"Stop."

An army of geese shot over my head.

"You can leave. I'll fend for myself. I always have. In fact, I grant you a divorce. I relinquish you from all sisterly responsibilities, including all family gatherings, holidays, funerals, and any organs I may need in the future."

"Stop it, please," she said, a look of deep regret gracing her face. She sat back down on the tombstone. She waited until she knew I was listening. "I don't know if Dad left or was kicked out, but at some point, he started showing up at the house, drunk."

"Before you went to live with him?"

"It was the summertime," she said, nodding. "I know because Mom always kept her bedroom window open, and I could smell the apple blossoms. The moment I heard his voice, I froze in my bed. The city was doing construction, and there were roadblocks with butterscotch caution lights that would blink all night. As he pleaded with her to open the door, I would attempt to memorize the pattern to ease my anxiety.

"Eventually, she would let him in. He wouldn't go away otherwise. Even though he was my father, he was now an intruder in our home. I tried falling back to sleep, but it was impossible. I would sneak down the hall and kneel behind the refrigerator. I had spent as much time behind the refrigerator as I did my bed that summer. Occasionally, I would venture out and peek into the living room. They would be on the floor in front of the stereo, glasses full, lights dim, talking. I remember once his pants were off, and I could see his exposed butt. No doubt the deal that was struck to get him to leave. I rushed back to my room and the comfort of the blinking construction lights, sick to my stomach.

"At some point, my mother met Sam, although how she found time amidst the chaos we were embroiled in still astonishes me. When Dad found out, it got worse. One evening, while she was making dinner, the phone rang. The second she hung up, we were in the car. We raced to Nancy's, then Samantha's, and finally to my grandparents, where we hid the car in their garage. I remember peering out from the window shades and watching my father's car creep slowly past. When we finally went home the following morning, all the flowerpots in our yard had been smashed. That was when I learned that a father was also a man, with all that entails, including occasionally being transformed into a fiend.

"On one of the nights, their arguing grew vehement, more animated and desperate than normal. I listened as my mother pleaded with him to leave. He refused. I inched my way into the middle of the kitchen floor. They were both stunned. It was as if I was a specter from beyond had appeared out of thin air. 'Please, Dad, just go,' I begged with all the courage a child can muster. I felt brave, grown-up, and proud. My father turned his head, drunk and slow. 'You too, huh?' This was a shock. Knowing nothing of the world of adults, I expected affirmation and praise for doing what was right and true. In an instant, my heart broke. I had betrayed my father. This is the man I've relentlessly defended my entire life."

The sun had now completely dipped below the horizon. The cemetery was silent and dark and still. I could not make out the expression on her face. I was immediately taken back to the strange conversation my father and I had on vacation about how Adele came into his care. Her words confessed to me that she knew these things or at least intimated them somewhere in her hard, tough heart.

"I don't know what to say. I'm confused and overwhelmed—"

"Quiet."

"Christ, this is a big deal," I said, but she was no longer listening, but staring hard into the black.

"What's over there?" she said, pointing into the darkness.

"I don't see anything," I said, but the moment the words left my mouth, I saw it – a wispy beam of light like water from a sprinkler, spreading outward, growing wider and more translucent the further it got from its source. Before I could react, a police officer was standing before us, a tower of blackness hidden by the cover of night and the radiance of the flashlight strategically aimed over our faces.

"Excuse me, the cemetery closes at dusk."

"I didn't know. I'm not from here."

"It states it explicitly on the sign at the entrance. Just you here? I thought I heard two voices."

As he was speaking, I became aware that Adele was not at my side. I scanned the area, but there wasn't any trace of my sister.

"Just me."

"Let's go," he said, motioning for me to walk in front of him. We made our way slowly past the mournful angels, lopsided crosses, and tombstones until we were out of the property. Placing the flashlight in his mouth, he removed the cement bricks with effort and closed the iron gates. "Have a nice evening." I stood a moment and feigned interest in my phone until the overhead light of his squad car illuminated its interior.

When Adele didn't immediately appear, I began hesitantly retracing my steps. I was nearly at the edge of the cemetery when I heard the quiet scuttle of footsteps that grew louder and more powerful until, from out of the darkness, Adele's form appeared. She was running full blast toward the iron fence, in a sort of crouched position, looking over her shoulder.

"I was not going to get busted by some small-town sheriff," she said, placing her foot on one of the crossbeams, hoisting herself up and over. Landing on the retaining wall, she concluded, "Let's get the fuck out of here."

We walked in silence for some time under the quiet protection of the stars.

"Look, my mother rejected me every day of my life until Dad took me. And he didn't want me either. When he started telling people how he rescued me, well, it was easier than the truth."

"Why would he lie in the first place?"

"You'd have to ask him. Best guess? To get back at her. I'm sure he wanted to believe it. Honestly, I never pressed him. I guess you're not the only one who couldn't address things directly," she said with a weary sigh.

"Hey, you were right. I had two years in his house to ask the hard questions and didn't. Maybe it was just a form of self-preservation. He just gets off so easy, though."

"He's not all bad. Whatever the intent or desire, he saved me from a wretched life. I am grateful to him, no matter how much that pisses you off. You don't have to hate him."

We followed the frontage road back past under the railroad bridge, up the incline, the gas station coming into sight.

"Did it ever cross your mind that you didn't need him the way I did? You already had a hero. I'm not excusing him. But he knew you were taken care of." Bumping shoulders with me, she said, "Would you know how to balance a checkbook without him? Or change a tire? And have you ever walked in front of a running car when you approach a busy street?"

"No," I said with a chuckle. "The way he would lay on the horn? It caught me off guard every time. I still have a condition."

"He would kill anyone that hurt us. Despite his flaws and missteps, he loves us, you know."

"All right, you made your point."

I thought about his insistence that you never take your star player out of the game. It was as close to a philosophy as I had ever heard him articulate. It said something about how he viewed the world. No matter what life threw at you or how dark it got, it was worth being a part of.

"Do you miss him? Scott?"

"Every goddamn day."

We crossed onto the gas station parking lot under the blazing light of its canopy. The man with the black patch over his eye, no doubt an emissary of Mr. Bones, if not the beast himself, gazed up from the register.

"Have you ever thought about it?"

"Doing that?" she asked. "Never. Never. No. Not for a second. I wouldn't give this shit existence the satisfaction. Fuck that. It'll have to take me kicking and screaming. You?"

"Bunches of times."

"I didn't know that." She pondered for a moment. "I'm glad you didn't."

Standing before the car, Adele pointed at me and, with an air of grand defiance, said, "We are going to stop in Lincoln on the way back."

"Whatever for? I hate that town. If I see that state ever again, it'll be too soon."

"I know where your car is."

"How?"

She smiled. "I'll tell you this, that bitch and her deadbeat husband aren't going to know what hit them. Nobody fucks with my sister."

I threw my arms around her neck and hugged her as tightly as I could.

"God, I am not the person for this," she said, turning her head away in mock disgust.

"Yes. Yes, you are," I said, refusing to let go.

"Alright, alright. We have lots to do and little time. Let's get out of here," she said. I was still holding on as she popped open the door.

*   *   *

I never heard from Chet or Darlene again or found out if they got the baby they so badly desired. Brayden moved to Charlotte, North Carolina, and became a therapist. He never much cared for Minnesota anyway. Many years later, my dad died of a stroke while walking his beloved dog, Coco. I can't say things had improved much between us. It didn't matter. I was always happy just to be around him. He is, after all, my dad. I rarely talk about the road trip with my sister because I end up crying most of the time. While in high school, McKenna discovered a passion for writing, and in 2025, she graduated summa cum laude from Loyola University and was awarded the *Eliza A. Drew in English for Best Poem – First Place* and the *W. Quay Grigg Award for Excellence in Literary Study*. Sitting in the bleachers, Adele at my side, I watched in awe as she crossed the stage, her arms raised in victory. Maybe one day, she'll write a book about the adventures of her mother and her crazy little family. Wouldn't that be something?

ABOUT THE AUTHOR

David Haight

DAVID HAIGHT was born and raised in Minneapolis, Minnesota. He was educated at Hamline University where he received a degree in English and Philosophy and later an MFA in writing where he was distinguished by the Quay W. Grigg award in Literary Study. He published his first novel *Overdrive* in 2006, his second *Me and Mrs. Jones* in 2012, his first collection of short stories *Lemon* in 2015 and his fourth book (and second collection of short stories) *Katharina (and other magnificent disasters)* in 2017. He is inspired most by writers James Joyce, Ernest Hemingway, Richard Yates, Don Carpenter, Arthur Rimbaud, and Friedrich Nietzsche. He lives in the Twin Cities with his wife Rachel, stepdaughter Carys and his daughter Morgan.

www.ingramcontent.com/pod-product-compliance
Lightning Source LLC
Chambersburg PA
CBHW060946050426
42337CB00052B/1542